Alcohol, gender and culture

Europeans, who constitute 12½ per cent of the world's population, consume 50 per cent of the recorded world production of alcohol and this consumption, sometimes social, sometimes ceremonial, plays a significant role in the cultural, religious, and social identities of the people of these countries. The majority of studies on alcohol have examined its use with the assumption that alcohol is a drug and have focused on large, often diverse groups ignoring up until recently the importance of cultural variation.

In *Alcohol, Gender and Culture* the contributors show how different groups define the proper use of alcohol, how State policies may affect drinking behaviour, and highlight how beverages and comestibles must be seen in relation to each other. From this it is shown how important socio-cultural distinctions are made between and within communities, gender relations, ethnic groups, and socio-economic groups, and within religious ideologies. What one drinks, how one drinks, with whom, and where, all influence not only how alcoholic substances are regarded but also how social relations are experienced.

It is seen that in those societies where alcohol is not viewed as a dangerous product, but is highly valued and constitutes part of everyday life, drunkenness is not immediately associated with the quantity of alcohol consumed, but rather is constituted within social relations. Could it be, then, that certain communities exhibit a cultural immunity to alcohol problems since drunkenness is not necessarily considered a social problem?

The contributors present material from Greece, Spain, France, Hungary, Sweden and Ireland showing how the social construction of drinking may provide an analytical tool with which to approach different socio-cultural groups. To demonstrate this further the first chapter concentrates on gender roles and drink in Egypt, providing a comparison with European attitudes to drink and drinking and illustrating how *any* cultural group can be compared to another by its attitudes to alcohol.

Alcohol, Gender and Culture is invaluable reading for students and lecturers of anthropology, cultural history and gender studies.

Dimitra Gefou-Madianou is Assistant Professor of Social Anthropology at the Panteion University of Social and Political Sciences in Athens.

EUROPEAN ASSOCIATION OF SOCIAL ANTHROPOLOGISTS

The European Association of Social Anthropologists (EASA) was in-augurated in January 1989, in response to a widely felt need for a profes-sional association which would represent social anthropologists in Europe, and foster cooperation and interchange in teaching and research. As Europe transforms itself in the nineties, the EASA is dedicated to the renewal of the distinctive European tradition in social anthropology.

Other titles in the series:

Conceptualizing Societies
Adam Kuper
Revitalizing European Rituals
Jeremy Boissevain
Other Histories
Kirsten Hastrup
Understanding Rituals
Daniel de Coppet

Alcohol, gender and culture

Edited by
Dimitra Gefou-Madianou

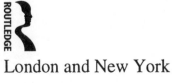

London and New York

First published 1992
by Routledge
11 New Fetter Lane, London EC4P 4EE

Simultaneously published in the USA and Canada
by Routledge
a division of Routledge, Chapman and Hall, Inc.
29 West 35th Street, New York, NY 10001

Typeset in Times by LaserScript, Mitcham, Surrey
Printed and bound in Great Britain by
Biddles Ltd, Guildford and King's Lynn

British Library Cataloguing in Publication Data
A catalogue record for this book is available from the British Library.

Library of Congress Cataloging in Publication Data
A catalog record for this book is available from the Library of Congress.

ISBN 0–415–08667–1

Contents

Contributors

Isabelle Bianquis-Gasser, Ph.D., is currently a Research Assistant at the University of Human Sciences in Strasbourg.

Gunilla Bjerén, Ph.D., is currently a Research Fellow at the University of Stockholm.

Henk Driessen, Ph.D., is currently an Associate Professor in Anthropology at the Catholic University of Nijmegen.

Dimitra Gefou-Madianou, MA, Ph.D., is currently an Assistant Professor in Anthropology at Panteion University, Athens.

Anna Marina Iossifides, Ph.D., is currently Lecturer Designate in Anthropology at Panteion University, Athens.

Karin van Nieuwkerk, Ph.D., is currently a Research Assistant at the University of Amsterdam.

Eleni Papagaroufali, Ph.D., is currently a temporary Lecturer in Anthropology at Deree College, Athens.

Adrian Peace, Ph.D., is currently a Senior Lecturer at the University of Adelaide.

Michael Stewart, Ph.D., is currently a Temporary Lecturer in Anthropology at Cambridge University and Research Fellow of Corpus Christi College, Cambridge.

Preface

This book is the outgrowth of a panel on 'Alcohol Commensality, Gender Roles and Religion in European Societies', part of the first EASA Conference in Coimbra, Portugal, during 3–7 September 1990.

The volume includes all papers presented for the first time and discussed at the Coimbra Conference. It presents recent ethnographic data on alcohol use in different Euro-Mediterranean countries, thereby allowing for cross-cultural comparisons and opening a discussion on related issues such as identity, power relations, commensality, religion and transformations.

Ten contributions, including the Introduction, are collected in this volume, reflecting ethnographic data from respective Euro-Mediterranean societies. Six papers focus on the Mediterranean area, mainly Greece, Spain and Egypt, and four papers on other European societies, namely Hungary, Sweden, Ireland and Alsace (France).

Acknowledgements

Many people have contributed in many ways to the publication of this book. I would first like to thank all the contributors who made the EASA panel discussion in Coimbra on 'alcohol commensality' such a lively and stimulating one, and who then took the time and effort to prepare their papers for publication. I should also like to thank Jens Hannibal and Maryon McDonald who as panel discussants offered their perceptive insights and comments. This book would not have been published, however, had it not been for the constant encouragement and support of Adam Kuper from its inception to its completion. I should also like to thank Dimitris Tsaoussis for his clear judgement, sound advice and continuous support, not only during this project, but throughout my academic life. With Marina Iossifides and Akis Papataxiarchis, I have shared many stimulating discussions concerning the central arguments of the book, and they have been especially supportive and encouraging throughout the project. Michael Herzfeld, Dwight Heath, Peter Allen, Linda Bennett, Jill Dubisch, Henk Driessen, Nia Georges and Stella Galani made helpful comments on earlier drafts of the Introduction. I would also like to extend my thanks to Jens Hannibal, Bruce Ritson, Marc Morival and Peter Shiöler, with whom I have worked over the past few years on various WHO and EEC committees. They have broadened my perspective and sharpened my understanding of alcohol-related issues. Heather Gibson, Katy Wimhurst and Jo Thurm at Routledge made the editorial process a pleasant experience. Sheila Bailey and Maureen Bloom have supported and assisted me throughout the organization of the panel at Coimbra and during the publication period. Many thanks also go to Antonis Papadis who did an excellent job in copy-editing the book. Michael Madianos shared with me the high and low moments of this effort and has offered me invaluable support and critical insights from the medical point of view. To him and to our children, Mirca and George, I am grateful for their love and belief in me. Most of all, the contributors and I would like to express our appreciation to the people in the communities all over Europe and the Mediterranean who, as informants, have inspired and assisted us in our observations and writings. Their trust and willingness to share their lives with us are reflected in this collection.

NOTE ON TRANSLITERATION

No uniform system of transliteration has been used in this book. The choice of transliteration was left to individual authors, many of whom rendered words and expressions as pronounced in the local dialect in the various European communities where they did their fieldwork, rather than as they appear in written standard Irish, French, Swedish, Hungarian, Egyptian, Spanish or Greek.

1   Introduction

Alcohol commensality, identity transformations and transcendence

Dimitra Gefou-Madianou

ALCOHOL USE IN AN ANTHROPOLOGICAL PERSPECTIVE

This volume focuses on the significance of the meaning of alcohol to societies and its relationships to individual and collective identity trans-formations and gender in Euro-Mediterranean societies.[1] However, all con-tributors have found it difficult to exclude consideration of many other important aspects of alcohol use in society, such as commensality, trans-cendence, and religious ideology which are also related to this central theme.

Although it would take us too far from our central concerns to undertake a systematic historical review of the literature and of the various ways the issue has been approached by anthropology and related disciplines,[2] a brief introduction to the extended literature on alcohol studies may help to place this collection in relation to what has already been said – or not been said – regarding the issues approached here; it may also stimulate new approaches for future research.

Reviewing the literature on alcohol studies, we can be sure that there are alcohol uses related to many aspects of human behaviour and to a variety of social activities. The uses of alcohol and the meanings attached to it vary widely, while the act of drinking is present in almost every society.

The link between alcohol consumption and culture was among the first introduced by the seminal work of Bunzel (1940) who systematically compared two communities in terms of how alcohol is related to other areas of culture. She found important differences in how alcohol use was asso-ciated with child-rearing practices and other institutions and showed how drunken behaviour was embedded in social life in one of the communities while condemned and destructive in the other.

Considerable advances in the study of beliefs and behaviours that relate to alcoholic beverages have come to light in recent years and this is especially true with respect to anthropological perspectives. An overview of the anthropological material shows how alcohol is embedded in social relations and sociocultural systems around the world, including for example factors such as race and ethnicity, health, religion, economics, politics, communication, sex and recreation, social change, criminality, anomie and family disruption (Heath 1987).

Social and cultural factors are acknowledged by many scientists of various disciplines as influencing the interaction of alcohol and human behaviour in many important ways (Bruun 1975, Davies and Walsh 1983). What anthropological approaches have revealed is the diversity of beliefs and reactions towards alcohol in various societies. This diversity which characterizes almost all kinds of attitudes towards alcoholic beverages ranges from teetotalism to excessive use and drunkenness, and from appreciation of its ecstatic and transcending power to expostulations of it as totally immoral.[3] What you drink, how you drink it, when, how much and with whom you drink, who has treated you, or how you obtained it, and in the health of whom you drink, may evoke diverse responses in different cultural settings. As Mac Marshall has put it:

> The cross-cultural study of alcohol presents a classic natural experiment: a single species (Homo sapiens), a single drug substance (ethanol), and a great diversity of behavioural outcomes. Among behavioural scientists, it is anthropologists in particular who seek explanations for human similarities and differences in natural experiments of this sort.
>
> (1979:1)

Over the past 40 years a number of readers on cross-cultural literature on alcohol, including those taking an anthropological approach, have been published.[4] Documenting the wide range of cultural habits related to alcohol these studies paved the way for the inclusion of sociocultural factors in the study of alcohol use and abuse (Everett *et al.* 1976, Marshall 1979, Douglas 1987); they also indicated that drunken comportment is a learned behaviour (MacAndrew and Edgerton 1969, Marshall 1979a). Comparable studies of ethnic differences in alcohol morbidity rates brought out the importance of socialization, social definition and social support in relation to alcohol (McCarthy 1959, Pittman and Snyder 1962, McClelland *et al.* 1972).

Most of the above-mentioned collections present cross-cultural data ranging from non-literate societies to highly technologically developed ones which exhibit different socioeconomic backgrounds and religions, and, more importantly, which have diverse backgrounds in respect to the social history of alcohol. In some of the societies alcohol, whether fermented, brewed or distilled, was known for centuries and was made from locally cultivated plants, while in others it was not originally known and was introduced by 'foreigners' eventually. This diversity allows broad cross-cultural comparisons and the formulation of some generalizations which contribute, on the one hand, to the analysis of the involved relationships between alcohol and human behaviour (Marshall 1979); on the other hand they do not contribute in-depth sociocultural and historical analyses to the study of alcohol.

All these collections have unquestionably contributed a great deal to the field of alcohol studies. Nonetheless, they present a number of limitations. Some of the collections present a compilation of reprinted papers covering a 25-year period and, although they offer an understanding of the development of alcohol studies, they do not allow for consistent comparisons on ethnographic data nor do they articulate with the recent theoretical anthropological issues.[5] Others adopt an interdisciplinary approach right from the beginning, stressing physiological/psychological, biomedical and cultural factors, thus allowing for a dialogue between different fields, such as epidemiology, sociology, anthropology, psychiatry and economics. However, by and large, they approach alcohol drinking and alcohol-related behaviour as a social problem and are aiming at preventive measures.[6] Similar limitations are found in the literature that focuses explicitly on intoxication and drunken behaviour, thus totally excluding 'normality' in drinking.[7]

A recent collection of works (Douglas 1987) does focus on 'constructive drinking', considering it a positive activity. It promises to provide 'perspectives on drink from anthropology'. A considerable number of the papers, however, come from disciplines other than anthropology.[8] Moreover, the collection does not focus exclusively on alcoholic beverages.

Most of the research on alcohol done by anthropologists so far has been criticized either for focusing only partly on the subject while the main concern of the research lies elsewhere, or for focusing on the 'cultural benefits' of alcohol and avoiding alcohol-related problems.[9]

A major debate has been taking place over the last eight years around the issue of 'problem deflation' in alcohol ethnographic research (Room 1984). Room has pointed out that anthropologists are emphasizing the positive aspects of alcohol use in a 'functionalistic way', thus underestimating alcohol-related problems which exist in all the societies studied. A number of anthropologists have reacted to this (Agar *et al.* 1984),[10] contending that alcohol use is apparently found to be a constructive and 'coherent' social act which presents many forms usually not of a problem type; they also note that what Room calls 'anthropological bias' and 'functionalistic' approach is the ethnographer's emphasis on context and meaning(s) of alcohol use in a given society and also on the links of alcohol use with other aspects of social life. Heath in particular criticized Room for assuming that alcohol use is problematic or can always cause social problems.[11]

It is evident however that after the 1960s most of the studies on alcohol concentrate on the medical model of alcohol-related problems. This may be attributed, first, to the failure of anthropologists and other social scientists to develop 'aetiological theories' of alcohol abuse or alcoholism; second, on the continually growing financial support given to studies which either 'directly or by inference propose biological solutions to alcohol abuse' (Roman, in Kuper and Kuper 1985).

In Europe, which has one-eighth of the world's population, 50 per cent of the recorded world alcohol production is consumed (Ahlström 1976). Alcoholic beverages have been favoured for centuries in European societies as the best means to achieve a transcendent state. Despite this, few of the ethnographic studies on alcohol have concentrated on European societies.[12] Most of them have followed the course of the ethnographic research of American and British anthropologists and have been conducted in non-literate societies.[13]

Ethnographic studies on alcohol in European societies are few and far between. The first studies were published in the 1960s (Honigman 1963, Gibson and Weinberg 1980, Pinson 1985, Thornton 1987).[14] The Irish tend to be the first in terms of the attention paid to their alcohol-drinking patterns, often in comparison to the Jews. It has been suggested that learning to drink in the context of family and religious rituals acted as a protecting factor, making Jews moderate drinkers, while lack of family rituals and the tendency for bar drinking combined with economic frustration made 'alcoholism' (Bales 1962) and excessive drinking acceptable among the Irish (Heath 1976).

These two examples however may also reflect the way these two ethnic groups have been acculturated into the American culture, for the first signs of 'alcohol problems' were identified among Irish migrants in the USA. When this association (Irish and alcohol) was established, many researchers, including ethnographers, started focusing on the 'Irish drinking problem'.[15] Some ethnographers who have studied Southern European and Mediterranean countries have brought to light observations on alcohol use which were by-products of research that was focusing on other issues (Arensberg 1937, Campbell 1964, Herzfeld 1985, Brandes 1980). Brandes and Herzfeld, however, have analysed important institutions for all-male gatherings such as bars and coffeehouses which constitute important points of departure for anthropological alcohol studies.

In the 1980s important ethnographic research was conducted in the area of alcoholism and its transmission to the offspring of 'alcoholic' persons in USA. Bennett (1989)[16] showed that undisrupted family rituals – surrounding dinner time, holidays and vacations – act as protectors against the transmission of 'alcoholism' to offspring.

A collection of ethnographic data on alcohol from five South-Central European countries was published by the *East European Quarterly* (1985). Some of the papers focus on an ethnohistorical approach to alcohol from ancient times up to the present; others emphasize the importance of public drinking institutions (bars, taverns, coffeehouses); still others concentrate on alcohol problem treatment systems.

The predominating literature on alcohol studies in European societies, however, comprises mostly epidemiological, public health and alcohol control studies undertaken by WHO,[17] EEC[18] and other major Foundations for alcohol studies in Europe.[19] The Scandinavians in particular have created a tradition from the beginning of this century in systematic epidemiological research aiming at the reduction of its consumption (Ahlström 1976, Skog and Waahlberg 1988).

Although these studies provide valuable information on the patterns of alcohol consumption, give an overall picture of quantity and types of drinks consumed by the different sex and age groups, and also present indices of morbidity and mortality rates, they do not allow for aetiological associations between the variables involved.[20] At another level they do not link this epidemiological material with sociocultural, historical and religious factors and the way they might influence alcohol consumption and problems. The underlying assumption in these studies is that alcohol is a drug and should always be treated as a problem.

Another puzzle these cross-cultural epidemiological studies exhibit is that they are usually dealing with large and diverse groups within Europe and sometimes even drawing comparisons with North American populations. Given the fact that considerable variation in patterns of alcohol consumption occur within a given country and that homogeneity within any country is more often the exception than the rule (Heath 1987), these comparisons may become problematic.

The World Health Organization, having wrestled with the prickly problem of defining 'alcoholism' and alcohol-related problems in a way that would be meaningful among the various member states that it caters for (WHO 1951, 1952), has come to acknowledge the importance of cultural variation. In a similar manner during the last decade it has approached the study of alcohol-related problems at the 'community' level, thus reducing tremendously the unit of analysis; examples of this effort both in cross-world cultures (Ritson 1985) and within European countries[21] have emphasized the importance of sociocultural factors in the study of alcohol-related problems as well as the meanings of alcohol in various communities.

The above ethnographic and epidemiological examples bring us to a consideration of alcohol in a great many cultures – the meaning of its use and abuse, conspicuous consumption or abstinence from it; the social construction of these concepts is still missing from the anthropological literature. Despite the vast literature on alcohol we still need the formulation of concepts and analytical tools to grasp the meanings of alcohol use in each society. As Madsen and Madsen (1969) have put it, 'we shall attempt to explain drinking behaviour as a consequence of cultural premise about reality . . .'.

Let us now turn to the focal issues of this volume, namely, gender, identity transformations, commensality and religious ideology. With regard to gender[22] and identity transformations,[23] little substantial research has been carried out in direct association with alcohol.[24] Douglas (1987) introduces the issue of gender and alcohol use, pointing out an interesting association between biology and culture. Heath, a contributor to Douglas's volume, notes, in his excellent historical review of the literature, the fact that men in many cultures drink whereas women tend towards abstinence. For the greater part however most of the contributors to Douglas's volume do not take up the issue of gender in relation to alcohol.[25]

In connection with alcohol commensality the existing literature has focused more on the solidarity acquired in public drinking places (Pittman and Snyder 1962, Gibson and Weinberg 1980, Beck 1985, Pinson 1985). However, the link between public drinking places and other important institutions of society (e.g. household, church) is missing.

The link between religious ideology and alcohol use is a complex one. Most of the studies in this area concentrated on Judaism.[26] They have shown how Jewish culture as influenced by the religion acted as an inhibitor of drunkenness and alcoholism. Along these lines Snyder (1978) explained the break between the traditional Jewish sobriety and the heavy alcohol use of some Jews in New York as a result of the distance from traditional orthodoxy and ceremonial participation. A number of other studies[27] noted, significantly, that prohibition or prevention policies have never been successful in societies 'except when couched in terms of sacred or supernatural rules' (Heath 1987:46). However, most of the studies in this field have an ethnohistoric character rather than an ethnographic one (Heath 1976).[28]

These studies have opened the discussion of alcohol to its relationships with gender, religion and commensality. However, from within the more general alcohol studies and those which take up the issue along more anthropological lines certain crucial questions demand further investigation:

1   Since forms and meanings of drinking alcoholic beverages are culturally defined we must ask what these meanings are and how they are linked to the entire culture and society.

2 Why is it that in the majority of the societies studied men may in certain contexts drink alcohol even in large quantities without cultural impunity whereas women for the greater part either do not drink or, drink less and very rarely in homosocial gatherings?

3 Given that gender roles are at least in part delineated by religious ideology (outlooks and beliefs), how is religion linked with the discourse created between alcohol and gender?

4 Within any given society it is important not only to understand the forms and meanings of a particular drink but to understand how different drinks in different contexts are interrelated. Moreover, is it possible that the meaning and form of the same alcoholic drink will, within the same society, vary from context to context?

5 How is alcohol drinking defined and regulated/controlled within a given society? Can a distinction be drawn between those communities in which the state plays a significant role in the regulation of alcohol production, distribution and/or consumption and those communities in which alcohol regulation is embedded in the overall social fabric?

6 Given the above, could the social construction of drinking provide an analytical and useful tool with which to approach a given society?

This collection does not claim to give answers to all these questions; however, all contributors provide recent ethnographic material on the cross-cultural perspective and on the variety of ways that alcohol production, distribution and the very act of drinking itself can be analysed and interpreted within the framework of commensality and rituals, gender roles and religions ideologies in different Euro-Mediterranean cultural settings.

ALCOHOL: AN ANTI-DOMESTIC DISCOURSE?

In most European societies men are the main consumers of alcoholic beverages while women form only a minority of consumers. In the Euro-Mediterranean cultures from which ethnographic data are presented in this volume, a distinction, sometimes sharp, is made between male and female domains in relation to drinking alcohol. This holds true both for north- western European countries, and for southern European and Mediterranean ones.[29]

Over the past ten years there has been an explosion in the area of gender studies.[30] In relation to alcohol, ethnographic material from Mediterranean societies has linked male sociability and alcohol drinking in coffeehouses with the gender discourses in these societies. Brandes first (1979) and a few years later Driessen (1983) examined male drinking in terms of gender relations within their respective communities in Andalusia, Spain. They noted that when, where, and how men drink in coffeehouses and bars serves to constitute their identity as men independently from household relations and to the exclusion of women.[31] Furthermore, both suggest that the rituals of male drinking and socializing together in coffeehouses and bars, although emphasizing masculinity, are directed toward obscuring male dependency on the female members of their family. By excluding women from coffeehouses men reinforce a doubtful female subordination. As Driessen has put it: 'Their vulnerable dominance over women is reinforced by the rites in coffee houses which exclude females' (1983:131).

Papataxiarchis (1988, 1991) in an eastern Aegean community also discusses male insecurity as exhibited in raki drinking sessions in the village coffeehouses. He contrasts these drinking sessions to kinship relations which exhibit rules of uxorilocality and female dominance within the household (matrifocality), a situation which forces men to seek refuge in the coffeehouses. He describes the coffeehouse drinking sessions as formulations of an anti-structure, an anti-domestic discourse within which male gender and male identity may be constructed. In a somewhat analogous case Iossifides (1991) discusses the construction of female identity in a discourse of anti-conjugal relations, yet reflecting kinship relations in a Greek Orthodox convent.

Essentially, then, these anti-domestic/anti-kinship discourses arise from within the commensal relations between men. Yet, the opposition between kinship and alcohol commensality is not so clear-cut. Men drink at weddings, funerals, baptisms, name-days, celebrations which are fundamental household rituals, and very much family-oriented ones. More importantly, women are often present at these drinking bouts, sometimes serving alcohol, yet not always themselves drinking it (Gefou-Madianou 1991). Despite the fact that women are either abstainers or drink less, in many cases they are providers of drinks (Bjerén and Stewart, this volume) or producers of the alcoholic beverages which they offer to men (Colson and Scudder 1988, Gefou-Madianou, this volume), a point which will be taken up further on.

What should be noted here is the fact that alcohol studies, up to now, have examined alcohol predominantly from a male point of view, seemingly regarding alcohol as a substance that naturally belongs to men. Thus, though the studies above are noteworthy in placing the drinking of alcohol by men within the context of gender, that is men in relation to women, there have been very few studies which examine alcohol consumption, production, and distribution from a woman's point of view. In this volume a number of papers address this imbalance. For example, female entertainers in Egypt, as van Nieuwkerk reports, find themselves caught between what are considered respectable practices for women and the public nature of their work. Drinking and smoking associated with public entertainment are considered highly improper for women in line with Islamic law. While men should also adhere to these laws, it is recognized that they will indulge occasionally during weddings or at night-clubs. Yet, it is seen that some female entertainers do drink and smoke in public as a means of denying their femininity. In this manner, van Nieuwkerk suggests, these women are able to present themselves as men among men and thus, paradoxically, protect their reputation as respectable women.

In a rather more defiant vein, Papagaroufali introduces us to the short-lived Women's Coffeehouse in Athens, Greece. Opened in 1982, this coffeehouse sought to challenge traditional practices in which coffeehouses and the consumption of 'strong' drinks in public were strictly male preserves. The opening of the coffeehouse brought to light conflicting discourses. Generational differences and outlooks between the founders of the coffeehouse highlighted different approaches and views concerning what it is to be human and a woman. Taking her cue from Myerhoff's (1986) 'definitional ceremonies' and Foucault's (1978) explorations of the 'games' of power and pleasure, Papagaroufali also examines how the Coffeehouse offered opportunities for women to confront male dominance publicly and, though short-lived, served as a locus of resistance. This confrontation, however, was not one-way, for it might be argued that women, by seeking to display their equality through the use of male symbols, simply reinforced the established order.

It might be said, then, that when women enter into a male-dominated public arena in order to work with or for men, or simply for their own pleasure, they either seek or are forced to adopt male behaviour including drinking. Given the examples cited above it might be suggested that female drinking in public either serves to challenge and confound socially accepted norms or paradoxically to protect women's reputation through the adoption of male habits. How female drinking in public is interpreted will depend in large part on the women's motivation for drinking and the manner and place in which this drinking occurs.

This is not to say, however, that women are associated with alcohol only as a means of redefining or protecting their social status *vis-à-vis* men (Papagaroufali, Stewart, van Nieuwkerk, this volume). Though they may in large part refrain from drinking socially constituted male drinks in male-defined spaces, women may consume other types of alcohol, as for example wine and even sweet liqueurs, which often have very high alcohol content. These drinks may be store-bought or made by women as part of their recognized domestic roles and are consumed largely in the home during family celebrations, when guests are visiting (Bjerén and Iossifides, this volume), or during all-female visits.[32] For example, Driessen (this volume) describes Andalusian women drinking alcohol in public places, but only when accompanied by family men (husbands).[33] In Greece (see Cowan

1990, Gefou-Madianou, this volume, Iossifides 1990), aside from ritual occasions such as baptisms, weddings and funerals, women drink liqueurs on formal visits or, in some instances, when a group of friends get together. Yet even then the drinking is done in moderation and in some contexts supposedly behind the backs of their husbands or brothers. Bjerén (this volume) notes changes in women's drinking patterns in Sweden such that women are now increasingly drinking wine together, both within the confines of home and in all-women groups out for a night on the town. Apart from some ritual occasions, these drinking sessions are more subdued and less directed towards getting drunk than all-male drinking.

What characterizes women's drinking then seems to be moderation in the quantities consumed and the domestic context within which it is consumed, whether this contact is same-sex or mixed. Moreover, within the domestic context, women in many societies (see Peace, Gefou-Madianou, Driessen, this volume) often encourage their men to go out to the bar, tavern or coffeehouse so as to get them out from under their feet. While women then seem to find their social role within the household capacious, men, though often owners and representatives of the household to the outside world, would appear paradoxically to be confined and restrained.

Given the above, we see how Brandes and Gilmore's thesis is supported. Male drinking, in bars and coffeehouses, serves to constitute their identity as men, obscuring as it does their dependency on the female members of their households. In short, men find themselves in a position of insecurity *vis-à-vis* women, in a position of 'vulnerable dominance'. It is a position they seek to overcome and possibly escape from through all-male commensal relations which take place outside the home and which deny women entrance.

Yet, is it only men who find themselves in positions of insecurity and vulnerability within a household context? Certainly women too, especially young newly married women, are not always fully secure in their new households. New brides, especially those in virilocal communities, may find themselves in foreign neighbourhoods, villages, or even regions, under the tutelage of domineering mothers-in-law and sisters-in-law.[34] Alone, often far from their relatives and friends, these women too must experience a deep sense of insecurity. Similarly, widows when faced with the prospect of raising children alone without the support of a man also find themselves highly vulnerable. Moreover, it is not only the structurally weak women within the system that are exposed. Within many societies women are not regarded as fully respectable until they are married. And once married, though their legal status may deem them equal to men, their social status often does not carry the required weight to fulfil all the functions necessary to the running of a household. Given this, could we not say that women too require a place of refuge? Why do they not also resort to communal alcohol-drinking practices? Why do we not see the development of female coffeehouses? Or, when we do, why do they seem false, a mimicry of the 'real thing'?

Finally, this very real male insecurity should not blind us to the fact that these all-male gatherings not only allow for the creation of male identity but also for the creation of a sense of solidarity and unity which would not otherwise be possible. Moreover, the use of alcohol, which may at times even lead to drunkenness, or more accurately to a state of 'spiritual intoxication', provides a means whereby men transcend their everyday selves.

MEN IN ALL-MALE GATHERINGS

We have already noted the inclination for the strict separation of the sexes in many aspects of everyday life. Even in cultures where social values are experiencing rapid transformation and women are beginning to frequent bars and taverns (though usually only when accompanied by a male relative), drinking habits between the sexes remain very distinct (see for example Driessen, this volume). These spatial and behavioural gender distinctions are often quite sharp.[35] Among Rom Gypsies in Hungary, for example, women may drink moderately, even in public, but should not under any circumstances drink to the point of drunkenness, a state that is by contrast highly valued among men (see Stewart, this volume). Similarly, in the town of Torsby, Sweden, women traditionally used to drink quantities of coffee, preferring to sit quietly while their husbands were drinking together on party occasions in the home. If they had any alcohol at all it was predominantly in the form of sweet liqueurs which were taken in moderation. This is still the pattern among older women.

It may be said then that men have a freedom of movement and autonomy in public which is denied to women. They may spend much of their leisure time both during the day and in the evenings, on weekdays and even holidays, in coffeehouses, taverns and bars socializing with other men. In these regular and long-lasting all-male gatherings a situation of camaraderie is developed and strong feelings of solidarity are experienced.[36] More importantly, through these commensal same-sex gatherings, men are seen to construct their 'real masculine identities'.[37]

Peace (this volume) links alcohol drinking with the production and reproduction of socially constituted occupations and gender differences in the small Irish fishing community of Clontarf. He shows how fishermen through their commensal drinking in bars reproduce their social identities within the community. Fishermen are characterized by an ethos of fierce egalitarianism, an egalitarianism which emerges from within the discourse of drinking. Moreover, as well as exchanging information vital to their work, these commensal settings enable men to display their physical toughness and to enhance their reputations through public displays of drinking and buying rounds. Through the exchange and consumption of alcohol men make competitive bids to prove their self-worth *vis-à-vis* other men.

> But by socializing effectively and drinking hard and well – and in knowing well that he can do both regardless of immediate circumstances out at sea – he is able to retain full confidence in his calibre as a fisherman and in his sense of self as a member of the pier domain.
>
> (Peace, this volume)

Thus, once a man has proved himself to be a 'man amongst men', he achieves a type of acceptance and, though he must continue to maintain this status, he is now regarded as an equal amongst equals.

It is in these 'egalitarian communities' that men are able to transcend their everyday, mundane roles. In the closed and bounded space of the coffeehouse, bar or tavern, and through the exchange and consumption of alcoholic drinks, men cross socioeconomic boundaries which in mundane situations separate them. The alcohol relaxes them, it breaks down internal constraints, allowing through the flow of alcohol, the flow of sentiment. What is important to note is that men drinking together in homosocial gatherings reach a state of *methy* – spiritual intoxication[38] – through drunkenness which is highly valued because it stresses sharing and egalitarianism. It facilitates 'transcendence' and is contrasted with the intoxication of the lonely drinker, or the habitual drunkard of the community, who are both condemned. It is important to note that the best *methisia* in Messogia, Greece (Gefou-Madianou, this volume) were experienced by people when there was a lack of retsina in the village due to vine phylloxera, and they were 'getting drunk' on 'water'.

In the wine-producing virilocal community of Messogia, for example (Gefou-Madianou, this volume), men's dominance over women and over household wine production is prominent. Men will often be found in coffeehouses drinking together or amongst the wine-producers, and between the months of October and April, in the *katoy* (wine cellar)[39] where the individual producer's wine barrels are kept. Contrasted with the coffeehouse gatherings where beer or wine is drunk, the *katoy* gatherings are of a more private and intimate character. To these *katoy* gatherings only owners of vineyards and cellars, the ones who know the 'secrets' of retsina, are invited. In the dark, humid, dusty and warm world of *katoy* where must is transformed into retsina, these male peasants through the drinking of retsina, sometimes to the point of *methy* (drunkenness), are transformed, achieving their true (masculine) identity. And though, like the fishermen of

Clontarf, they should, as men, be able to drink quantities of alcohol they should also always maintain their self-control.[40]

Stewart (this volume) presents a similar case. Among the Rom Gypsies of Northern Hungary, the consumption of alcohol lies at the heart of social life. The Gypsies are under continual pressure by the government to conform and use the drinking of beer or wine in the communal gathering of men as a means of expressing their identity. The drink loosens them up allowing for the creation of *voja* (good mood),[41] the symbolic expression of communal life and 'the Gypsy way of doing things'. Stewart goes on to note the opposition made between beer, wine, and water. Water, associated with the household, is seen as a conductor connecting those things which should be kept distinct and separate. Brandy and spiced wine, on the other hand, with their burning qualities are associated with purification and health, and with the creation of boundaries. Strictly speaking, then, it is not simply the effects of alcohol but the social construction of the sharing of certain drinks under certain circumstances which is essential for the creation of social existence and social identity among the Rom.

It seems therefore that there is in some societies a culturally defined 'need' for all-male gatherings in which alcohol plays a central role. In these alcohol drinking gatherings men transcend or go beyond the confines and constraints of the everyday world. Their talk becomes sentimental, their bodies more expressive. They hug one another with greater freedom, laugh, cry, and dance in ways that are said to express their true sentiments, their true selves.[42]

Moreover, in these gatherings, a systematic destruction of capital is taking place. Buying rounds for others,[43] conspicuous drinking, gambling and losing a great amount of money, and also conspicuous squandering of alcohol,[44] are all forms of this systematic destruction. These 'anti-productive' behaviours and attitudes serve to emphasize an egalitarian ethos among men; an ethos which concerns moral attributes rather than material assets. It is worth noting that this 'spiritual intoxication', which is highly valued and desirable among men, can only take place in collectivity; that it is unpredictable in character and stresses sharing, egalitarianism and intimate relationships among the men who achieve this state of *methexis* (communion).[45] It is through this experience that men construct their male identities and obtain 'power' to control their immediate circumstances. As Peace notes:

> As fishermen imbibe heavily and become inebriated they do not thereby lose control . . . or their sense of judgement. On the contrary it is precisely under such circumstances that they are in a position to grasp effectively the fluid and complex realities of their world.
>
> (Peace, this volume)

This state of 'spiritual intoxication', however, contrasts drastically with the drunkenness of the lonely drinker – someone who drinks in isolation, an act that is condemned in many societies (Ireland, Portugal, Spain, Italy, Greece).[46] Moreover, it is significant to note that in many Mediterranean societies drinking excessively is not always associated with drunkenness, whereas drinking alone, even in lesser quantities, is (Papageorgis 1987, Papataxiarchis 1988, Madianou, this volume). To drink and to eat are by definition acts which imply commensal relations. They cannot or rather should not take place alone, individually. They are acts enmeshed within the collectivity.

Durkheim in his seminal work on suicide makes a similar point when comparing suicide among Catholics, Protestants and Jews. The collectivity which arises within Catholicism and the unity expressed within the Jewish church contrasts with the individualism evidenced in Protestantism. Durkheim argues that the suicide rate is lower among Catholics and Jews because of 'their lesser religious individualism'. He introduces the concept of 'immunity' to suicide for both Catholics and Jews; an immunity based on 'the greater integration of the Catholic Church' (1951:401–2) and the 'strong unity of the Jewish Church . . . governing all the details of life and leaving little free room for individual judgement' (p.160). As for the Protestants and their association with suicide, he concludes 'that the superiority of Protestantism with respect to suicide results from its being a less strongly integrated church than the Catholic church' (p.159).

WOMEN IN ALL-FEMALE GATHERINGS

Let us now turn to women's relationship with alcohol. Women's same-sex gatherings contrast markedly with those of men. Though women may drink alcohol together, they do not seek, for the greater part, to step out of their 'confining' everyday roles. For example, Park (1990) describes how New Zealand women have become alcohol users as part of their more general attempt to attain equality in the public and domestic spheres. None the less women, unlike men, do not drink in bars but at home, in small groups mostly with other female relatives and friends. The drink, usually home-made wine, is accompanied by food and is considered to be 'good' alcohol as opposed to the beer and spirits preferred by men.

Papagaroufali (this volume) presents an extreme example. In the short-lived Women's Coffeehouse in Athens, Greece, older feminists, having prepared food, would without hesitation invite their husbands to the Women's Coffeehouse to drink and eat together, thereby replicating the commensal activities found in household rituals.[47]

Many researchers throughout Europe have noted this household-oriented nature of all-female gatherings as well as their kinship, neighbourhood, and community orientation[48] (Honigmann 1965, Thornton 1987, Gibson and Weinberg 1980, Hirschon 1989). Moreover, these gatherings have been found to exhibit antagonistic characteristics which have often been attributed to the fact that women act as representatives of their households rather than as separate individuals. Thus, not only do they seemingly acquire their identity through the male members of their household but they compete with one another in the presentation of their house, the goods that are produced within it and its members, of whom they are the caretakers (Dubisch 1986).

There is, however, another aspect in these female homosocial gatherings, that of conviviality and solidarity. Though ethnographic material suggests that women do not achieve a state of transcendence in these gatherings, whether there is drink or not, there is evidence to suggest that strong bonds are created as well as an atmosphere of conviviality. Rather than drink, it is chat which is emphasized (Peace, this volume). For here women talk, giggle, laugh, gossip, tell secrets, share tips on beauty and fertility treatments, exchange cooking recipes and significantly discuss men's behaviour (du Boulay, 1976).

Yet, despite the fact that these gatherings are often deplored by men and sometimes women as simply time-wasting gossip sessions, it has been noted that they are largely 'productivity bound'. That is to say, women participating in these gatherings are at the same time busy embroidering, crocheting, needle pointing, or preparing or selling foods, agricultural or other goods. In that important respect, these gatherings contrast with the unproductive and at times anti-productive nature of all-male drinking gatherings, for in the bars, taverns and coffee-houses men will be found drinking, gambling, or simply passing the time (op. cit.).

For example, Stewart (this volume) describes how Rom Gypsy women prefer to take their drink back to their stand when selling things in the market, rather than drink with the men at the bar. This in effect serves to interweave drinking with work rather than making the drink a central activity.

Park (cited above) notes how those women who are increasingly working outside the home will on their way home stop at the bar for a drink. Yet, they do not consume their drinks in the bar. Rather, they will buy the alcohol and take it home. In this manner, they seek to maintain their image as good mothers, sisters, wives, caretakers, in short as 'good women'.

Thus we see that women's all-female gatherings are embedded within household and domestic discourses and that though men are absent, and often chased from the house, they are still present in the talk (about men) that goes on in these gatherings. Moreover, in relation to alcohol consumption, it seems that for women's same-sex gatherings the drinking of alcohol is not of central concern. Rather it is the getting together, the exchange, the commensal chat that is valued and sought after. Female identity seems to be achieved from within the household in many European, mostly rural or semi-urban societies.

Within this context it is understandable that, as has been noted, excessive drinking and drunkenness among women is generally deplored. Women who do drink heavily are considered social misfits and are stigmatized; their drinking is often interpreted as a lack of self-control and self-respect[49] and even regarded as dangerous, an indication of uncontrolled sexuality.[50] It may be for these reasons that excessive drinking among women is seen as threatening to the household since through their promiscuity women expose the household to public criticism and in extreme circumstances leave the household open (as they open their bodies) to infiltration by strangers and the possibility of illegitimate children (Hirschon 1978, Giovannini 1981, Dubisch 1986, Park 1990).

This presumed link between excessive female drinking and uncontrolled sexuality may be contrasted with, granted, rather limited suggestions which not only link certain types of alcohol with fertility but place women in pivotal roles as distributors (see Bloch and Parry 1982).[51] In the ethnographic material from the virilocal community in Messogia, Greece, for example, women are the producers and keepers of sweet wine. They are the ones who offer it to their husbands to assure the procreation of male offspring and thus the continuity of the household. Moreover, not only is it highly desirable and 'blessed' for men and women to have conjugal relations in the vineyards, but sweet wine made by women with grapes taken from vineyards belonging to the men of the household, 'cut' with soil from these vineyards, and often 'watered down' with retsina, a male product par excellence, serves to unite the sexes through the actions and under the jurisdiction of women. Though women control its production and distribution, sweet wine is created with 'male' products and has as its primary objective the fertility of the household through its consumption by men from the hands of women.

Is it possible then that women do not wish, or do not find the need, to transcend their everyday roles, in the manner that men do?

WOMEN COOK, MEN DRINK: COMMENSAL HOUSEHOLD RITUALS

There are, however, house-based gatherings at which both men and women are present and in which alcohol again plays a central role. The heterosexual discourse constructed during rituals which are household-oriented emphasizes the unity of men and women. This discourse, though present in many European societies (Bjerén, Peace, Driessen, Gefou-Madianou, this volume), seems to hold a prominent role in Mediterranean societies where households are deeply embedded in community networks through strong family, kinship and community ties.[52] Family rituals[53] which involve drinking and eating together as well as household rituals[54] join – in many cases around the same table – members of the extended family who do not necessarily live under the same roof, together with members of the broader community, all within the realm of the household. These commensal gatherings serve to create bonds between different groups, often overriding major social and economic distinctions. Yet, competition among individuals and between households may also be expressed and experienced during these drinking rituals. For example, what the hostess is wearing, the type of food served, or how much this particular ritual cost as compared with a similar ritual celebrated recently can all be points of discussion, criticism and competition. Thus, though these rituals emphasize the unity of the family and also that of the household with the broad community, and though they may serve thereby to transcend occupational, class and status differences, they also serve to create and re-create boundaries between the close and extended family, between neighbours and neighbourhoods, as well as defining broader community relations. As Douglas has noted, drinking and eating household rituals define 'different degrees of hierarchy, inclusion and exclusion, boundaries and transactions across the boundaries' (1975:249).

Women in these household rituals are either denied drink or drink in moderation. In this sense they may seem to play a secondary role to men (see also Dubisch 1986). Women, however, cook, thereby transforming a 'natural' product into food, a cultural artefact. This food is an indispensable part of household rituals contributing significantly to their successful outcome. In many societies in fact drinking cannot take place without the presence of food (Mediterranean societies: Ahlström 1976, Gili-Miner *et al.* 1992, Mercês de Mello *et al.* 1992, Gefou-Madianou 1988 and 1992; New Zealand: Park, but this applies only to women).

Furthermore, the association between alcohol and food is highly prominent in religious discourses, particularly those within the Judaeo-Christian tradition. In Greece, for example, many researchers have noted the link drawn between the family meal, the Last Supper, and the Communion Meal which in the Greek Orthodox and Catholic Church symbolizes unity and power[55] (Drower 1956, Campbell 1964, Hirschon 1989, du Boulay 1991). Central to this role are women who cook and distribute the meal, who provide the table with food (Dubisch 1986).

This link between food, drink, women and religion has been noted, again by many Mediterranean researchers. Gefou-Madianou (this volume) in her discussion on sweet wine notes that this wine may either be given to men to assure fertility or taken to the church along with home-made bread to be used as elements in the Holy Communion. Through this wine and bread which are made and brought to the church by women, consecrated by the priest and partaken of, ideally at least, by all members of the community, women serve as unifying forces, linking the household with the divine, with the community, and with the broader Orthodox community (see also, for Spain, Christian 1972; for Portugal, Pina-Cabral 1986; for Greece, Hirschon 1989, Dubisch 1986, 1991:7, Iossifides 1990, and Gefou-Madianou, this volume).

It may be said then that women hold pivotal roles since through the food they cook and serve they create a discourse which allows them to unite categories that are often kept distinct.[56] This cooking discourse unites men and women, households and the broader community, and also the mundane and spiritual worlds.

MEN, WOMEN, WINE AND RELIGION

The association between women, wine, and religion is also marked in Iossifides' (this volume) material on the practices within a Greek Orthodox convent. Here, in this all-female world, women seek to transform their material fallen state in order to achieve eternal life. It is seen that the body serves to symbolize on the one hand the material world in opposition to the spiritual, while on the other it serves as an aspect of the divine. Ultimately, it is only through the uniting of the body and the soul that salvation and eternal life after death are achieved. This unity is most strikingly expressed in the ritual of Holy Communion central to which is wine.[57] Wine is seen to portray blood, life, the Holy Spirit, the divine, and is associated with men.[58] Combined with bread which is the body, the mundane world and associated with women, unity with the divine is assured. In the secular world of the village the uniting properties of wine are found again in the exchange relations within the male domain of the coffeehouses.[59] Yet the truly unifying and reproducing aspects of wine, which in Holy Communion unite male and female, divine and mundane, and promise life after death, are found in a secular context only in the household production and consumption of wine.

Bianquis-Gasser (this volume) also notes the symbolic relationships between household wine production, religious beliefs and human life-cycles in Alsace, France. Her material, however, focuses on the male wine producers, who through wine are able to unite the divine and the mundane. Compelling symbolisms and associations are made between genders, death and procreation as well as between men and the transcendent. Two distinct cycles are noted in the production of wine: the vine cycle which refers to the actual cultivation and care of the vines, and the wine cycle which refers to the fermentation process. Interestingly, in the vine cycle women and men work in complementary roles to care for the crop, while during the nine-month wine cycle when the wine is fermenting in the cellars, like a child in the womb, women are prohibited entrance, just as they are prohibited, in the end, from imbibing the potent and transforming drink. These two cycles are closely associated with the religious and yearly cycles as they are with the impregnation of women and the birth of children. Thus, human and divine cycles are united within the central domestic task of wine-making.

OPPOSITIONS AND UNIFICATIONS

We see then that alcohol serves to create, mediate and unite different categories while in no way dissolving those categories. In the first instance household is opposed to coffeehouse and bar, men are opposed to women. But the boundaries are not impermeable for, as noted, women may and do drink within household or 'work' contexts (such as the market stall); men and women may drink together in family and household gatherings or rituals; and equally they are united within Church rituals. As Bourdieu notes:

> The union of contraries does not destroy the opposition (which it pre-supposes), the reunited categories are just as much opposed, but now in a quite different way, thereby manifesting the duality of the relationship between them, at once antagonism and complementarity . . . which might appear as their twofold 'nature'.
>
> (1977:125)

Thus it is through opposition and unity that men and women continually seem to be defining and redefining one another. Women offer food and drink in the home. But men too will, in the home, in certain contexts serve food and drink (Campbell 1964, Dubisch 1986, Bjerén, this volume). It is a man, a priest, who offers and mediates between the divine and the mundane in official religious contexts. But as noted throughout the Mediterranean it is women who will go to the church as representatives of their households. There from the hands of a priest they will receive the blessing, a blessing which will suffice for the household as a whole. In this manner women appropriate divine powers enabling them, like priests, to spiritualize the household and to unite it with the divine. Finally, in the work of Gefou-Madianou (this volume) we see that though women's sexuality may threaten the household, they are none the less necessary for its continued existence. And though women are excluded from male drinking sessions as well as denied participation in the preparation of retsina, due to their supposedly dangerous physiology (menstruation, childbirth), they are also seen as the means whereby this potentially dangerous sexuality can be transformed into life-giving fertility. Through the making (cooking) of sweet wine and significantly through its distribution to men, women are able to ensure that their threatening sexuality is transformed into esteemed fertility. In this instance it is men and not women who act as mediators, as the transforming and linking element between two distinct categories.

CHALLENGES AND REALITIES

As we have already noted in the discourse generated from exclusively male gatherings,[60] personal and collective identities are constructed and social boundaries are created, aiming at or defining local and ethnic identities: local communities in relation to other ethnicities; local communities in relation to neighbouring ones; one occupational group in relation to another within the same community (Peace, Stewart, Gefou-Madianou, this volume, Papataxiarchis 1991).[61]

For example, a differentiation in the intimacy, solidarity and emotions expressed between groups within the same community may be observed. This differentiation may evolve due to job competition, class, or status differences of the members (as well as the stability of the group itself).[62] For example, among the fishermen in Clontarf, Ireland, Peace (this volume) describes an overt everyday competition expressed among drinking groups in bars (today's friend – tomorrow's enemy), which in large part stems from job competition and the unpredictable nature of their occupation.[63]

In many societies refusal or avoidance by men of different 'classes' to drink with one another often indicates a lack of solidarity, but may also serve as a vehicle to express hostility in an 'institutionalized' manner through, for example, accusations or excuses: 'he had drunk a lot'.[64] Drinking may also serve as a manifestation of and a preparation for public arguments and 'rebellions' between different interest groups: wage labourer versus landlord; wine producer against Athenian merchant.[65] What is important to note is that, though these instances of 'challenging the system' may be manifested in an individualized, self-oriented manner, that is one man standing up to speak against the landlords, in reality the individual expresses the sentiments which arise from within his (often drinking) group.[66] More importantly, members of different groups, even competitive drinking groups, will identify themselves as a person in a group when dealing with those they deem outsiders.[67]

Some of the societies discussed in this volume, however, do not offer their members opportunities for the creation of such discourses;[68] they do not offer opportunities for same-sex gatherings which may lead to the construction of individual identities through collectivity.[69] In these societies it is often the state which regulates to a large extent the production, distribution, taxation, importation and consumption of alcoholic beverages.[70] It is also noteworthy that in these societies there is often a social history of temperance movements which have led to feelings of guilt in relation to the consumption of alcohol. Thus, though alcohol consumed in strict moderation is tolerated, though usually only during leisure hours,[71] in general it is felt that its consumption easily leads to a myriad of social problems: family disputes, illness, absenteeism from work. Those who wish to drink are often forced to do so privately, in secret, which may further reinforce their guilt since drinking alone is deemed an even greater evil.[72] None the less, people do drink, despite their feelings of guilt, despite the strict measures taken by the state, despite views which see alcohol as a socially and morally destructive substance. It may be for these reasons that alcohol is regarded as an ambivalent substance.[73]

Bjerén (this volume) notes that there are strict state regulations which restrict alcohol consumption and opportunities for all-male gatherings around drink. For example, in the whole town of Torsby, Sweden (4,000 inhabitants) there are no pubs or bars. There are only a couple of places licensed to serve alcohol. The price of alcohol in these establishments makes social drinking prohibitively expensive except in a very limited form. Young men meet these restrictions by bringing their own drink to dancing places, which of course is strictly against the rules, and drinking 'outside the place you intend to visit, or on the sly inside the place by topping up your soft drink under the table from a bottle brought in pocket or bag, or during visits to the toilet . . . ' (Bjerén, this volume). Some men will also drink clandestinely at football matches. This set-up minimizes all-male drinking commensality in the community context. The idea of transcendence of the everyday self is rather linked to ideas of male togetherness in nature, beyond the regular 'women-infested' community. Fishing and hunting in the vast pine forests covering the entire Torsby region is associated with ideas of masculinity and drink. In short, little space is left between the household and the state for men to construct their personal identities in a collectivity within the community[74] in contrast to many Mediterranean communities. What may be suggested here is that in communities such as Torsby, Sweden, men are essentially forced to seek out the wilds of nature to drink with other men in an atmosphere conducive to the construction of the male identity.

Moreover, we may even hazard the suggestion that through the cultivation of the raw products that constitute alcohol, along with its production, the producer comes to identify with the product. He develops a different type of relationship, an almost intimate relationship, with the alcohol which enables him to view alcohol not with fear and guilt but with pride, an essential element of his self-respect and social standing, a relationship which contrasts with alienation.[75] In societies where alcohol is highly valued and praised, even considered sacred, and constitutes an inseparable part of everyday social life drunkenness is not necessarily considered a social or personal problem. Could it then be suggested that certain communities have acquired a 'cultural immunity' to alcohol 'problems' based on the ways in which alcohol is interwoven into the matrix of the personal, social and religious lives of the people of these societies?

We may be able, then, to explain why, despite centuries of use in some societies (e.g. Greece, Italy and Spain) where there have been opportunities for commensality both single-sex and mixed, there has not developed a negative discourse around alcohol. Alcohol is not seen as a dangerous or even ambivalent product but rather as a substance which, as we noted before, is embedded in the social and personal identities of the people who use and produce it.[76]

Given this, how are we to measure possible alcohol-related problems? What analytical categories are we to use to define them? How can the epidemiological and clinical indices used for alcohol-related problems – morbidity and mortality of liver cirrhosis, accidents, absenteeism, criminality – come to an agreement with the native's point of view? That is what indigenous people consider a 'problem'.

This leads to another serious question which EEC countries will be facing in the coming years; how will the harmonization in alcohol production, distribution and consumption, and, more importantly, the EEC intervention policies for the regulation and control of alcohol use, influence those societies which have succeeded for centuries in 'regulating' alcohol use according to basic aspects of culture without state interference (Gefou-Madianou 1992)?

We are not, in this volume, dealing with the question of the existence or absence of alcohol-related problems in the societies concerned; nor are we discussing the 'scientific criteria' used in defining these 'problems'. As Dolgin *et al.* in their introduction to *Symbolic Anthropology* explain: 'Our concern is not with whether or not the views a people hold are accurate in any 'scientific' sense of the term . . . in social action, that which is thought to be real is treated as real' (1977:5). What we have tried to explore is how societies and individuals in these societies formulate their social everyday reality in terms of alcohol use.

Through this ethnographic exploration, which focuses mostly on the meaning of alcohol in different Euro-Mediterranean societies, we aim to contribute to the formulation of 'other' analytical tools in approaching both the 'reality' and the symbolism (metaphors) of this controversial issue, alcohol, and stimulate future research in the field. As Lakoff and Johnson put it:

> Each culture must provide a more or less successful way of dealing with its environment, both adapting to it and changing it. Moreover, each culture must define a social reality within which people have roles that make sense to them and in terms of which they can function socially. Not surprisingly, the social reality defined by a culture affects its conception of physical reality. What is real for an individual as a member of a culture is a product both of his social reality and of the way in which that shapes his experience of the physical world. Since much of our social reality is understood in metaphorical terms (symbolically), metaphor plays a very significant role in determining what is real for us.
>
> (1980:146)

Thus, it is tempting to see the meaning of alcohol in society as Geertz sees the meaning and aim of symbolic anthropology: 'the enlargement of the universe of human discourse' (1973:14).

NOTES

1 Nine of the papers reflect field work from European Societies and only one is based on field work in Egypt. This paper will provide comparison with Europe on all aspects of drinking.
2 A systematic review of the literature has been undertaken elsewhere: Gefou-Madianou, in preparation.
3 Heath (1976).
4 P. McCarthy 1959, Pittman and Snyder 1962, MacAndrew and Edgerton 1969, McClelland *et al.* 1972, Everett *et al.* 1976, Marshall 1979, Douglas 1987.
5 Marshall 1979; his reader reprinted papers published within the period 1954–77.
6 Pittman and Snyder (1962); the idea for their book originated with the Committee on Alcoholism of the Society for the Study of Social Problems. Also the book by Everett *et al.* originated from a conference on human scientists and world-wide social problems in 1973, and the publication was supported by the National Institute on Alcohol Abuse and Alcoholism.
7 McAndrew and Edgerton 1969.
8 Of the fourteen papers, eight are written by anthropologists while only three of them reflect ethnographic accounts of alcohol use. See also Marshall (1989).
9 See Room (1984).
10 ibid. pp.178–186: comments on Room's paper in *Current Anthropology*.
11 ibid. p.181.
12 Some historical studies have been done (Harrison and Trinder 1969, Harrison 1971) which stressed the ambivalence exhibited by the temperance and prohibition movements.

13 See Anderson *et al.* (1946) and Horton (1943); for Latin-American ones see Bunzel (1940); for native American Indians see Waddell (1973), Westermeyer (1979) and Mars (1987); for Pacific Islanders see Marshall and Marshall (1975) and M. Marshall (1979a); for Eskimos see Honigmann and Honigmann (1965); also for African societies see Colson and Scudder (1988) and Ngokwey (1987).

14 Honigmann (1963) has done a study on drinking rituals in a German-speaking central European village in Austria, and emphasized the importance of drinking rituals and ceremonies in maintaining a moderate pace in drinking among the people of the community. Pinson (1985) studied an Icelandic community in terms of how public drinking and drunkenness construct friendship bonds between persons. Gibson and Weinberg (1980) studied wine symbolism in a Swiss Alpine village and pointed out that wine constitutes a symbol which expresses and preserves the primary tenets of peasant identity: egalitarianism, self-sufficiency and autonomy. Thornton (1987) studied *sekt* versus schnapps in an Austrian village and found that drinking schnapps together guarantees mutual support and solidarity in the community, while drinking *sekt* does not.

15 Bales (1962), Robins *et al.* (1962), Snyder (1962).

16 See also Bennett (1985) and Bennett *et al.* (1988).

17 Bruun *et al.* (1975), Mäkelä *et al.* (1981), Single *et al.* (1981), Grant (1985), Anderson (1990), Porter *et al.* (1986), Plant *et al.* (1990), Plant (1989), Skog and Waahlberg (eds) (1988), Partanen and Montonen (1988).

18 Davies and Walsh (1983).

19 They are mostly Scandinavian: The Finnish Foundation For Alcohol Studies; The National Institute for Alcohol Studies, Helsinki; The Swedish National Board of Health; The Swedish Council on Alcohol and other Drugs; The International Council of Alcohol and Addiction in Geneva.

20 In Sweden, the strict alcohol control policy measures have managed to reduce the per capita alcohol consumption over the years 1970–80 and to keep it stable over the decade 1980–90. Although Sweden's per capita alcohol consumption is much lower than that of any of the EEC countries, its death rate from liver cirrhosis is higher than in UK, Ireland, the Netherlands and Denmark (Davies and Walsh 1983: 213–14). This was partly explained by the fact that when Swedish people drink, they drink excessively and in order to get drunk (Bjerén, this volume). Also, in Denmark, the rate of death from liver cirrhosis is lower than in the rest of EEC and Scandinavian countries, while its per capita alcohol consumption is higher and its alcohol control measures are milder compared to the same countries (Davies and Walsh 1983, p.60).

21 WHO – Collaborative Study on 'Community Response to Alcohol-Related Problems', WHO-Euro, in press.

22 Berg has announced a new reader on *Gender, Drink and Drugs* edited by M. McDonald, but it is not yet in circulation.

23 See Loizos and Papataxiarchis (1991a and b).

24 See Brandes (1979), Gilmore and Gilmore (1979), Driessen (1983) who indirectly bring the issue to their gender studies.

25 Recent ethnographic material from Eastern Aegean offers clear links to drinks, drinking and masculinity (Papataxiarchis 1988, 1991).

26 Snyder's (1962) and Keller's (1970).

27 See Yamamuro (1954), Carstairs (1954), Singer (1972), Leacock (1964).

28 This, of course, was raised long before by Immanuel Kant (Jellinek 1941) in his anthropological lectures during 1772–1796 where he stated that 'Jews do not get drunk, as a rule, at least they carefully avoid all appearance of it because their civic position is weak and they need to be reserved'.

29 See Peace for Ireland, Bjerén for Sweden, Bianquis for Alsace, Stewart for Hungary, Driessen for Spain, Gefou-Madianou for Greece, and van Nieuwkerk for Egypt (this volume).

30 See Reiter (1975), MacCormack and Strathern (1980), Caplan (1987).

31 See also Hansen (1976) and Gilmore (1977, 1985).

32 See also Cowan (1990), Kerewsky-Halpern (1985); see also Stewart (this volume) for public consumption of sweet liqueurs among Rom Gypsy women.

33 Plant (1990) offers another explanation: to a large extent alcohol problems amongst males and females reflect social and economic influences such as the general acceptability of drinking in specific contexts and the price and availability of alcohol.

34 Campbell (1964), Dimen (1986), du Boulay (1986).

35 Greek and Mediterranean ethnography stresses this fact (Herzfeld 1985, Hirschon 1989, Dubisch 1986, 1991, Loizos and Papataxiarchis 1991a and b, Peristiany 1966, Davis 1973, Gilmore 1987, Brandes 1980).

36 See the work of Robbins (1979) on the Naskapi Indians of Quebec; also the work of Mars (1987) on longshoremen in the Port of St John's in Newfoundland, Canada; the work of Clinard (1962) on public drinking houses Mid-West USA; Bruun's work (1959) in Finland; also the work of Allen (1985), Herzfeld (1985), Loizos and Papataxiarchis (1991a) in Greece and Beck's work on coffeehouses in the Balkans (1985). Also T. Gregor explores this subject in his study of a prestigious Bohemian men's club in San Francisco (1987).

37 Most probably the first presentation is by Gilmore and Gilmore (1979) and Brandes (1980, 1981) to be followed by Driessen (1983), and many others already referred to above.

38 *Methy* = spirit, the gracefulness of spirit; enthusiasm; expression of deep feelings; *methysi* (plural *methysia*): a) *elaphra methy* (light drunkenness) = a state of *kefi* (see below), happiness, slight intoxication. b) *hypervoliki methy*, *kraepali* (drunkenness) = inebriation, debauchery, Dionysian orgy; extreme expression of feelings (see *Antilexicon* 1962, Th. Vostanjoglou, Athens). See also MacAndrew and Edgerton (1969) for an excellent account on how drunkenness is learned; also Dennis (1975), Papataxiarchis (1988), and Frake (1964) for 'drinking talk'.

39 *Katoy* literally means the basement of the house; it is a place where the wine barrels are kept. It can also be a separate construction next to the house (see also Gefou-Madianou's chapter).

40 Campbell (1966) describes how a man loses his honour if he cannot hold his drink.

41 *Voja* (good mood) could be compared with *kefi* (pleasure and delight; humour; a healthy state) as well as a state of slight intoxication (Papataxiarchis 1991: 170).

42 The atmosphere in these all-male gatherings resembles the one described during the ritual gatherings of the *dervisses* of the Bechtassi Order (Myrmiroglou 1940).

43 See Mars (1987); also Peace (this volume).

44 See Robbins (1979); also Gefou-Madianou (1988), where she presents examples of conspicuous drinking: men celebrating in homosocial public

gatherings during the town saint's festival would buy rounds of beer for their group members; after drinking for some time they start squandering the beer; they open the cans in such a way that the beer spurts out and is spilled on the ground; they exhibit wealth and power by piling up the empty beer cans on the table; they also pour quantities of wine on the ground when someone from their group (*parea*) is dancing.

45 *Methexis* (koinonia, metalipsis): communion; people participating in a ritual and reaching a state of extreme egalitarianism and communication through sharing in collectivity (Vostanjoglou op. cit.).

46 See Bales (op. cit.) for Ireland; Mercês de Mello *et al.* (1992) for Portugal; Gili-Miner *et al.* (1992) for Spain; Cooper and Heath (1987) and Lolli *et al.* (1958) for Italy; and Blum and Blum (1965, 1970) and Gefou-Madianou (1992) for Greece.

47 By contrast, the younger generation of feminists deplores such activities. Shunning the domestic role, they seek, with questionable success, to achieve a 'male' type of transcendence through alcohol drinking: see above.

48 Tapper (1983) in her work in a Turkish town points out the class orientation of women's household gatherings; they tend to invite and be invited by the wives of their husbands' friends.

49 See Bjerén (this volume).

50 See Stewart (this volume).

51 Bloch and Parry introduce the disjunction of fertility to sexuality by discussing instances where this dissociation is accomplished by denying or suppressing 'the biological fact that human reproduction is the consequence of human sexuality', and in other cases by associating female sexuality with death. By fertility they understand the broader terms of 'fecundity' and 'productiveness' (1982: pp. 7, 18, 19).

52 See, for example, Campbell (op. cit.), Herzfeld (op. cit.), Hirschon (op. cit.), Dubisch (op. cit.).

53 By family rituals I mean everyday and/or Sunday meals, important Christian holidays (e.g. Christmas, New Year, Easter) *Apokries* (carnival), or the village saint's festival, during which members of extended families, who do not necessarily live under the same roof, exchange visits.

54 The distinction between family and household rituals is needed; though they both take place in the household, the first do not involve an invitation and are less formal while the second involve reciprocity and some kind of competition and hierarchy: e.g. baptisms, engagements, weddings, nameday dinner parties.

55 Wine represents life in the Orthodox Church (Drower 1956); for a meal to be complete bread, which symbolizes the body, and wine, which symbolizes the blood of Christ, are both needed. Campbell emphasizes the importance of both in wedding feasts among the Sarakatsani shepherds who drink excessively for four days and who also consider wine 'the life fluid' (1964: 117).

56 Much in the manner of the discourse which is created through the consumption of alcohol. In Mediterranean societies households and coffeeshops hold a very important role in community lives. Household drinking gatherings offer opportunities for these two antagonistic worlds to unite.

57 It might be said that, though the nuns live in an all-female context, they can only receive the divine food and drink from the hands of a male priest, thereby portraying the spiritual unity between men and women through priest and nun. In monasteries, especially those in isolated areas such as Mount Athos, which

prohibit entry to women, this uniting of genders might not be so clearly marked. Monks receive Holy Communion from male priests. Yet it should be noted that the patron of Mount Athos is the Virgin Mary. It is she who in many narratives is said to have kept over-inquisitive women from landing on the shores of this male refuge.

58 You could simply note the difference between wine in Iossifides' material and sweet wine in Gefou-Madianou's material.

59 A link between the monastery and the coffeehouse has been made by Loizos and Papataxiarchis (1991). Both constitute loci for same-sex gatherings and both seek the true spiritual self.

60 See Peace for bars on the pier, Gefou-Madianou for coffeehouses and wine cellars, Bjerén for home and Stewart for open-space alcohol drinking, all included in this volume.

61 See also Komninou and Papataxiarchis (1990).

62 The reason for the refusal by men of different classes, as well as brothers, or fathers and sons, to drink together in bars or coffeehouses is explained by this; their status expresses hierarchy (Peace, Iossifides, Gefou-Madianou, this volume).

63 In a bounded occupational group like fishermen in Ireland it is essential to maintain some kind of equality. The pressure to spend capital in drinking spells which last for days on the pier may be explained by the pressure to avoid differences in wealth which would lead to differences in interests (Peace, this volume). The same holds true for the wine-producing community in Messogia, Greece, where low-income wine producers depend on each other's families for periods of intensive labour like *trygos* (harvesting grapes).

64 See Dennis (1975), Robbins (1979).

65 See Gefou-Madianou (this volume).

66 ibid.

67 Peace (this volume) gives a good example of fishermen in contrast with farmers or local authorities.

68 See Bjerén (this volume); also Ahlström (1976).

69 As Bourdieu puts it (1977:203): 'the personification of collectives' or 'collective consciousness: by crediting groups or institutions with dispositions which can be constituted only in individual consciousness, even when they are the product of collective conditions'.

70 The Protestant ethic holds that alcohol is so repugnant spiritually that it is not allowed even symbolically in the Communion rite (Mandelbaum 1965).

71 See Gusfield (1987); also Bjerén (this volume).

72 ibid.

73 ibid. See also Simmons (1962); see also Tsaoussis (1980) for a similar discussion concerning illicit drugs. Abraham Myerson (1940) gave an accurate definition of 'social ambivalence' in regard to alcohol: 'a condition which limits the development of stable attitudes toward drinking, restricts the meaning of the act to a hedonistic alternative, and insulates it from effective social controls. The upshot when drinking takes place is purported to be the kind of extreme and uncontrolled behavior the effect of which is to intensify the conflict and polarization of attitudes, activating a vicious circle of cause and effect' (p.17).

74 See Marx and Engels on the free development of individuals in *German Ideology*: they consider that the individual is created through opposition and in

collectivity which is historically determined; lack of it may lead to alienation (1970: 117).
75 See Bourdieu (1977: 203).
76 It is not that these communities are unaware that alcohol may lead to 'drunkenness' and inebriation, nor that they have not found ways to regulate its abuse, often through rituals or even social condemnation. The criteria used locally are in many cases 'different' from those used scientifically. Drunkenness, for example, is highly valued and socially desirable in certain social rituals that take place in same-sex gatherings in various communities that are discussed in this volume, especially Greece.

REFERENCES

Agar, M., Bennett, L., Heath, D. and Marshall, M. 'CA comment on alcohol and ethnography: a case of problem deflation?' (by Robin Room) in *Current Anthropology* 25, p.178–84.

Ahlström-Laakso, S. (1976) 'European drinking habits: a review of the research and some suggestions for conceptual integration of findings' in M.W. Everett, J.O. Waddell and D.B. Heath (eds) *Cross-Cultural Approaches to the Study of Alcohol: An Interdisciplinary Perspective*, The Hague: Mouton, 119–132.

Allen, P. (1985) 'Appollo and Dionysus: alcohol use in modern Greece', *East European Quarterly*, Vol. XVIII, No 4, pp.461–480.

Anderson, P. (1990) *Management of Drinking Problems*, WHO Regional Publications, European Series, No 32, Copenhagen: WHO.

Anderson, R.K., Serrano, G. and Payne, G. (1946) 'A study of the nutritional status and food habits of Otomi Indians in the Mezquital valley of Mexico', *American Journal of Public Health*, 36, pp. 883–903.

Arensberg, C.M. (1937) *The Irish Countryman*, New York: Macmillan.

Bales, R.F. (1962) 'Attitudes toward drinking in the Irish culture' in D.J. Pittman and C.R. Snyder (1962) (eds), *Society, Culture and Drinking Patterns*, (op. cit.) pp.157–187.

Beck, S. (1985) 'Changing styles of drinking: alcohol use in the Balkans', *East European Quarterly*, Vol. XVIII, No 4, pp. 395–413.

Bennett, L. (1985) 'Treating alcoholism in a Yugoslav fashion', *East European Quarterly*: Issue on 'Ethnography, Alcohol, and South-Central European Societies', Vol. XVIII, No 4, pp.495–519.

Bennett, L. (1989) 'Family Alcohol and Culture' in M. Galanter (ed.) *Recent Developments in Alcoholism*, New York: Plenum.

Bennett, L., Wolin, S. and McAvity, K.J. (1988) 'Family identity, ritual and myth: a cultural perspective on life cycle transition', *Family Transitions*, New York: The Guildford Press.

Bloch, M. and Parry, J. (eds) (1982) *Death and the Regeneration of Life*, Cambridge: Cambridge University Press.

Blum, R. and Blum, E. (1965) *Health and Healing in Rural Greece*, Stanford, California: Stanford University Press.

Blum, R. and Blum, E. (1970) *The Dangerous Hour: The Love of Crisis and Mystery in Rural Greece*, London: Chatto & Windus.

Bourdieu, P. (1977) *Outline of a Theory of Practice* (translated by R. Nice), Cambridge: Cambridge University Press.

Brandes, S.H. (1981) 'Like wounded stags: male sexual ideology in an Andalusian town' in S.B. Ortner and H. Whitehead (eds) *Sexual Meanings: The Cultural Construction of Gender and Sexuality*, Cambridge: Cambridge University Press.

Brandes, S.H. (1979) 'Drinking patterns and alcohol control in a Castilian mountain village', *Anthropology* 3:1–16.

Brandes, S.H. (1980) *Metaphors of Masculinity: Sex and Status in Andalusian Folklore*, University of Pennsylvania Press.

Bruun, K. (1959) 'The significance of roles and norms in the small group for individual behavioral changes while drinking', *Quarterly Journal of Studies on Alcohol*, Vol. 20, pp.53–64.

Bruun, K., Edwards, G., Lumio, M., Mäkelä, K., Pan, L., Bopham, R., Room, R., Schmidt, W., Skog, O.-J., Sulkumen, P. and Osterberg, E. (1975) *Alcohol Control Policies in Public Health Perspective*, The Finnish Foundation for Alcohol Studies, Vol. 25. Distributors: Rutgers University Center of Alcohol Studies, New Brunswick, N.J., USA; The Finnish Foundation for A.S., Helsinki, Finland.

Bunzel, R. (1940) 'The role of alcoholism in two central American cultures', *Psychiatry*, 3, pp.361–387.

Campbell, J. (1964) *Honour, Family and Patronage: A Study of Institutions and Moral Values in a Greek Mountain Community*, Oxford: Clarendon Press.

Campbell, J. (1966) 'Honour and the Devil' in J. Peristiany (ed.) *Honour and Shame*, Chicago: University of Chicago Press, pp.139–170.

Caplan, P. (ed.) (1987) *The Cultural Construction of Sexuality*, London: Tavistock.

Carstairs, G.M. (1954) 'Daru and bhang: cultural factors in the choice of intoxic-ant', *Quarterly Journal of Studies on Alcohol*, 15, pp.220–237.

Christian, Jr., W.A. (1972) *Person and God in a Spanish Valley* (new edn 1989), Princeton, N.J.: Princeton University Press.

Clinard, M.B. (1962) 'The public drinking house and society' in D.J. Pittman and C.R. Snyder (eds) *Society, Culture and Drinking Patterns*, London: Southern Illinois University Press, pp.270–292.

Colson, E. and Scudder, T. (1988) *For Prayer and Profit. The Ritual, Economic and Social Importance of Beer in Gwembe District, Zambia, 1950–1982*, Stanford, California: Stanford University Press.

Cooper, A.M. and Heath, D. (1987) 'Italian drinking patterns: model for theories and policies'. Paper presented at the International Conference on Alcohol and Social Science, Torino, Italy, 30 Sept.–3 Oct. 1987.

Cowan, J. (1990) *Dance and the Body Politic in Northern Greece*, Princeton, N.J.: Princeton University Press.

Davies, P. and Walsh, D. (1983) *Alcohol Problems and Alcohol Control in Europe*, London and Canberra: Croom Helm; New York: Gardner Press.

Davis, J. (1973) *Land and Family in Pisticci*, London: Athlone.

Dennis, P.A. (1975) 'The role of the Drunk in an Oaxacan village', *American Anthropologist*, Vol. 77, No 3, 1975.

Dimen, M. (1986) 'Servants and sentries: women, power and social production in Kriovrisi' in J. Dubisch (ed.) *Gender and Power in Rural Greece*, Princeton, N.J.: Princeton University Press.

Dolgin, J., Kemnitzer, D.S. and Schneïder (1977) 'As people express their lives, so they are . . .' (Introduction), in J. Dolgin, D.S. Kemnitzer and Schneïder (eds) *Symbolic Anthropology: A Reader in the Study of Symbols and Meanings*, New York: Columbia University Press, pp.3–44.

Douglas, M. (1975) *Implicit Meanings: Essays in Anthropology*, London: Routledge & Kegan Paul.

Douglas, M. (1987) *Constructive Drinking: Perspectives on Drink from Anthropology*, Cambridge: Cambridge University Press.

Driessen, H. (1983) 'Male Sociability and Rituals of Masculinity in Rural Andalusia', *Anthropological Quarterly*, 56:116–24.

Drower, E.S. (1956) *Water into Wine*, London: John Murray.

du Boulay, J. (1976) 'Lies, mockery and family integrity' in J.G. Peristiany (ed.) *Mediterranean Family Structures*, Cambridge: Cambridge University Press, pp.389–406.

du Boulay, J. (1986) 'Women – Images of their nature and destiny in rural Greece' in J. Dubisch (ed.) *Gender and Power in Rural Greece*, Princeton, N.J.: Princeton University Press.

du Boulay, J. (1991) 'Cosmos and gender in village Greece' in P. Loizos and E. Papataxiarchis (eds) *Contested Identities*, Princeton, N.J.: Princeton University Press, pp.47–78.

Dubisch, J. (1986) 'Culture enters through the kitchen: women, food and social boundaries in rural Greece' in J. Dubisch (ed.) *Gender and Power in Rural Greece*, Princeton, N.J.: Princeton University Press.

Dubisch, J. (1991) 'Gender, kinship and religion: "Reconstructing" the Anthropology of Greece', in P. Loizos and E. Papataxiarchis (eds) *Contested Identities*, Princeton, N.J.: Princeton University Press.

Durkheim, E. (1951) *Suicide: A Study in Sociology* (translated by J.A. Spaulding and G. Simpson), London: Free Press, Macmillan.

Everett, M.E., Waddell, J.O. and Heath, D.B. (eds) (1976) *Cultural Approaches to the Study of Alcohol: An Interdisciplinary Perspective*, The Hague and Paris: Mouton.

Foucault, M. (1978) *The History of Sexuality Vol. 1. An Introduction* (translated by R. Hurley), New York: Vintage Books.

Frake, C.O. (1964) 'How to ask for a drink in Subanun', *American Anthropologist*, Vol. 66: 6, pp.127–32.

Geertz, C. (1973) *The Interpretation of Cultures: Selected Essays*, New York: Basic Books.

Gefou-Madianou, D. (1988) 'Alcohol consumer's consciousness: an anthropological approach'. Paper presented at the CEC meeting on 'Alcohol: Methodological Issues in Community Studies', Brussels, 14–15 April; also (1989) Report No 88, Prepared for the Commission of the European Communities – Directorate General: Employment, Social Affairs and Education.

Gefou-Madianou, D. (1991) 'L'Etude Anthropologique de l'Usage des Drogue: L'Usage de l'Alcool en Greece' in *Retrovirus*, t. IV, Mars 1991 No 9.

Gefou-Madianou, D. (1992) 'Country report – Greece', WHO Collaborative Study on *Community Responses to Alcohol-Related Problems*, WHO Document No ICP/ADA 017, Copenhagen: WHO (in press).

Gibson, J.A. and Weinberg, D. (1980) 'In vino communitas: wine and identity in a Swiss alpine village', *Anthropological Quarterly*, 53, No 2, pp.111–121.

Gili-Miner, M., Giler-Ubago, J. and Tinto, A. (1992) 'Country report – Spain', WHO Collaborative Study on *Community Response to Alcohol-Related Problems*, WHO Document No ICP/ADA 017, Copenhagen: WHO (in press).

Gilmore, D. (1977) 'The social organization of space', *American Ethnologist*, 4: 437–51.

Gilmore, D. (1985) 'The role of the bar in Andalusian rural society: observations on political culture under Franco' in *Journal of Anthropological Research*, Vol. 41, pp.263–277.

Gilmore, D. (ed.) (1987) *Honour and Shame and the Unity of the Mediterranean*, A special publication of the A.A.A. No 22, Washington, D.C.: American Anthropological Association.

Gilmore, M. and Gilmore, D. (1979) 'Machismo: A psychodynamic approach', *Journal of Psychological Anthropology*, 2:3, pp.281–299.

Giovannini, M. (1981) 'Woman: A dominant symbol within the cultural system of a Sicilian town', *Man*, Vol. 16, pp.408–426.

Grant, M. (ed.) (1985) *Alcohol Policies*, WHO Regional Publications, European Series No 18, Copenhagen: WHO Regional Office for Europe.

Gregor, T. (1987) 'Men's Clubs: No Girls Allowed' in Spradley and McCurdy (eds) *Conformity and Conflict: Readings in Cultural Anthropology*, Boston, Toronto: Little, Brown and Co., pp.177–183.

Gusfield, J. (1987) 'Passage to Play: rituals of drinking time in American society' in M. Douglas (ed.) *Constructive Drinking: Perspectives on Drink from Anthropology*, Cambridge: Cambridge University Press.

Hansen, E.C. (1976) 'Drinking to prosperity: the role of bar culture and coalition formation in a modernization of the Alto Panadés' in J. Aceves *et al.* (eds) *Queens College Papers in Anthropology*, 2, pp.42–51.

Harrison, B. (1971) *Drink and the Victorians: The Temperance Question in England, 1815–1872*, London: Faber and Faber.

Harrison, B. and Trinder, B. (1969) 'Drink and sobriety in an early Victorian country town: Banbury 1830–1869', *English Historical Review*, supplement 4: 1–72.

Heath, D. (1976) 'Anthropological perspectives on alcohol: an historical review' in M.W. Everett, J.O. Waddell and D.B. Heath (eds) *Cross-Cultural Approaches to the Study of Alcohol*, The Hague: Mouton.

Heath, D. (1986) 'Anthropology and alcohol studies: current issues', *Annual Review of Anthropology*, 16:99–120.

Herzfeld, M. (1985) *The Poetics of Manhood: Contest and Identity in a Cretan Mountain Village*, Princeton, N.J.: Princeton University Press.

Hirschon, R. (1978) 'Open body/closed space: the transformation of female sexuality' in Shirley Andener (ed.) *Defining Females*, New York: John Wiley and Sons, pp.66–88.

Hirschon, R. (1989) *Heirs of the Greek Catastrophe: The Social Life of Asia Minor Refugees in Piraeus*, Oxford: Clarendon Press.

Honigmann, J. (1963) 'Dynamics of drinking in an Austrian village', *Ethnology* 2, pp.157–196.

Honigmann, J. and Honigmann, I. (1965) 'How Baffin Island Eskimos have learned to drink', *Social Forces*, 44, pp.73–83.

Horton, D.J. (1943) 'The functions of alcohol in primitive societies: a cross-cultural study', *Quarterly Journal of Studies on Alcohol*, 4, pp.199–320.

Iossifides, A.M. (1990) 'Earthly Lives and Life Everlasting: Secular and Religious Values in two Convents and a Village in Western Greece', Ph.D. thesis, Department of Anthropology, London School of Economics and Political Sciences, London.

Iossifides, A.M. (1991) 'Sisters in Christ: Metaphors of Kinship among Greek Nuns' in P. Loizos and E. Papataxiarchis (eds) *Contested Identities*, Princeton, N.J.: Princeton University Press.

Jellinek, E.M. (1941) 'Immanuel Kant on drinking', *Quarterly Journal of Studies on Alcohol* 1, pp.777–78.

Keller, M. (1970) 'The great Jewish drink mystery', *British Journal of Addiction*, 64: 287–296.

Kerewsky-Halpern, B. (1985) 'Rakia as ritual in rural Serbia', *East European Quarterly*, Vol. XVIII, 4, pp.481–494.

Komninou, M. and Papataxiarchis, E. (eds) (1990) *Community, Society and Ideology: C. Karavidas and the Question of Social Sciences*, Athens: Papazisis.

Lakoff, G. and Johnson, M. (1980) *Metaphors We Live By*, Chicago and London: The University of Chicago Press.

Leacock, S. (1964) 'Ceremonial drinking in an Afro-Brazilian Cult', *American Anthropologist* No 66, 344–54.

Loizos, P. and Papataxiarchis, E. (eds) (1991) *Contested Identities: Gender and Kinship in Modern Greece*, Princeton, N.J.: Princeton University Press.

Loizos, P. and Papataxiarchis, E. (1991a) 'Gender, sexuality, and the person in Greek culture' in P. Loizos and E. Papataxiarchis (eds) *Contested Identities*, Princeton, N.J.: Princeton University Press.

Loizos, P. and Papataxiarchis, E. (1991b) 'Introduction: gender and kinship in marriage and alternative contexts' in P. Loizos and E. Papataxiarchis (eds) *Contested Identities: Gender and Kinship in Modern Greece*, Princeton, N.J.: Princeton University Press.

Lolli, G., Serriani, E., Golder, G. and Luzzatto-Fegiz, P. (1958) *Alcohol in Italian Culture: Food and Wine in Relation to Sobriety among Italians and Italian Americans*, Monograph No 3, New Haven: Yale Centre of Alcohol Study.

MacAndrew, C. and Edgerton, R.B. (1969) *Drunken Comportment: A Social Explanation*, Chicago: Aldine.

McCarthy, R. (ed.) (1959) *Drinking and Intoxication: Selected Readings in Social Attitudes and Controls*, Glencoe, Ill.: Free Press.

McClelland, D., Davis, W., Kalin, R. and Wanner, E. (1972) *The Drinking Man*, New York: Free Press.

MacCormack, C.P. and Strathern, M. (eds) (1980) *Nature, Culture and Gender*, Cambridge: Cambridge University Press.

Madsen, W. and Madsen, C. (1969) 'The cultural structure of Mexican drinking behavior', *Quarterly Journal of Studies on Alcohol* 30(3):701–18.

Mäkelä, K. *et al.* (1981) *Alcohol, Society, and the State, vol. 1: A Comparative Study of Alcohol Control*, Toronto, Canada: Addiction Research Foundation.

Mandelbaum, D.G. (1965) 'Alcohol and culture', *Current Anthropology*, Vol. 6, No 3, pp.281–293.

Mars, G. (1987) 'Longshore drinking, economic security and union politics in Newfoundland' in M. Douglas (ed.) *Constructive Drinking: Perspectives on Drink from Anthropology*, Cambridge: Cambridge University Press.

Marshall, M. and Marshall, L. (1975) 'Opening Pandora's bottle: reconstructing Micronesians' early contacts with alcoholic beverages', *Journal of the Polynesian Society* 84:441–65.

Marshall, Mac (ed.) (1979) *Beliefs, Behaviours and Alcoholic Beverages: A Cross-cultural Survey*, Ann Arbor: The University of Michigan Press.

Marshall, Mac (1979a) *Weekend Warriors, Alcohol in a Micronesian Culture*, California: Mayfield Publishing Company.

Marshall, Mac (1989) Book review: 'Constructive drinking: perspectives on drink from anthropology', in *American Ethnologist*, Vol. 16, No 3.

Marx, K., and Engels, F. (1970) *The German Ideology Part I, With Selections from Parts II and III and Supplementary Texts*, Introduction to a Critique of Political Economy, C.J. Arthur (ed.), New York: International Publishers.

Mercês de Mello, M.L. *et al.* (1992) 'Country report – Portugal', WHO Collaborative Study on *Community Response To Alcohol-Related Problems*, WHO Document No ICP/ADA 017, Copenhagen: WHO (in press).

Myerhoff, B. (1986) '"Life not death in Venice": its second life' in V.W. Turner and E.M. Bruner (eds) *The Anthropology of Experience*, pp.231–261.

Myerson, A. (1940) 'Alcohol: a study of social ambivalence', *Quarterly Journal of Studies on Alcohol*, Vol. 1, p.13–20.

Myrmiroglou, V. (1940) *The Dervisses*, Athens: Ekati.

Ngokwey, N. (1987) 'Varieties of palm wine among the Lele of the Kasai' in M. Douglas (ed.) *Constructive Drinking: Perspectives on Drink from Anthropology*, Cambridge University Press, pp. 113–21.

Papageorgis, C. (1987) *'Peri Methys' – About Drunkenness*, Athens: Roes.

Papataxiarchis, E. (1988) 'Kinship, friendship and gender relations in two East Aegean village communities (Lesbos, Greece)', Ph.D. thesis, Department of Anthropology, London School of Economics and Political Science, London.

Papataxiarchis, E. (1991) 'Friends of the heart: male commensal solidarity gender, and kinship in Aegean Greece' in P. Loizos and E. Papataxiarchis (eds) *Contested Identities: Gender and Kinship in Modern Greece*, Princeton, N.J.: Princeton University Press.

Park, J. (1990) 'Only 'those' women: women and the control of alcohol in New Zealand', *Contemporary Drug Problems*, Vol. 17, No 2.

Partanen, J. and Montonen, M. (1988) *Alcohol and the Mass Media*, EURO Reports and Studies 108. Copenhagen: WHO Regional Office for Europe.

Peristiany, J. (ed.) (1966) *Honour and Shame: The Values of Mediterranean Society* (Midway reprint 1974), Chicago: University of Chicago Press.

Pina-Cabral, J. (1986) *Sons of Adam, Daughters of Eve: the peasant worldview of the Alto Minho*, Oxford: Clarendon Press.

Pinson, A. (1985) 'The institution of friendship and drinking patterns in Iceland', *Anthropological Quarterly*, Vol. 58, pp.75–82.

Pittman, D.J. and Snyder, C.R. (eds) (1962) *Society, Culture, and Drinking Patterns*, Carbondale: Southern Illinois University Press.

Plant, M. (ed.) (1989) *Alcohol-Related Problems in High-Risk Groups. Report on a WHO Study*, EURO Reports and Studies 109, Copenhagen: WHO Regional Office for Europe.

Plant, M., Goos, C., Keup, W. and Österberg, E. (eds) (1990) *Alcohol and Drugs Research and Policy*, WHO-Europe, Edinburgh: Edinburgh University Press.

Plant, M.L. (1990) 'Women and alcohol: A review of international literature on the use of alcohol by females', WHO-Europe, EUR/ICP/ADA 020.

Porter, L., Arif, A.E. and Curran, W.J. (1986) *The Law and the Treatment of Drug- and Alcohol-Dependent Persons*, Geneva: WHO.

Reiter, R.R. (ed.) (1975) *Toward an Anthropology of Women*, New York: Monthly Review Press.

Ritson, B.E. (1985) *Community Response to Alcohol-Related Problems. Review of an International Study*, Public Health Papers No 81, Geneva: WHO.

Robbins, R.H. (1979) 'Alcohol and the identity struggle: some effects of economic change on inter-personal relations' in M. Marshall (ed.) *Beliefs, Behaviors, and*

Alcoholic Beverage: A Cross-Cultural Survey, Michigan: University of Michigan Press, pp.158–190.

Robins, L.N., Bates, W.M. and O'Neil, P. (1962) 'Adult drinking patterns of former problem children' in D.J. Pittman and C.R. Snyder (eds) *Society, Culture, and Drinking Patterns*, Carbondale: Southern Illinois University Press.

Roman, P. (1985) 'Alcoholism' in A. Kuper and J. Kuper (eds) *The Social Science Encyclopedia*, London and New York: Routledge & Kegan Paul.

Room, R. (1984) 'Alcohol and Ethnography: A case of Problem Deflation?' *Current Anthropology*, Vol. 25, No 2, pp.169–191.

Simmons, O.G. (1962) 'Ambivalence and the learning of drinking behavior in a Peruvian community' in D.J. Pittman and C.R. Snyder (eds) *Society, Culture, and Drinking Patterns*, Carbondale: Southern Illinois University Press.

Singer, K. (1972) 'Drinking patterns and alcoholism in the Chinese', *British Journal of Addiction* 67, pp.3–14.

Single, E., Morgan, P. and de Lint, J. (1981) *Alcohol, Society and the State, Vol. 2: The Social History of Control Policy in Seven Countries*, Toronto, Canada: Addiction Research Foundation.

Skog, O. and Waahlberg, R. (eds) (1988) *Alcohol and Drugs: The Norwegian Experience*, Switzerland: ICAA.

Snyder, C.R. (1962) 'Culture and the Jewish sobriety: the ingroup–outgroup factor' in D.J. Pittman and C.R. Snyder (eds) *Society, Culture and Drinking*, pp.188–225.

Snyder, C.R. (1978) *Alcohol and the Jews*, Carbondale: Southern Illinois University Press.

Tapper, N. (1983) 'Gender and religion in a Turkish Town: a comparison of two types of formal women's gatherings' in P. Holden (ed.) *Women's Religious Experience*, London and Canberra: Croom Helm.

Thornton, M.A. (1987) 'Sekt versus schnapps in an Austrian village' in M. Douglas (ed.) *Constructive Drinking: Perspectives on Drink from Anthropology*, Cambridge: Cambridge University Press.

Tsaoussis, D. (1980) 'Ta Narkotika san kinoniko provlima' (Drugs as a Social Problem), *Eklogi (Issues in Social Welfare)*, Vol. 52, pp.81–92.

Waddell, J.O. (1973) 'Drink friend! Social contexts of convivial drinking and drunkenness among Papago Indians in an urban setting', in *Proceedings of First Annual Institute of Alcohol Abuse and Alcoholism*, New York.

Westermeyer, J. (1979) 'The drunken Indian: myth and realities' in M. Marshall (ed.) *Beliefs, Behaviors and Alcoholic Beverages: A Cross-cultural Survey*, Ann Arbor: The University of Michigan Press.

WHO (in press) *Responding To Alcohol Related Problems* (based on the WHO Collaborative Study: Community Response to Alcohol-Related Problems) D. Gefou-Madianou, U.J. Hannibal, J. Moskalewicz, B. Ritson, M. Rud and T. Van Iwaarden (eds), ICP/ADA 017, Copenhagen: WHO Regional Office for Europe.

WHO Expert Committee on Mental Health (1951) 'Report on the first session of the alcohol subcommittee', WHO Technical Report Series 42, Geneva: WHO.

WHO Expert Committee on Mental Health (1952) 'Second report of the alcoholism subcommittee', WHO Technical Report Series 48, Geneva: WHO.

Yamamuro, B. (1954) 'Notes on drinking in Japan', *Quarterly Journal of Studies on Alcohol*, 15, pp.491–498.

2 Female entertainers in Egypt
Drinking and gender roles

Karin van Nieuwkerk

In Egypt, drinking and entertainment usually go hand in hand. There are not many public places solely for drinking. Bars in hotels are one of the few exceptions, but only foreigners and the upper class can afford to have a drink there. Drinking is done either in night-clubs or at home on festive occasions. At both places, there is a programme with singing, dancing, and music for the drinker as well.

Drinking is strongly condemned in Islam. This view is shared by most Egyptians, yet more strictly applied to women. For women, it is considered immoral and unfeminine. Despite the strong condemnation of alcohol, many men and even some women do sometimes drink. Female entertainers are particularly associated with drinking. Although they do not always do it themselves, they are often viewed as 'inciting' others to drink and related 'vices'.

I conducted field work on the position and status of female entertainers in Egypt. Drinking and performing in places where alcohol is served is one of the factors negatively influencing their reputation. Female entertainers, however, have their own reasons for engaging in this 'unfeminine activity'.

I shall try to clarify the relation between drinking, entertainment and gender. Firstly, I shall summarize the religious views on drinking and entertainment as regards both sexes. Secondly, I shall describe the two main contexts of drinking and entertainment, night-clubs and popular weddings. Lastly, I shall discuss the relation between drinking, gender and respectability as perceived by female entertainers themselves.

RELIGION, DRINKING AND ENTERTAINMENT

In Islam, alcohol is strictly forbidden, *harâm*. At the time of the Prophet, the people of Mecca and Medina were used to drinking wine to the extent that many of them made mistakes in the ritual prayers of the newly established religion. Moreover, drinking went hand in hand with other 'vices' such as gambling and entertainment. This resulted in a revelation prohibiting wine and gambling as the work of Satan.[1]

Sharab, the Arabic verb to drink, pertains to smoking as well as drinking. The frequent use of the water pipe for tobacco and hashish was probably what made smoking similar to drinking. No Qur'ānic verse explicitly referred to the permissibility of tobacco and hashish. Legal scholars tried to prohibit the use of hashish by analogy,[2] stating that its effect was similar to that of alcohol. Both of them changed the consumer into an intoxicated person, according to the accepted fourteenth-century definition: 'someone whose orderly speech is confused and who spills his hidden secret, or someone who does not know heaven from earth or length from width' (Rosenthal 1971:107). The lawfulness of tobacco, like that of coffee, especially shortly after their introduction in the early seventeenth and sixteenth centuries respectively, was debated as well (Chelebi 1957: 51–60, Hattox 1985). Yet, since there was no legal ground in the Qur'ān, hashish and tobacco were put in the category of the rejected, *makrûh*, not of the forbidden, *harâm*.

Smoking is very common among men and, just as offering tea and coffee, a cheap way of socializing and establishing contact. Drinking is less frequently done and is not a regular habit among most men. Yet, many men do drink on special occasions such as weddings and some men occasionally visit a night-club. Although drinking is forbidden in Islam and condemned for both sexes, in practice it is less frowned upon in men since, as Egyptian women often say:'whatever a man does, a man is a man, nothing is shameful for him'. Smoking, in belonging to the category of rejected things, leaves even more leeway for social and ideological interpretation. In practice, restriction is applied only to females.[3] For women accordingly, both smoking and drinking are considered extremely improper and only a few fearless women engage in them publicly. Now and then an older market woman can be spotted smoking a cigarette or a water pipe. 'Ordinary' women, however, can smoke only at home if their husbands allow them to. Drinking is very rare and seldom done in public.

Of all mood-changing substances, alcohol is considered the worst. Moreover, it was and is served in places where other bad things happen, particularly singing and dancing. According to the seventeenth-century Muslim scholar, Chelebi, who summarized the religious views on singing and music, three categories of music could be distinguished: coming from birds, from the human throat and from instruments. He stated that in Islam:

> The exponents of the sacred law have categorized it is perfectly permissible to listen to the melodies produced by birds, and have allowed those produced by human throats, subject to certain conditions and rules. But

. . . to listen to the instruments that are blown or struck is never permissible.

(Chelebi 1957: 38)

Certain instruments were forbidden because they were supposed to incite drinking. The *kûba*, an oblong drum, for instance, was prohibited because of the association with wine, licentious songs and dissolute people. With respect to the human throat, if it produced songs about wine and debauchery, it was not permissible to listen to them (*idem*:39).[4]

In addition to the contents of songs, the lawfulness of singing was to a large extent related to the sex of the singer. Up to the beginning of the twentieth century, most female singers and female musicians only performed in front of women. If they had a male audience, they were usually separated from them by a screen or were heavily veiled. Yet, as the eleventh-century scholar al-Ghazâlî clarified, listening to the voice of concealed female performers was still forbidden if it could evoke tempting images. Looking at female singers and other female performers was always unlawful. Excitement aroused by looking was considered more powerful than excitement aroused by listening (al-Ghazâlî 1901:235–237). Accordingly, female singing and, even more so, female dancing in front of a male audience were categorized as *harâm*.

The underlying reason for the prohibition of alcohol, other stimulants and female entertainment is that the state of intoxication or excitement is incompatible with the worship of God. The love of God should be restricted to Him alone and cannot be shared with anyone or anything else (*idem*: 233). This would disrupt the order of God and cause *fitna*, chaos. Women in general and female entertainers in particular are assumed to provoke men easily into abandonment and negligence and are thus feared for their disruptive potential (Mernissi 1975, Sabbah 1984).

Since drinking and female entertainment were strongly linked, they adversely affected each other. The reputation of entertainers was lowered because they were associated with participating in drinking and performing for a drunken audience. Drinking became suspicious because it was done in places where other 'vices' such as 'sexual excitement' occurred. The coincident drinking and light-hearted amusements in present-day Egypt occur particularly in night-clubs and at popular weddings.

DRINKING AND NIGHT-CLUBS

The first night-clubs were founded around the turn of the twentieth century. In the twenties and thirties, their number quickly increased and a concentration of foreign bars and Egyptian night-clubs developed in the centre of

Cairo. The main task of female entertainers was to sit and drink with customers. Usually they first sang or danced on the stage and if they were admired by a client he ordered them to sit at his table and opened bottles of champagne, whisky or beer for them. Some of them walked around and invited themselves for a drink. This system of sitting and drinking with customers was called *fath*, from the Arabic verb 'to open'. It was the most profitable part of the job, for the night-club owner as well. Therefore some female entertainers were mainly engaged in 'opening' and were reluctant to leave the tables for the stage. According to a journalist of an Egyptian art magazine, one of the night-club owners had to hire four new girls in order to fill the stage because his regular girls refused to perform (*Magalla al-Funûn* 24–7–1933:20). Sometimes they were said to be too drunk to dance. The female entertainers received a percentage of the profits accrued from their own offered drinks and the amount they made the customers consume. Their salary as performers was low since it was expected that they would supplement it with gains from drinking. Probably at least half the income was earned from *fath*.[5]

During the First World War, Cairo became a war base and a garrison populated with British, Australian and other troops. In the interbellum period, British troops remained stationed in order to protect British interests in the Suez Canal. Cairo was thus full of soldiers and officers who spent their evenings in night-clubs. The continuing bad economic situation during the World Crisis started to spark off criticism. Spending lavishly in times of need was under attack (*al-Malâhî al-Musawwara* 22–7–1932:7). In 1933, the government made a half-hearted attempt to restrict belly-dancing and *fath*. The foreign bars and night-clubs were left undisturbed since they were protected by the Capitulations, the legal agreements which gave foreigners the right to be tried in their own consular courts. Egyptian owners and journalists, united in a nationalist spirit, strongly opposed the legal inequality (*Magalla al-Funûn* 10–12–1933:13, *Kawâkib* 1–1–1934: 3). The patriotic protest had a short-lived effect since soon all owners and performers evaded the regulations once again. The observance depended heavily on the vigilance of the police, resulting in periods of open sitting and drinking with customers alternated with hidden *fath* and whisky in tea cups (*Rûz al-Yûsif* 12–3–1934: 32).

The Second World War brought another boom to the night-clubs. Pyramid Street became a new and more luxurious area for nightlife, but the clubs in the centre were filled with British officers as well. In order to please them, the dancer Shûshû Barûdî renamed belly-dancing 'the dance of the Allies and the Success of Democracy' (*Rûz al-Yûsif* 2–12–1943:18). As during the First World War, the sight of soldiers in search of bars, night-clubs and brothels was a thorn in the side of the population, particularly of the Muslim Brothers 'who were outraged that their poorer women were opting for a life of sin through the lure of British gold' (Marsot 1985:100).

After the war, a new campaign was launched against prostitution and night-clubs. In 1949, prostitution was made a criminal act. In 1951, sitting and drinking with customers was officially forbidden. A new article added to the law on public places stipulated that 'it is not permitted to allow women who are employed in a public place, nor those who perform theatrical acts, to sit with the customers of the shop nor to eat, drink or dance with them'. Under Nasser's reign, belly-dancers were seen as a bad advertisement for Arab Muslim womanhood. They were required to wear modest costumes. The naked midriff was no longer permitted, it had to be covered with material (Buonaventura 1983:108–109). The new regulations were generally evaded once more. The belly was covered with skin-coloured chiffon and later with net leotard, a token piece of material. *Fath* went on, and red lamps and ringing bells warned the girls of a vice squad raid.

Fath was eventually abolished under Sadat. In 1973, a new system of registration and licences was initiated. To obtain a licence, female performers had to pass an examination by which they proved to be real singers or dancers. In addition, they were listed by the police and became taxable. Dress prescriptions were sharpened, and side slits had to be closed up to the knees. Behaviour with customers was restricted. Not only were sitting and drinking with customers things of the past, but the government made dancing, laughing and talking with customers punishable as well.

In the present night-clubs, drinking on the part of entertainers is effectively abolished. This is the exclusive domain of the customers. Tips became the most profitable source of income for performers and owners. In contract to the past, entertainers are thus no longer supposed to make customers consume, but to provide the best ambiance for giving tips. Good performers manage to 'bewitch'[6] the customers by their good voices, stirring melodies or passionate dances. Yet, particularly the less talented entertainers, working in the cheaper clubs, use their time on stage for shaking hands, talking, joking and making dirty remarks in order that the men take out their purses. In combination with drinking alcohol, this behaviour is thought to put customers in the right mood to be lavish with tips. Especially, dancing with a revealing costume is said to 'bewitch' the drunken customer and to stimulate his generosity. Drinking thus turned from a direct way of earning money into an indirect source of profit.

During the last few years, the increasing pressure of fundamentalists has caused a new puritanical wave. Night-clubs were among the first things to be burnt down when a riot of soldiers occurred in 1986. Especially, the combination of sex, alcohol and the large amounts of money easily spent provoked rage among the financially weak. On 25 and 26 February, soldiers, who had their camp nearby and lived off a meagre salary, sent several night-clubs up in flames. Recently, the closure or replacement of the night-clubs of Pyramid Street has been under debate. When the street received its destiny as an entertainment area in the forties, it was at the margins of the city. Nowadays, due to the overpopulation, the city has expanded enormously and the night-clubs are situated in a new residential quarter. The governor of the area therefore preferred to relocate the night-clubs far off in the desert (*al-Wafd* 10–9–1989).

DRINKING AND POPULAR WEDDINGS

Although most weddings and other festive occasions provide drinks and entertainment as well, they are less under attack. Men drink and watch forbidden spectacles but, in contrast to night-clubs, weddings are not institutionalized and last only for one night. Weddings are celebrated in different places according to class. The higher class usually have their parties in the prestigious five-star hotels. The middle class usually celebrate their weddings in the more respectable night-clubs or in an army or sports club. In these clubs it is forbidden to serve beverages other than soft drinks.

The weddings of the lower and lower-middle classes are usually celebrated in the street. Red lights are hung up between the houses and chairs and tables are put in the street. A wooden platform enclosed by multicoloured cloth serves as a stage. Women usually watch from the balconies, or they have a seperate part of the alley for the first few hours of enjoyment. After about twelve o'clock it becomes an all-male happening until the call for morning prayer. Beer and water pipes filled with hashish, the cheaper stimulants, are usually available in large quantities.[7]

The entertainment programme is frequently interrupted by the ritual of giving tips. The tippers come on stage and yell their congratulations for the family of the bride and groom in the ear of the man with the microphone. They continue, while waving a banknote of ten pounds, by greeting their friends and colleagues. The ritual is concluded with a *salâm*, a musical salutation consisting of a popular song, while the money quickly disappears into the bag of the musicians. The *salâm* is usually interrupted by the next tipper who wants to give his greetings and congratulations. Guests who have just arrived have a right to be announced and greeted by a short musical salutation as well. Consequently, the party is usually rather hectic.

The consumption of hashish and beer is favourable for the entertainers in that it increases the tips. Probably the former habit among entertainers of starting the evening by sprinkling beer on the stage, in order to bring about prosperity, should be seen in this light. Yet, as a result of excessive consumption, the parties quite often end up in quarrels. Under the influence of alcohol or drugs, someone can easily feel provoked or insulted if somebody else gives a bigger tip. Lack of respect paid to their tip or excess of time spent on the salutations of others is another source of anger. Competition, old rivalries between neighbourhoods and personal conflicts are often fought out at popular weddings.

Most popular entertainers in Cairo were descended from several families who used to live together in Muḥammad 'Ali Street. Their music shops, coffeehouses and agencies for parties were in the main street and they lived in the small back alleys. They constituted a group of cooperating families and frequently intermarried. They spoke a professional jargon or secret language if they wanted to be incomprehensible to outsiders. Particularly in order to avoid embarrassment or unwanted problems with drunken guests, they communicated in secrecy.

At the beginning of the twentieth century, wedding celebrations were strictly segregated. Women were prominent on the entertainment market and female singers, dancers and musicians were in great demand. Female entertainers who performed only for women were called *'awâlim*. They formed groups that regularly worked together under the leadership of an experienced performer, the *ustâ*. She taught singing and dancing to family members and new girls, and kept an eye on their conduct. After a long period of training and experience with customers and the market, a woman could establish herself as an independent *ustâ* with her own performing group.

As the century progressed, weddings were less strictly segregated and the *'awâlim* started to work for men as well. Usually they performed the first hours in the women's quarters and left as soon as possible for the men's party downstairs because, as several performers said: 'the tambourine by the women was always empty'.[8] The *'awâlim* lingered on in the countryside, but about the 1960s this tradition disappeared.[9] Nowadays the parties are mixed, although there is usually a special section for women and they leave before midnight. Female entertainers work without an *ustâ* and her regular performing group, but under the leadership of different male or female employers.

Since the 1970s, during Sadat's open-door policy, many changes occurred in the circuit of popular entertainers. The opening to the West, the rise of a new class of rich people and the growing prosperity brought about a flourishing period for entertainers. The increased profits attracted many people from outside the profession and resulted in a breaking down of the monopoly of the Muḥammad 'Ali Street families. Since, as many Muḥammad 'Ali Street performers say, the trade is an 'inn without doorkeeper' (*'wikâla min ghêr bawwâb'*), anyone can enter the profession. Consequently, newcomers bought a belly-dancing costume or a *tabla*, a drum, and became entertainers. The 'intruders', as they were called by the original performers, were said to have lowered the artistic and moral level of the trade since they did not observe the codes of honour used by the Muhammad 'Ali Street families.

During the eighties, when the boom came to an end, the Muhammad 'Ali Street performers found that 'where the hogs are many the wash is poor'. People today are economizing on parties and entertainment. Moreover, parties in the street, although quarrels were always a recurrent phenomenon, are nowadays plagued by rising criminality. In particular hard drugs, introduced in the early eighties when Egypt became a transit country for heroine and cocaine, is a new problem. Due to lack of safety some female entertainers from Muhammad 'Ali Street decided to leave the trade altogether. As a former female entertainer said: 'The weddings are not like they used to be. In the days of beer and hash everything was fine, but now with the new generation and hard drugs, I don't like it any more.'

FEMALE ENTERTAINERS:[10] DRINKING, RESPECTABILITY AND GENDER

In the past, if female performers behaved improperly, for instance, if they drank beer on stage, they were punished by a fine or a beating. Zeinab, a former *ustâ*, described a respectable girl as follows:

> She does not accept a cigarette or beer. She works and sits on her chair afterwards. She respects herself and does not talk with customers or asks them 'give me a water pipe, or give me hash', that brings trouble. If a girl is impolite and does not respect herself on stage, then I'll beat her. If she is doing dirty things, I'll send her away. If you are *gada'*, a tough guy, and I accept a cigarette, beer, and then hash, and we talk together, the whole evening you talk to him, and you dance for him . . . that becomes a story . . . it is better to repress bad things from the beginning.

Muhammad 'Ali Street performers presented themselves as non-smoking and non-drinking and thus respectable. They said it was unthinkable that they would work in night-clubs, particularly as the clubs used to be in the time of *fath*. Since they were *baladî*, that is, belonging to the 'traditional' popular class,[11] they could not drink and sit with customers or open bottles of alcohol. Samîra, Zeinab's sister-in-law and a former entertainer as well, said: 'We worked and went home afterwards, we were straight and good and did not laugh or flirt with customers. We did not drink wine or whiskey.' In the mid-sixties, when Zeinab was still working as a dancer and singer in Muhammad 'Ali Street, she signed a contract with a night-club.

She was ill-informed about the practice of sitting and drinking with cus-tomers. When she found that it was not like what she was used to, she shouted at the owner 'go to hell, you like me to open bottles, you want me to be drunk the whole evening. I come to dance, I don't want this *fath*. I am *baladî*. I belong to the popular weddings', and she tore up the contract.

The older performers of Muḥammad 'Ali Street use their image as respectable non-smokers and non-drinkers to distinguish themselves not only from night-club performers, but from the new generation of popular entertainers as well. Everything a respectable girl did not do in their time, these intruders indulge in and thus defile the reputation of the trade. 'They dance as if they have stomach cramps. Moreover, they go with men, are drunk and do everything which God forbade (*bitû' harâm*)', is the opinion of many older performers. Some female entertainers admitted to drinking, but only at home: 'I might like to drink beer, but only at home. If I would drink beer or whiskey on the stage, then people might think that I could do other bad things as well.' Yet most entertainers of the older and younger generation try to dissociate themselves altogether from the image of being smokers and drinkers, saying: 'I do not drink or smoke, I do not do what most performers do'.

It is understandable that they try to uphold their reputation by denying smoking and drinking since the fact that they dance and sing in front of a male audience already makes them disreputable in the eyes of many Egyp-tians. Yet most of their statements implicity reveal the opposite of their intention. That is, by saying that smoking and drinking were punishable, they indicate that there were women engaging in this 'immoral' activity. By stressing that *they* do not do it and are exceptional in their abstention, they declare that it happens on a large scale, at least among others.

The conditions of their work make it likely that many do and did occasionally smoke or drink. The explosive atmosphere of drunken and competing men, trying to attract the attention of female performers, some-times puts the women in a position where it is wiser to accept than to pour oil on the fire. Zeinab related that men often offered her beer and cigarettes. She usually tried not to accept by saying that she did not smoke or drink, or if she was seen smoking she said that she could not change her brand. Samîra's strategy, however, was to accept cigarettes and beer, and to simulate drinking and smoking in order to avoid problems. A female entertainer described, for instance, the situation of a drunkard who gulped down a bottle of cheap spirit and started to dance with two knives on the stage. After injuring a female performer he said: 'I am sorry, I am drunk'. In awkward situations of drunkenness or quarrels it might be unwise to reject an invitation and it is thus no surprise that Magda, an experienced dancer, said: 'Sometimes I am in a position that I have to drink'.

Observation of their behaviour on stage reveals that most of them smoke cigarettes. One of my informants was inseparable from her water pipe whether at home or on stage. She smoked only tobacco, although other female entertainers regularly had a puff from a water pipe with hashish belonging to their male colleagues. A few of them drank while in front of the audience. Although they are occasionally forced to accept beer or cigarettes, they often do it of their own accord, particularly smoking.

As noted at the beginning, smoking and drinking are not just improper, they are seen as unfeminine. A young dancer explicitly explained her abstention from smoking and drinking in this way. She said: 'it does not fit women, femininity means that a woman does not drink beer or alcohol, and does not smoke a water pipe, these things belong to men'. Many female performers, however, display this type of 'male' conduct. How can their 'deviant' behaviour be explained? What is their own rationale for behaving in a 'masculine' and 'improper' way?

Although they probably simply like the taste of cigarettes and alcohol, I think that smoking and drinking on the part of quite a few female entertainers should be understood in the light of a broader complex of 'masculine' behaviour. The fact that they work in a public place puts them into a male world. Earning a living or, as is often the case, being the breadwinner of the family is not the common pattern for women. A female singer called herself 'the son of her father' because she provided for him. The ideal female role, quite often aspired to by female entertainers as well, given their hard working conditions, is being a dependent housewife. The nature of their work, especially at popular weddings, makes tough, masculine behaviour a prerequisite. Female entertainers, particularly the past generation of leaders, were seen as *gid'ân* (plural of (m) *gada'* or (f) *gad'a*), noble, tough and courageous, a word usually applied to men. A dancer described herself as having a rude tongue and most were quite able to defend themselves with terms of abuse. If it was necessary, a few tough women resorted to violence as well. Zeinab, for instance, related:

> I was *gad'a*, honest, courageous and tough, I was haughty and respectable. I did not like to talk or make jokes with people. I immediately beat the person who talked to me. I carried a knife with me. Once I used it in self-defence. That was only once; after that time whenever they saw me they said: '*ahlan ya fitiwwa*', 'hello bruiser'.[12]

Female entertainers are not the only women working in occupations where it is necessary to defend themselves in a strong masculine way. A dancer, almost kidnapped by a gang of young men, fled into a nearby house after the wedding was finished. It happened that only women were present inside. When the gang of men tried to enter the house, she became scared, afraid that a few women would not be able to protect her. But to her surprise, they all took a big knife and ran into the street and chased the men. Later the dancer heard that these women were hashish dealers. 'And those types are stronger and tougher as men,' she concluded. Hashish dealers and female entertainers are extreme examples of a larger group of independent women working in a male space. Other lower class working women, for instance market women, are confronted with the same ambiguity of being out of place and thus risking being seen as disreputable women. This brings me to another reason for their 'male' behaviour.

It is not always danger that prompts the entertainers to describe themselves as tough, strong, ready and able women. It also presents an image of respectability: 'If a woman is not strong in this trade, she will be lost', Magda said. A weak woman will lose respect because she is expected to engage in affairs with male colleagues and customers. *Baladî* women working, or even walking, in the male public space should react strongly if a non-related man bothers, let alone touches, them. Only women with sharp tongues able to beat the assaulter with a slipper, are viewed as capable of protecting themselves without going astray. This conduct of being tough and ready to defend themselves by verbal or physical abuse thus protects them from being considered the 'easy-going type'.

Female entertainers have to counter even stronger suspicion about their respectability. Exhibiting the body for money in public is quite near to selling the body for money, according to most Egyptians. Consequently female performers, particularly dancers, have to challenge the image of being prostitutes.[13] Defending the integrity of their body is not enough. They have to deny the femininity of their body. By presenting themselves as a man among men, they try to remove the suspicion of prostitution. Being a man, how could they be suspected of having affairs with other men, to wit, clients or colleagues? Or as Ibtisâm, a dancer in her early forties, remarked: 'I used to drink beer and to smoke hash, but we were all polite, we were as men together. There were no women and men, we were all men.' By denying their femininity and assuming masculinity they protect their reputation as women.

CONCLUSION

Drinking and smoking seem to be incompatible with the female gender identity and most women abstain from them in public. Yet, there are a few striking exceptions, particularly female singers and dancers. For the night-club performers drinking was part of their job and their main source of income. Female entertainers working at popular weddings usually smoke and some of them drink while on stage in front of the audience as well.

Although they are occasionally forced to accept cigarettes or drinks, they often exhibit this 'male' conduct of their own accord. In addition to smoking and drinking, they display masculine behaviour in other respects. Already the fact that they are in the male public space and earn money is not part of the ideal female role of dependency. They even refer to themselves as men in order to indicate the fact that they are breadwinners. Besides, the conditions of their work make it sometimes necessary to use verbal and physical abuse so as to be perceived as fearless, strong persons and thus ward off troublesome men. Moreover, by denying their feminity and presenting themselves as a man among men they protect their reputation as respectable women. They thus uphold their respectability as women by using the male gender in public.

NOTES

1 *Khamr*, usually translated as wine, includes different kinds of alcohol. The prohibition did not preclude discussions about what could be considered 'wine' or 'alcohol'. Beverages which were not fermented for more than three days, for instance, were excluded. For discussions on Islam and *khamr* see *Encyclopaedia of Islam*, pp.994–998, Heine (1982).

2 Analogy, *qiyâs*, is one of the four roots of the sacred law (*sharî'a*).

3 There are restrictions, however, on young men about smoking in front of their father, 'out of respect'.

4 Wine was an important theme for verses and poetry. A genre of poetry was named after wine, *khamr*, the *khamriyya*. See *Encyclopaedia of Islam*, Khamriyya, pp.998–1009. For the permissibility of listening to songs see also the discussion on 'listening to music', *al-samâ'*, *Encyclopaedia of Islam*, *ghinâ'*, pp.1072–1075, Farmer (1973), Robson (1938).

5 In 1934, a journalist from the art magazine *Rûz al-Yûsif* estimated that dancers earned 16–20 pounds a month from performing and 24–48 pounds from drinking. A glass which normally costs about 4 piastres was 15 piastres in the night-clubs. Champagne was raised from 50 to 150 piastres. The profits of a glass of 15 piastres, of which the cost price was 2 piastres, 5 went to the performer and 8 to the owner (*Rûz al-Yûsif* 19-3–1934:30).

6 The word *sha'wâza*, bewitchment, is often used to describe the effect of female entertainers on men.

7 There used to be a clear class distinction with regard to the consumption of stimulants. The upper class drank alcohol, the lower class smoked hashish. Lately, this has changed because hashish has become more expensive. Nowadays, the cheaper forms of alcohol such as beers or local cheap spirits and some hashish are consumed at popular weddings. In lower class night-clubs beer is usually served, and whisky in the more expensive clubs.

8 The performers would collect tips, *nu'ât*, in the tambourine or sometimes they spread a handkerchief on the bride's lap on which female friends and relatives put their contributions before the eye of the bride. The tips were shared equally among the female entertainers.

9 According to an article in the art magazine *Dunyâ al-Fann*, many *'awâlim*

started working in the night-clubs, initially veiled and fully dressed (9–3–1948:19). Yet my informants categorically deny this. With a few exceptions of performers saying that they did work in night-clubs but never sat with customers, which is supported by the above-mentioned article, most of them claim that they never worked there at all.

10 I concentrate on performers at popular weddings. Drinking on the part of night-club performers has become a private matter since the abolition of *fath*.

11 The word *baladî* is difficult to translate. It refers to *balad*, the place one comes from and belongs to. Depending on the context, it means country, nation, town or village. In a more narrow sense, it refers to the 'conservative' lower class as opposed to the 'modern' Westernized middle class. In this context, it is usually translated as 'popular' or 'traditional'.

12 A *fitiwwa* is the strong man of a neighbourhood. He uses his strength for good purposes, in contrast to the *baltâgî*, who abuses his strength and power.

13 Night-club dancers in particular are perceived as prostitutes, which is understandable in the light of the past practice of *fath*. Public drinking, which was part of their job, is more closely connected to prostitution than the mainly smoking and occasionally drinking behaviour of popular entertainers. I do not have the impression that smoking on the part of women in Egypt is solely a 'strong symbol of prostitution' as Jansen mentions for Algeria. Market women, who occasionally smoke cigarettes or a water pipe in public as well, are, unlike entertainers, not associated with prostitution. I think it indicates male behaviour, which is improper for women, but not necessarily prostitution. Besides smoking, Algerian prostitutes also take over other male behaviour, particularly, the male spatial idiom (Jansen 1987:175–190).

REFERENCES

Buonaventura, W. (1983) *Belly Dancing*, London: Virago.

Chelebi, K. (1957) *The Balance of Truth*, London: G. Allen and Unwin.

Farmer, H.G. (1973) *A History Of Arabian Music to the XIIIth Century*, London: Luzac and Company.

Ghazâlî, al- (1901) 'Emotional religion in Islam as affected by music and singing'. Translated by D. B. Macdonald, *JRAS* 1901:195–253.

Hattox, R.S. (1985) *Coffee and Coffeehouses. The Origins of a Social Beverage in the Medieval Near East*, Seattle and London: University of Washington Press.

Heine, P. (1982) *Weinstudien*, Wiesbaden: O. Harrassowitz.

Jansen, W. (1987) *Women without Men: Gender and Marginality in an Algerian Town*, Leiden: E.J. Brill.

Marsot, A.L. al- Sayyid (1985) *A Short History of Modern Egypt*, Cambridge: Cambridge University Press.

Mernissi, F. (1975) *Beyond The Veil: Male–Female Dynamics in a Modern Muslim Society*, Cambridge, Massachusetts: Schenkman Publishing Company.

Robson, J. (ed.) (1938) *'Tracts on Listening to Music'*, London: The Royal Asiatic Society.

Rosenthal, F. (1971) *The Herb: Hashish versus Medieval Muslim Society*, Leiden: E.J. Brill.

Sabbah, F.A. (1984) *Woman in the Muslim Unconscious*, New York: Pergamon Press.

3 Uses of alcohol among women
Games of resistance, power and pleasure

Eleni Papagaroufali

This chapter constitutes an attempt to explore the links between female gender identity and alcohol consumption in the urban context of Greece. Towards this end, I focus on instances of convivial alcohol drinking performed by highly self-conscious women, whether in the company of men or not, in the city of Athens, in the early 1980s. The consumption of specific drinks, with specific companions, at specific places, and the historically specific moment, encompasses issues pertaining to the situational and contextualized social construction of selves and sentiments. I regard these drinking practices as sites of resistance enacted by women against the established ideas about female gender, sexuality and pleasure in contemporary Greece.

The ethnography of women's social drinking, though sketchy and incidental, has given us some clues about the ways gender relations of power and discrimination are expressed and reaffirmed even in the domain of entertainment: in many civilizations, women, as opposed to men, are excluded from taking strong alcohol and prohibited from experiencing the pleasures that accompany relative tipsiness (Douglas 1987:7, Kondo 1990:324, Ngokwey 1987:117–18).

In contemporary rural Greece, gender differences/discriminations also pervade social everyday and celebratory drinking practices and the locations used on these occasions (e.g. Cowan 1990, Friedl 1967, Herzfeld 1985, Papataxiarchis 1991). Hot, pungent substances (e.g. 'ouzo'), also called 'manly' (Cowan 1990:67), are drunk by men only, mostly in the coffeehouse, a place traditionally forbidden to women. Women are expected to 'like' drinking 'womanly' (ibid.) drinks (e.g. fruit-flavoured liqueurs) or 'sipping' beer and wine – diluted with soft drinks – at pastry shops and 'tavernas' (i.e. restaurants) or during visits, in the presence of male chaperones. These gendered drinking preferences are generally perceived as tying 'naturally' to gender – natural – traits, i.e. male fierceness, female passivity/mildness, respectively.

Hence drunkenness is not tolerated in women – as opposed to in men – and is avoided by them, because of its 'publicly discernible symptoms' (ibid.:115), the cultural meanings attached to them – when related to female nature – and the repercussions ensuing: the loss of bodily control or the open release of enthusiasm and sensuality (due to drunkenness) are connected with the non-natural, thus dangerous, meaning seductive, aspect of female nature/sensuality and thus viewed as socially 'degrading' both women themselves and their families. As a consequence of all this, Greek women, as opposed to men, are not only treated as more or less 'invisible' to use Myerhoff's terms (1986:263), that is to say, marginal to the production of sociable high spirits (on this, see Cowan's *kefi*, op. cit.:107) but are also kept as such through surveillance. In fact, violations of the standards of modesty and/or passivity required from women in celebratory situations are easily noticed because females are 'constantly watched' or 'surveyed' (ibid.:199, on this, see also Handman 1981:115–18). Anticipated sanctions against this 'immoral' behaviour are still severe – gossip, angry scenes at home, verbal and physical retaliation from male family members (ibid.:82). Cowan, in her recent book, has eloquently demonstrated not only how these restrictive sexual stereotypes are 'incorporated' by women 'through the habitus'(ibid.:114) but also how real feelings, preferences, and desires are consciously hidden behind sedated bodies for fear of experiencing 'self-destruction' (ibid.:204).

The sexual ideology underlying all these restrictions and defining femaleness is still widespread in Greece despite, or parallel to, the many equality-based institutional reforms established by the Greek state due to its full entry to the European Economic Community (EEC). According to this ideology women are 'naturally' different from men and one such difference is that women's sexual needs or sensuality can (thus ought to) be physically controlled by them, whereas men's cannot (thus ought not) (see also Cowan op. cit.:15 and Hirschon 1978). Yet during the decade of the 1980s, in Athens, as opposed to provincial/rural areas, women's alcohol drinking behaviour has been less strictly surveyed, for two main reasons. First – and mainly – because women's mobility in this city has increased and cannot be easily held in check.[1] Second, because the egalitarian ideology of the West (EEC) was more felt in the capital than the provincial areas.[2] Thus, urban women of all ages (though mainly young) and socioeconomic status (though mainly of middle class) could be seen alone or with girlfriends, or male companions, drinking all kinds of alcoholic spirits, diluted or not, in all kinds of places.[3] A relative tipsiness in everyday and celebratory sociability was definitely more tolerated – even found to be amusing – than in provincial settings, yet this tolerance depended and still depends on where, when, and with whom this was taking place.

In this chapter, I am concerned with a particular category of Athenian women: feminists organized in that part of the women's movement which was denied – by the government – the right to participate in gender-equality-oriented decisions and institutional reforms introduced by the country's full entry to the EEC. (In the early 1980s the women's organization that participated in such decisions/reforms was the one affiliated to the government.) At that time, the women presented here engaged in specific forms of drinking in order consciously to resist, even subvert, Greek men's cultural power (including male-dominated government's power) over women's desires, pleasures and sentiments, all over Greece, rather than merely to profit from the freedoms gradually offered (and sold as commodities) by the big city. Hence I describe their drinking practices – everyday and celebratory – as performative stategies through which women enacted and exposed, to outsider-witnesses, demands for the acknowledgement of their own naturalness and legitimacy. I demonstrate that alcohol was consciously 'used' by them as a powerful 'medium' for the redefinition of female identity and the recasting of relations of power and pleasure between women and men.

THEORETICAL BACKGROUND

In a recent article, Abu-Lughod cautions researchers of resistance against 'romanticizing' (1990:42) it – that is, reading it in a one-sided way as a sign of human freedom and/or change – and thus risking the danger of 'fore-closing . . . the workings of power' (ibid.) and/or domination, inherent to resistance. Following this precaution (admittedly based on her reading of Foucault's power theory) the author herself ends up with the opposite result: she forecloses resistors' romanticism – as opposed to the re-searchers' – and demonstrates how they are 'unwittingly enmeshed' (ibid.:52) in complex sets of power relations and/or structures productive of domination. In this study of resistance, I try to avoid this 'either–or' schema and look for potentials of 'both reproduction and transformation' (Comaroff 1985:6) of established gender relations of power produced by the drinking/resisting practices of the specific women. Towards this end, I explore these practices both as what Myerhoff has called 'definitional ceremonies' (1986:266) and Foucault 'games' or 'perpetual spirals of power and pleasure' (1978:45).

On the one hand, the notion of 'definitional ceremony' has drawn my attention to the performative dimension of seemingly trivial practices – in this case alcohol drinking – through which people enact (as opposed to merely assert) not only 'what they think they are' but also 'what they [think they] should have been or may yet be' (Myerhoff 1986:262). According to

Myerhoff, definitional ceremonies deal with the problems of cultural 'invisibility' or 'marginality' imposed on a group – in this case women – 'by a more powerful outside society' (ibid.:267) – in this case the male-dominated society of Greece. They are 'strategies' – formal or informal, spontaneous or planned, discursive or non-discursive – that 'provide opportunities for being seen and . . . garnering witnesses to one's own worth, vitality, and being' (ibid.). Imaginative interpretations of selves projected through these strategies are shown to be equally 'convincing' with non-imaginative ones and both of them, sometimes, successful in 'reversing, to some degree, political invisibility' or marginality (ibid.:262).

On the other hand, my reading of Foucault's power theory[4] has kept me alert to the recognition that the development of such 'strategies' or resistances is inseparable not only from power but also from the pleasure that comes while power is produced by acts of resistance to another power – the one producing resistance.

More specifically, three of Foucault's central and interrelated propositions about power and resistance are relevant to this presentation: first, that both constitute a multiplicity of mobile and transitory forces exercised from below' (1978:94–95, 102); second, that they are interdependent (ibid.:95); third, that both power and resistance may produce 'pleasure' (ibid.:95) and be (re-)produced by it – as opposed to by force and repression only.

The first assertion urges researchers to stop looking for fixed 'binary and all-encompassing opposition[s] between rulers and ruled' (ibid.:94) and/or for 'single locus [loci] of great Refusal[s]' (ibid.:95–96); it is suggested that both the reproduction and denial of power are constantly negotiated in domains seemingly marginal to the exercise of great power and revolution – e.g. the domain of entertainment in this presentation. The second assertion discourages researchers from expecting people either to comply with, or resist, power; rulers' power techniques may be 'reversed' (ibid:101) into resistors' weaponry for some time – and vice versa – depending on the situation. According to the third assertion, pleasure may be felt and detected in the imposition, denial, even acceptance of power relations entailed in various micropractices (ibid.:45). In this, so-called, 'game' of power and pleasure (ibid.:45), the concept of 'pleasure' is politicized, that is, put on a par with 'power' and 'resistance'. Also, both its sources and definition are expanded: pleasure is not only to be found in activities a priori defined as pleasurable (e.g. dancing, eating, drinking).[5]

On the whole, in this chapter, taking cues from both Myerhoff and Foucault – among others – I attempt to discern in these women's drinking practices – from the casual to the most eventful – instances of 'limited victories' (Myerhoff op. cit.:272) against the Establishment, or of 'transitory cleavages' (Foucault op. cit.:96) in it, at the same time that these

practices are, or appear to be, 'enmeshed' in the Establishment (on the eman-
cipatory forces of the Establishment see also Frazer 1989, Giddens 1979).

The task is difficult because the discourses, practices, and emotions
produced in the opposition enactment 'can never be pristine or transcendent', to use Kondo's words (1990:302). Instead they are the results of
culturally available meanings and the open-ended, power-laden enactments
of them in everyday situations (ibid.). As will be shown in this ethnography,
women's redefinitions of gender enacted through drinking and of pleasures
felt through them are not only multiple, even contradictory, but also very
similar to, or the same as, their 'oppressors'' own. Resistors are shown to
use oppressors' discursive and non-discursive means in reverse, for their
own purposes. The extent to which these reversals are successful, that is
subversive, depends largely on the persuasive force/appeal they have to
performers themselves and to outsider-witnesses in the historically specific
time, situation, and context.

My major suggestions in this chapter are, first, that these short-term,
small-scale, localized resistances must be 'rescued' not just 'for the record'
(Abu-Lughod op. cit.:41) but because they may constitute what Foucault
describes as the 'multiplicity of mobile and transitory points of resistance',
the 'strategic codification' of which 'makes a revolution possible' (op.
cit.:96). Second, that these instances of women's convivial drinking in a
male-dominated society should not be seen as analogous to the experience
of men's convivial drinking, that is, as instances of either gender re-
affirmation, or power production, or pleasure production (e.g. Herzfeld
1985, Mars 1987, Ngokwey 1987). They must be seen as instances of a
specific kind of pleasure felt by marginals in the process of their producing
and enacting power against the established culture and towards the formation of an alternative counterculture more appropriate to their own
experiential reality.

THE WOMEN'S COFFEEHOUSE: BACKGROUND

In Greece, the coffeehouse is an 'exclusively male preserve' (Herzfeld
1985:52), indirectly forbidden to both rural and urban women for the
purpose of entertainment. Female urbanites who trespass on this male
stronghold – alone or in the company of males – still feel intimidated by
men's stares and forced to control their bodily postures.

In 1982, the members of a women's organization established the
Women's Coffeehouse in central Athens. This constituted the enactment of
two opposed feminist discourses that had developed between two
generations of women, differing in marital, socioeconomic and educational
status, and in political experiences.

The creators of one discourse were mostly middle-class housewives in their early/mid fifties and early sixties. The majority were high-school graduates who had participated in the Resistance Movement of the Second World War as well as the women's movement prior to the establishment of the military dictatorship in Greece (1967–73); many of them had also been old members of a political party of the Left. These women believed that females are the 'same' as males in all aspects due to their commonly shared 'human substance'. On the basis of this belief they rejected gender discriminations imposed on Greek women through biologically determined explanations. They viewed women's biology/nature as being no more predetermined than men's: women, like men, are entitled to the right to choose to become parents. By the same token, they believed that women's sexuality is no more 'passive', vulnerable or 'treacherous' than men's: women have the same sexual needs as men and are thus equally entitled to the right to choose partners and sexual preferences. Their main – feminist – vision comprised the redefinition of both sexes into 'human beings' (vs gender-role-players) and of their relations into 'human relations' (vs hierarchical, authoritarian, power-fraught ones). Towards this end they stressed the necessity for the establishment of institutional/legal reforms that would provide men and women with the same rights and obligations and would gradually secure them their equality or 'humanness' in all expressions of daily life, including the sexual one. The tactics proposed toward these goals revolved around the notions of 'logic' or 'reason' viewed as central to the 'human' (vs animal) nature of women and men: if feminists' 'duty' is to rediscover and maintain 'homogeneity' between genders, they must use 'reasonable' means, i.e. peaceful protests, formal negotiations with governmental bodies toward legal reforms, collaboration with men, and 'instruction' of men and women on gender issues. Thoughts and acts that, in their view, 'trespassed' reason were considered 'non-human', 'abnormal', 'not real(-istic)', thus 'irresponsible' and 'non-persuasive'.

For these women, the Coffeehouse represented 'a public place of women's own', open to men as well. The latter could 'have a drink', 'attend lectures', and thus be 'instructed' about the feminist cause: the (re-)humanization of both sexes.

The creators of the opposite discourse were mostly followers (vs members) of the Left, middle-class university graduates, working outside home, single/divorcees but also married, between their late twenties and mid-thirties. Many of them had participated in the feminist movement abroad (during postgraduate studies) and in anti-dictatorial organizations in Greece and Europe.

These women also rejected biological–anatomical differences as a basis of gender discrimination. Yet they did not share the belief in 'sameness' of the two sexes nor did they use it as an argument to support the issue of gender equality. Instead, they believed that 'individual differences' or 'particularities' exist among women and between women and men, in terms of 'inner needs', meaning 'all kinds of desires, instincts, senses, feelings and emotions'. For these women, the 'complete' experience/expression of these needs constituted the so-called 'real' (vs culturally determined) state of biology and/or sexuality. Their main vision was to transform themselves into 'whole' persons (vs alienated gender-role-players) and their relations into 'relations of substance' (vs of hierarchy, competition, and dominance). Towards this end they stressed the necessity to liberate their sexuality from the roles men have imposed on women in order to 'objectify' and/or 'dominate' them. The tactics proposed resonate their repudiation of logic/reasonable means (thus of the importance of equality-oriented legal reforms) and their admiration of spontaneity: if women plan to become whole persons or subjects (vs objects) they must discover, release, and/or immediately satisfy their inner needs, even in public, and at the risk of open verbal and non-verbal confrontation.

For them, feminists should be persons who 'have the guts' to follow their desires (vs 'duty') and live against and outside the accepted standards of their society: to 'do things for themselves' and, thus, 'be themselves'.

These members consented to the establishment of the Coffeehouse in order to: provide 'all women' with a public place of their own; make them conscious of their 'particular needs and problems' through information (vs 'instruction') offered there; and give them the chance to practise 'new forms of politics against men's oppression through the exchange of personal experiences of it'.

A few days before the opening of the Coffeehouse, the members of the Administrative Council (AC) of the organization invited the media to announce the aims of their undertaking. During the next few days, the 'event' was advertised with pictures and short articles by the newspapers and magazines; some presented it as revolutionary, whereas others presented it as a new form of ghettoization – because of its name. The AC members, obviously vexed by the second commentary, made their own comments on this presentation. One woman of the older generation – in her late fifties – said:

> Let them think what they please . . . Women cannot tolerate being excluded from certain places arbitrarily defined as 'male'. We chose this name to show people that we are equivalent to men, thus, equally free individuals. That from now on women like men may do what they please, that is, drink, smoke, play cards and *tavli* (backgammon), in public, without feeling embarrassed by men's 'famished' stares and offensive jokes. Besides, it'll be open to men. . . . That's not a 'ghetto'!

Despite its name, the Women's Coffeehouse looked more like a pastry shop or a bar than a men's coffeehouse; it was cleaner, more elegant and 'sophisticated'. The walls, brightly coloured, were full of posters showing women participating in women's movement protests, internationally, and armed women who had participated in the war-time Resistance movement. Also, historical and sociological books, related to the woman question, were displayed on shelves to be sold.

The place was open all day long – like traditional coffeehouses – and run by two members of the organization who worked on commission. Various kinds of coffee, soft drinks, and alcoholic beverages of Greek and European origin were served: ouzo, beer, brandy, whisky, vermouth, vodka, gin. Wine was not served. Cheese-pies and snacks (*mezedes*) were also available.

Many women, both members of the specific organization (mostly representatives of the younger generation) and non-members (advocates of this organization) visited the coffeehouse on a daily basis. They were women of various ages (though mainly young), socioeconomic status (though mainly middle class), political persuasions (though mainly leftists) and sexual preferences (mainly 'straight' but also lesbians). They used to come either alone, or in pairs, or in large groups, quite often 'accompanying' men. Sitting at small round tables designed for four, they talked and laughed loudly, played cards and *tavli*, and smoked. Sometimes single women or small groups would join larger ones to talk about a common issue or play cards.

OUZO-DRINKING AT THE WOMEN'S COFFEEHOUSE

The kinds of beverage drunk on all these occasions depended, to some extent, on the time of day, the season, the size and composition of the group as well as the mood of each individual. In the winter, at around 10.30–11.00 a.m., women started with hot coffee or tea and, later on, continued with ouzo accompanied by snacks. At that time of day, they used to come alone or in twos or threes, mostly girlfriends. In the evenings, women used to come in pairs – with boyfriends – or in all-female or mixed large groups; in both cases, most of them would begin and end with ouzo. Beer and European aperitifs diluted with cold fruit juices were almost always preferred in the summer, when the Coffeehouse was open for one month only.

Before they left, each woman and/or man paid their share – *refene*; treats (*kerasma*) were observed rarely, on special occasions, e.g. name days.

Despite the variety of drinks available, ouzo, a drink generally considered 'manly', was the most popular among younger women. Scattered comments on various kinds of beverage, usually made by women at the time of ordering in the form of suggesting to each other what to have or even teasing each other about what they were going to have, revealed to me some of the reasons underlying this preference. One main reason had to do with the name of the place and its meaning for Greeks. A woman teasing another for ordering Martini said once: 'For God's sake, Maria, you came to a Coffeehouse to drink Martini? We are not in America, you know . . . Have at least a beer, or better an *ouzaki*. It will make you feel much better.'

'Feeling much better with ouzo' as opposed to other popular drinks, such as beer and wine, was frequently stressed. It meant the arousal of specific sensations that were produced by its particular qualities – i.e. taste, smell, strength – qualities that were highly valued and desired by the specific women. According to the latter, while beer and wine 'go straight from mouth, to throat and stomach', ouzo has an 'imposing' taste and strength: it has to be 'entertained' for a while, first into the mouth and, then, let go slowly. During these moments 'lips get hot, cheeks become red and eyes glitter'; the 'area of the head gets high' and the body 'as a whole' gradually 'succumbs' to the same 'sense of loss'.

Following the description of Vassiliki, a young member, 'it feels as if it imprisons my mind, thus frees me from logic, and then lets me feel whole. . . . A mysterious sensation starts from mouth to head and then all over me. . . . I wish I could be like that continuously!' The fact that ouzo has to be drunk slowly[6] – as opposed to beer – and unaccompanied by food – as opposed to beer and wine – seemed to play a significant role in women's preference, for 'food keeps you more real so to speak. . . . It reminds you of your flesh. . . . It doesn't let alcohol penetrate your "being" and feel "immaterialized", vanished. . . '.

Furthermore, these women preferred ouzo to other beverages because they believed that this drink, in spite of (or because of?) its production of non-logic tied more to 'serious discussions' and/or 'deeper feelings' as opposed to 'mere jokes and teasings' viewed as 'superficial' and 'partial'. Most important, they believed that the specific qualities of ouzo aroused so-called erotic feelings in them, leading to the production of 'substantial' communication with each other, that is, as 'whole persons'. The concept 'erotic' was carefully dissociated from its usual cultural connotation, i.e. 'purely sexual'; instead, it was associated with a kind of so-called 'esoteric energy' and/or 'dynamics' viewed as involving the 'being as a whole'.

The distinction between a purely sexual, but partial, disposition and an erotic more complete one, was described by women as particularly felt in cases of drinking ouzo with men, at the Women's Coffeehouse – as opposed to other drinks, persons, and places. According to Georgia, a young member in her early thirties,

When I have a drink here with my man (*me ton thiko mou*) it feels different from, say, a taverna, or a pub, or a bar. There, it's the sexual component of our relationship that is implicitly brought out. . . . It usually constitutes an introduction to our having sex, although sometimes it's the epilogue. . . . Here, it's the friendly, Erotic aspect – Erotic with capital 'E' – felt by me, at least, I don't know about him. . . . I don't know why this is so, but I like it more because it's more complete. . . . It is a situation I provoke, one could argue. It's like inviting him on the purpose to make him know us [women]. I think: 'let him see for himself that women also play real games while drinking and smoking'. . . . Or that alcohol does not necessarily lead a man and a woman to 'bed' only. . . . We have many more needs than sex. . . . There's a lot more than that inside us. . . . Men have to understand that once and for all.

Furthermore, women's comparisons of their drinking at the Coffeehouse with men's were also based on the same contrast – that is erotic/whole vs sexual/partial and competitive. The following statement belongs to Christine, a woman in her mid-twenties and is quite revealing:

Men who go to the coffeehouse get drunk and then go home and force their wives to make love. . . . This is a continuation of the competition enacted at the Coffeehouse. For this is what they do there. . . . They compete with each other as to who will pay first, who will win at *tavli* and things like that. This is not the case with us in here. Here, when we drink, we function like 'communicating vessels' [she laughs]. We enjoy ourselves and each other's company. . . . We come here to forget about competition rather than repeat it.

Women who formed large groups (at least six people) used to stay much longer than those who came alone or with one or two other people to 'have an ouzo'. Within three to four – even five – hours, round after round of ouzo made women's heads and bodies look quietly uncontrolled: sitting back in their chairs, with legs open or unfolded on other chairs, women leaned on each other's shoulders, kissed each other, and laughed and talked loudly. Their cheeks became red, their lips swollen, their eyes were glittering and their bodies perspired and produced a 'womanly' smell. From time to time, one of them would stand up, go to the bar, have a chat with the woman in charge, make a phone call, and bring back another round of drinks. Each new round started with a toast (*ante yia mas*). Indeed, they looked like 'communicating vessels'.

During such moments, despite the presence of men, no woman seemed to conform with the etiquette habitually required of women on these occasions. Men, on the other hand, always in the company of women, were behaving 'properly': no loud voices or laughter were heard from them. Seated opposite their partners (as opposed to by their side) they seemed to feel comfortable in general, although their postures were somehow reserved.

Yet the presence of men at the Women's Coffeehouse was welcomed and encouraged for reasons that recall the vision shared by women of the younger generation, that is, to live against and outside the accepted standards of their society, even in public, and at the risk of open confrontation. The following statements are quite revealing.

Maria (late twenties):

> I don't mind seeing men in this place. In fact, I come with my boyfriend here quite often. After all, they are only visitors! I think it's important for these jerks [laughter] to visit once in their life a place which is dominated, so to speak, by women but is neither a brothel nor a monastery.

Ketty (late twenties):

> The other day I asked my father, in case my boyfriend George called, to tell him I was going to be at the Women's Coffeehouse until 6.00 p.m. He looked puzzled. My brother asked what was 'that'; I said it was a coffeehouse run by women. He asked me whether they were lesbians and what we were doing there. I replied we were 'everything' and were doing the same things 'they' were doing at the coffeehouse. Then I asked him to join me and see for himself. He murmured 'women!' in a half-contemptuous way and refused my invitation. My father said: 'It's not a bad idea provided that you don't overdo it and make yourselves ridiculous!' When George called he was told by my father about 'the Coffeehouse'. He met me there. . . .

In sum, women of the younger generation, during their everyday sociability at the Coffeehouse, consciously used the qualities of a strong drink, ouzo, to 'provoke' the production, release, and satisfaction of senses and feelings supposed to be found 'inside them' but perceived as being 'suppressed' by alienating forces of their male-dominated society.

Through this drinking experience, women felt, on the one hand, they were 'losing their logic', perceived as repressive and, on the other, (re)discovering another 'self', the so-called Erotic/whole/complete individual self as opposed to the sexual/partial one – attributed to men in the process of drinking. This 'self' was sought for and dreamed-of ('I wish I could be like that all the time') because it materialized – tentatively – these women's desires or visions: to see themselves and be seen as 'whole' individual people or 'subjects' as opposed to 'objects' of men's sexual pleasures – objects assigned various 'labels' ('We are everything' vs 'whores', 'nuns', 'wives', 'lesbians'). This 'self', both desired and experienced at the moment of drinking, was also consciously displayed, through discursive and bodily signs, to each other, to female customers, and male friends. The latter were directly and indirectly invited for a drink (for an *ouzaki*) to constitute the 'audience' necessary for the women's performative enactment of actual and desired truths about themselves and the dissemination of these truths. Taken into a context that sounded familiar, in the first place, because of the attributes women had arbitrarily borrowed from the male world of sociability – i.e. 'coffeehouse', ouzo-drinking, cards and *tavli*-playing – men were unexpectedly faced with the demand to see women neither as inferior to them (e.g. 'sexual objects') nor as the same as them (e.g. 'purely sexual') but as erotic/whole individuals, independent of restrictive labels, thus 'different' from each other and from men in terms of internal feelings, emotions, desires.

Younger women then developed a strategy towards gender redefinition that was based on the following tactics: first, they (together with older women) appropriated symbols of manliness for their own purposes, that is, they dressed the Coffeehouse with female clothes. Through this strategic reversal of meanings they rejected the equation of the coffeehouse – including the drinking and other activities in it – with 'maleness', an equation so far taken for granted, in Greece, as 'natural'. Second, they made this new interpretation known to people, through the media, in order to produce audiences and show themselves the way they wished or dreamed to be seen: drinking, playing cards, smoking, relaxing, kissing, perspiring, smelling, feeling erotic/high. Through this tactic, these women not only refused to let people – in particular men – watch or survey, thus control, their social drinking behaviour but also reversed this practice – for their own purpose. In fact, at the Women's Coffeehouse, it was they, in their capacity as owners/hosts/'insiders' (on the powerful aspect of being 'inside', see Herzfeld 1985:155) who watched/surveyed/controlled the others, who in this case, were seen as 'visitors only', thus 'outsiders': the latter had to sit, drink, behave, and entertain themselves in ways more or less prescribed by the women, and were thus more restrained than them. Finally, they let men (and women) 'see and decide for themselves' whether to approve, even adopt, their experience – loss of logic, Eroticism. Through their distance from 'visitors' – a tactic repudiated by older feminists – these women declared their own repudiation of another 'label' also attributed to women, that is, to be 'seductive' through alcohol drinking.

In short, in the midst of an activity a priori defined as pleasurable, these women produced and used power by means of consciously violating culturally established powerful meanings about female naturalness and/or sexuality and the ways these are expected to be expressed in cases of sociability – in particular the social drinking of alcohol and 'afterwards'. Yet, during this power-laden process of gender redefinition, I suggest, these women felt pleasures other than, or parallel to, or combined with, the ones described as deriving from convivial alcohol consumption *per se* – communitas/togetherness, release of senses, 'eroticism'. To put it another way, these women seemed also to feel pleasures that came of the very act of exercising the power that questioned cultural sexist discriminations, brought them to light, and rejected them; the pleasure that came of the power that 'travestied', to use one of Foucault's terms (op. cit.:45), or reversed and thus ridiculed and resisted a specific expression of Greek male power over women. Thus, the redefinition of female gender on these women's terms – i.e. erotic/whole – through drinking in the specific context entailed also elements of competition, individualism, domination, even revenge, that is, elements that may have been felt as 'pleasant' but that were not included in their vision of 'relations of substance' – in fact they were contradictory. Yet the performance as a whole seemed to be successful on a daily basis because the audience seemed to accept, even approve this situation: men accepted being treated as 'visitors' and were willing to meet women at the Women's Coffeehouse to share the 'erotic' vs sexual effects of alcohol drinking.

In the following case of convivial drinking, the contradictions underlying feminist women's performative assertions of selves came to the fore in the form of tension and conflict. Yet the performance *per se* was successful: no one from the audience had known what had happened 'backstage'; everyone seemed to have a good time and approve of the way the celebration was enacted.

WINE-DRINKING AT THE WOMEN'S COFFEEHOUSE

In 1983, the Woman's Day was celebrated by the specific organization with a party at the Coffeehouse, following a protest march against male violence – from psychological violence to rape. The idea of having a party belonged to AC members of the older generation. It was announced in advance to two newspapers of the Left so that it became known to 'everyone'; the announcement invited 'women and friends' to celebrate the Woman's Day 'with wine and food'.

Wine, though not served at the Coffeehouse on an everyday basis, was chosen on this occasion for 'the warmth and fervour it produces in groups', in one woman's terms. Protesters included members of this organization (of both generations) and of groups of 'autonomous' women (i.e. not affiliated with any political party); male friends from both sides also participated. Women wore white masks on their faces to denote their conviction that 'rapists do not see who/how women victims are, they just rape'. Members carried placards reading 'all men are potential rapists'. After the resolution of protest was handed to one representative of the Ministry of Justice, most protesters, male and female, walked to the Women's Coffeehouse.

The place was already occupied by female customers who had read about the party and were already served. At the entrance, members of the AC greeted their guests and showed them in. The kitchen was full of bottles of wine and plates of food. The crowd gradually divided into three large groups seated around tables that were placed one next to the other. One group included regular members, women of the older generation, with male companions; the other comprised younger women, members of the organization and of 'the autonomous' group, together with some male friends; the third constituted customers. Before food and drinks were served, a woman (member of the AC in her late fifties), carrying a glass of wine, made a toast to the 'Equality of the Two Sexes' and gave a short speech about the history of this Day. After that, women of the first group stood up in line and one after the other brought wine and plates to serve their male guests. In the second group, males and females, one after the other, went to the kitchen and served themselves. The AC members helped everyone with serving but did not sit at any table. Carrying glasses of wine, they sipped a few drops, and passed by each table to see if everyone was served. Everyone seemed to have a good time – divisions were not obvious to a casual observer. Some women of the younger generation wore their masks and played with male friends; the latter offered them wine but women refused to unmask and drink it: 'I'll drink it when it pleases me, don't push me', I heard one woman saying. Very soon – half an hour after the party had begun – a group of twelve young women, members of the organization, stood up and got ready to leave. I asked them why they were leaving so soon. Anna, indicating some of the women of the older generation, answered on the part of the rest:

> Look at them! Half an hour ago they were saying 'all men are potential rapists!' and, now, they are serving them wine like ancient Greek servants, slobbering over them. Yah! We'll go some other place to have a real wine and food party of our own.

I asked her what she meant by that. Her answer was as abrupt as the previous one: 'Wine-drinking is a ritual, it's a communication of each other's souls, not a theatre. . . . "Wine loosens tongues", as they say, it doesn't bind them.' Katherine, one of those who remained, apparently less outraged than the others but equally embarrassed, took her glass, went to the 'servants' and told them scoffingly: 'Come on, girls, let men be your cup-bearers for once in your life. After all, we are feminists.' Men seemed annoyed while women laughed loudly. One of them (Demy, 55) replied:

> Katherine, this place is ours, they are our guests. It's both an obligation and a pleasure for us to make them feel at ease. After all, wine-drinking is a liturgy. . . . Let's be the priests for once in our lives and let them be the flock [laughter].

Another woman (Jenny, 45), also laughing, murmured: 'Let's intoxicate them to make them come to their senses for once in their lives and teach them how to be humane'.

As the teaser was going away, an AC member approached her and asked her, rather ironically, why 'they' had left. She answered, playing the same tune: 'they thought the wine was sour'. The woman answered back: 'I can't stand these women's selfishness. All they want is to act on their own pleasure. . . . How are these people [indicating men and customers] going to believe in us if we act like that? They must be psychologically unbalanced.'

The celebration went on for another two hours. Except for a few celebrants no one else had noticed the women's departure. Some women (of the older generation), while sipping and serving wine, showed their partners the posters on the walls and explained what these were depicting. All, before they left, met with AC members, gave them money, and exchanged impressions about the appeal the event might have had to their 'guests'. Within the next week, younger women accused the older ones of subservience to men, hypocrisy to themselves and women, and emotional barrenness. The latter, in their turn, charged the former with individualism/selfishness and 'abnormality'. On the other hand, within the same week, a popular women's magazine reported on the protest march and the party. The description presented both women and men protesting against (male) rapists and drinking wine at the Women's Coffeehouse. Male interviewees suggested that such celebrations might be repeated. None of the readers would ever know exactly what had happened during this wine-drinking event. On the contrary, the Women's Coffeehouse would be perceived as a symbol of women's freedom and the unity of men and women/equality of the two sexes.

But what exactly had happened at that wine party? If, indeed, all these women believed that 'all men are potential rapists', what was the purpose/meaning of their bringing them to the Women's Coffeehouse to share food and wine with them? Was this an act of older women's 'subservience' to men? Or was it part of a strategy to make men see women the way the latter wished to be seen?

In my view, the older women's invitation of men for wine at the specific space and time was made for the purpose of displaying to them their own vision – i.e. rehumanization of genders – and self-interpretations through 'reasonable' means. Hence, of all beverages, they chose wine because its sociable qualities were considered more appropriate for mixed company – that is, less 'manly' than ouzo – and for recreational talks. They used alcohol in ways that suited the realization of their performance and the 'staging' of the context: they themselves only 'sipped' wine and thus kept in full control of their bodies and minds; at the same time, they 'served' men as much wine as they pleased and kept talking to them about their Coffeehouse and the pictures hanging on its walls. The images projected fitted in with these women's feminist beliefs and visions about their gender and gender relations: they saw and displayed themselves as being the 'same' as men – i.e. pictures of armed partisan women in the Resistance Movement of the Second World War; priests; society reformers. Men's 'intoxication' by these women was part of their 'plan' to fuse in, and claim, through this drinking event, roles of the past gained by women and highly valued by them, though not necessarily experienced by all of them, i.e. participation in war; dreamed-of dignities for women in the future, e.g. female, not only male, priests; and lived-in roles of the present, i.e. feminists as instructors/rehumanizers. Women's 'serving' men wine in that context took the form of a power or resistance technique against stereotypes rather than of 'subservience'. This act, regarded so contemptuously by feminists, was consciously used, in this case, as a means to convince men about women's 'sameness' with men in terms of potentialities. In this event of convivial drinking, these women, like women in the previous case, drew pleasure not so much from drinking wine with men as from using a kind of power that, on the one hand, questioned and resisted the power so far monopolized by men and, on the other, asserted itself in showing-off and fooling this power. Stated otherwise, the redefinition of female gender on these women's terms – sameness of rights and obligations – in the specific context entailed the reversal of a role hierarchy for which men had been severely accused by all feminists: in women's fantasy – enacted through wine-drinking – priests were only female, rather than both female and male, and flocks were only male, rather than male and female.

Younger women who left the party did so because they disagreed with the interpretations of selves and pleasure conveyed by the older women's drinking behaviour; they thought these women reproduced their subservience to men and identified their own pleasure with pleasing men. Younger women who remained, after they found out what the older women were up to, disagreed with the latter's techniques of 'seduction' and role reversal; they accused them of being hypocritical and of reproducing hierarchy.

The conflict that developed between the two trends was one of self-interpretation as women – one stressing the issue of sexuality, the other the issue of rights – and of tactical choices towards the redefinition of gender relations. At the same time, this conflict revealed the contradictory character of each trend's interpretations: the realization of the younger women's concepts of individual wholeness/relations of substance denied older women the right to please themselves as they wished and required the support of all other women, that is, 'sameness' of attitudes rather than difference of freedom of choice. On the other hand, the materialization of the older women's concepts of sameness/ rehumanization was made possible through the enactment of individual (true and imaginative) wishes, the reproduction of hierarchy of roles, the exclusion of women who thought differently as 'abnormal'. Both developed obvious competition with each other and latent competition with men. Yet the fact that none of the guests became aware of this conflict and that the magazine conveyed the message of equality of the sexes and freedom of each proved the degree of success of all these women's performative skills through drinking: no one would ever know what had happened 'backstage'.

In the instances of gender redefinition through alcohol drinking so far presented, the goal underlying women's performances was to show their male audience they were other than 'objects' of men's sexual and other desires/pleasures. In the following case, women drink to redefine their gender as sexual subjects.

THE PLEASURE OF CONQUEST

In the early 1980s, in Athens, while it was not very unusual for women to go with female friends to a taverna to have wine or beer, and food, it was less common for them to go to a bar alone or with girlfriends to have a drink. Quite often, single women who belonged to one of the categories presented here – i.e. feminists of the younger generation – practised the second kind of drinking for a specific purpose: they went to a bar, alone or with another female friend, to make new male acquaintances. These women used the male terminology for this practice, that is *kamaki* (literally 'harpoon'), and the proposition often heard, 'let's go to a bar for a drink', meant 'to go for *kamaki*'. A key motivation behind this act as a whole was to do things they liked on the basis of their own initiative. This included going alone to places where women – as opposed to men – 'normally' go accompanied by men/boyfriends; to 'harpoon' the man they liked instead of being harpooned by a man who liked them; even to order the kind of drinks they themselves liked without any male intervention whatsoever. Because alcohol-drinking was the primary medium used for purely sexual communication with men, women were very cautious about the manner in which drinks were drunk. The following statement of one of these women shows their sensitivity to (and knowledge of) the power relations that develop between the two genders even within the etiquette usually required and followed on such occasions of everyday sociability:

> When I go to a bar with a man, the waiter [usually also a man] asks him what 'we' want, and he asks me what I want. I feel sort of obliged to follow this order and tell him what I want and he, then, tells the waiter what I and he want. Sometimes, after I have heard my partner's choice, I find myself changing mine. . . . That is, I take the same drink as him, because I feel that my disposition should fit his. . . . This is not the case when I come alone or with a girlfriend. And when a man joins us, he brings his drink with him, or quite often orders the same as the woman with whom he is going to have the affair.

The *kamaki* process entailed sitting at a table, ordering an alcoholic drink of Western origin, chatting with a girlfriend – when one was not alone – and, simultaneously, 'searching for faces'. Once a woman located a man she liked, she began staring at him while drinking. She might have more than one drink before the man decided to respond to the 'message'. Once he started responding either by smiling, or by exchanging stares, or by making a toast, the woman invited him to her table – it was unusual for her to go to his table, invited or not. The man brought his drink and, soon, ordered another drink, the same as the previous one or the same as the woman's. The acquaintance entailed exchanging information about each other, drinking and laughing, most of the time ending in bed after a couple of hours.

The experience as a whole was included among those so-called states of wholeness/completeness, meaning the release/satisfaction of inner needs. Yet the assertions consciously performed through this planned drinking activity were uttered by these women more specifically: 'women, like men, have sexual urges that cannot be naturally withheld'; 'sex is something that women may obtain from men rather than the opposite only' being the case; 'men may become objects of women's sexual pleasure if the latter so wish'.

Going to a bar for a drink was considered by these women to be 'exciting' despite their awareness that the probability of 'going steady' was minimal, for most of these men thought of them as 'easy', whereas the possibility of feeling a 'sense of void', following the completion of this process, was maximal. Yet, according to a woman, 'what counts is the pleasure of conquest, no matter how temporary it may be'.

In this case, like the previous ones, women chose the practice of alcohol-drinking as a suitable context to reverse, and thus violate, established male roles for their own purposes. They 'invited' men through alcohol ('for a drink') primarily to make them see women the way they wished to be seen – drinking, smoking, flirting, sexually active – and, secondarily, to share drinks. At first sight, the men's response seemed 'traditionally' male or Greek: they responded to women considered 'easy'. In fact, they became participants in a rather new game of power and pleasure consciously organized by political actors, feminists – of the younger generation. The latter, in their effort to redefine their gender and the relations of pleasure between men and women, presented themselves as sexually active, and violated, in public, cultural stereotypes about female passive and treacherous sexuality. At the same time, they violated their own concepts of wholeness/relations of substance, for these did not include the 'pleasure of conquest' or of dominance! Yet what counted in this performance, as in the previous ones, was the new message enacted 'on the stage' rather than what was happening 'backstage' – in women's thoughts and hearts. The male audience responded positively to this violation, no matter what they thought of it.

CONCLUSION

In this chapter I have shown how a particular category of Greek women, i.e. feminists, used alcohol as a medium to resist, and retell, the 'Establishment' telling of their experiences as females. Actual and imaginative interpretations of gender, performed through the social drinking of alcohol, were shown to be, on the one hand, multiple, because of differences in gender ideology and visions: feminists envisaging women's sexual liberation displayed their gender as sexually 'different' from men's and from male-dominated cultural definitions – that is, as whole/erotic (vs partial/purely sexual) and as sexually active (vs sexually passive). Feminists concerned with women's emancipation from ascribed gender roles displayed their femaleness as 'same' with maleness in terms of capacities related to public activities rather than sexual ones – that is, as priests, warriors, society reformers. On the other hand, women's gender redefinitions, enacted through alcohol-drinking, proved to be self-contradictory, that is to entail such characteristics as competition, power- and hierarchy-production, normally attributed to men, and thus repudiated by these women's visions.

At this point, I have argued that these women drew great pleasure from these contradictory experiences – actually they defined their own concept of pleasure through them – because these, in fact, constituted the 'moments' of violation, or resistance, or reversal, or transformation, of the 'Establishment' and the legitimation of these women's actual and dreamed-of interest: to become culturally visible the way they 'wished'.

In other words, I have seen these women's pleasure as coming (in fact, as being consciously provoked) more from their power-laden, performative strategies of counterculture, articulated through the medium of drinking, than from the physical and sociable effects of alcohol consumption usually perceived as 'pleasant' even by women themselves – i.e. communal relations/'communicating vessels', 'loosening of tongues'/release, relaxation. I grounded this argument, first, on women's 'confessions' (e.g. 'the pleasure of conquest is what counts most'); second, on the fact that in that period (early/mid-1980s) the presence of these women in the decisions made about institutional changes oriented to the equality of sexes was stubbornly denied by the government; third, on the fact that in the atmosphere of that 'Europeanization'-oriented period ('equality for all, liberty for each') it would not be very difficult for Athenian middle-class women to enjoy the 'established' pleasures of convivial drinking – already known to men – at least in secret.

What was still difficult for women to enjoy, and what was enjoyed through the drinking performance in front of an audience more or less positively predisposed, was the right to express and please themselves the way they wished, rather than the way their 'Europeanizing' society was about to preordain for them. The 'staging' of the Women's Coffeehouse and the conscious 'conquest' of males at a period of actual and promised reforms, oriented to the equality of sexes, signalled women's criticism of them and refusal to accept what was being decided for 'their' pleasure by the male-dominated government, 'backstage'. Hence, they established their own 'counter-stages' or 'counter-backstages'.

To be sure, within a few years, the Women's Coffeehouse closed while traditional ones, as well as bars, pubs, and cafeterias, multiplied all over Athens and Greece. Was then the Women's Coffeehouse 'reproducing' the male establishment and its contradictions by means of 'reversing' it, and got 'absorbed' by it, in the long run? I would not think so. In my view, all the above-mentioned instances of women's drinking were but what Foucault calls 'perpetual spirals of power and pleasure' (Foucault op. cit.:4) or multiple, cleavage-producing 'points of resistance', spread over time and space at varying densities, waiting for 'a strategic codification capable of making revolution possible' (ibid.:96). Or, to use Myerhoff's terms, women's redefinitions of gender through alcohol drinking were indeed 'victories' but 'limited' ones (ibid.:272).

NOTES

1 In Athens, there are still middle-class women who are not permitted by their husbands to go out with women friends, but who succeed in doing so by saying, for example, they are going shopping (Papagaroufali 1990).

2 By the mid-1980s, the 'equality for all and liberty for each' discourse (including gender-s) had become the dominant one among political parties and movements: these differed only in stressing, primarily, one over the other of the two
   concepts (equality or liberty) while, simultaneously, assuming the existence of
   the unstressed one(s) as parallel or complementary. The women's movement
   did not evade the abstract character of this ideology and its inherent contradiction (i.e. be both equal and individually free to choose), concealed by its
   abstractness. As I have shown elsewhere, the veracity of these women's
   visions, though freed from biological determinist explanations of gender differentiation, was based on 'substantialized'/'naturalized' concepts (human/
   whole individuals; human relations/relations of substance) denuded of historically specific referentials, and thus reified. Consequently, these women not
   only retained the nature–culture opposition (imposed on them by society) but
   also constructed new, similar ones to interpret their position in society and the
   reformation of it; thus, they confronted tensions and conflicts that came of
   contradictions concealed by substantializing concepts. As will be shown, the
   tactics to their resolution tended to include practices similar to, even identical
   with, what were seen as 'male' ones, that is contradicting their feminist
   ideology because the latter did not specify social traits/practices (e.g. of
   'human relations'); instead it was denuded of them (Papagaroufali 1990).

3 In Greece, strong alcoholic spirits of Western origin became popular in the
   1970s, first in the cities among the upper class, as a celebratory drink, particularly among young males and females of all ages. Symbols of 'modernity',
   these drinks have reached the countryside as well and are largely consumed by
   men – especially whisky. Nowadays, the places where these beverages are
   available, in various combinations, are a multiplicity of bars and pubs with a
   European look, and 'cafeterias' (a hybrid combination of a bar and a pastry
   shop, Cowan 1990: 73–74) established mostly in the cities but also in rural
   towns. Nevertheless, wine, beer and aniseed-flavoured ouzo still remain the
   typical drinks of the lower classes in both urban and rural areas. They are still
   served in men's coffeehouses (ouzo) and tavernas (beer and wine), although
   one may also drink beer and ouzo in the above-mentioned 'modern' places –
   ouzo being served in goblets, instead of in small glasses, 'on the rocks' and
   with pistachios, instead of with snacks.

4 The readers of Foucault's power theory who have one-sidedly insisted on his
   suggestion that power tends to be reproduced and resistance coopted due to the
   'productive' (vs 'repressive') nature of modern power techniques (Foucault
   1980:119) are misreading him (e.g. Abu-Lughod 1990). Insistent references to
   his sentence '. . . resistance is never in a position of exteriority in relation to
   power' (Foucault 1978:95) present part of his theory and 'misunderstand the
   strictly relational character of power relationships' (ibid.: 95). In my view,
   Foucault gives 'resistance' an equally 'powerful' position with 'power': he
   asserts that power 'depends' (ibid.:95) on resistance and vice versa. Also, he
   stresses that, although resistance is 'inscribed' in power (or because of it?), it
   does not function 'only as a reaction or rebound, forming with respect to the
   basic domination an underside that is in the end always passive, doomed to
   perpetual defeat', but produces mobile and transitory 'cleavages' in society
   (ibid.:95). His illustration of social relations as 'perpetual spirals' (ibid.:45) of
   power, resistance, and pleasure break with any representation of relations as
   simply contrasting each other.

5 Pleasure is usually presented as an abstract feeling implicitly or explicitly tied to situations a priori defined as pleasurable, i.e. states of leisure, or of 'playful'/irrational experiences (e.g. singing, dancing, laughing, drinking), or of communitas-producing kinds of sociability (e.g. Gusfield 1987). Although it is also acknowledged that pleasurable practices (e.g. dancing) may be wedded to asymmetrical social relations and, in fact, mask them (see e.g. Cowan 1990, following Bourdieu), the interconnection *per se* between the two and the possibility that pleasure comes from the imposition/denial/acceptance of such asymmetries is not equally – or simultaneously – studied. For instance, although Cowan informs us that women participating in the *patinadha* dance-event 'are aware of, and take pleasure in, its exhibitionist character' (op. cit.: 114), she does not explore how/why this happens. This approach tends to be tautological (pleasure stems from pleasurable situations and v.v.) and treats 'pleasure' *per se* as either apolitical or semi-political, that is merely 'co-existing' with political relations of power.

6 Traditionally, ouzo is served in small glasses (3–4 cm high at most) and is accompanied by a glass of water in case one wants to dilute it a little (the small glass cannot contain more than a few drops of water). It is drunk rather slowly, because it is strong, with or without snacks (vs food) and repetitiously, one glass after the other.

REFERENCES

Abu-Lughod, L. (1990) 'The romance of resistance: tracing transformations of power through Bedouin women', *American Ethnologist* 17, 1:41–55.

Comaroff, J. (1985) *Body of Power, Spirit of Resistance*, Chicago: The University of Chicago Press.

Cowan, J. (1990) *Dance and the Body Politic in Northern Greece*, Princeton, N.J.: Princeton University Press.

Douglas, M. (1987) 'A distinctive anthropological perspective' in M. Douglas (ed.) *Constructive Drinking: Perspectives on Drink from Anthropology*, Cambridge: Cambridge University Press.

Foucault, M. (1978) *The History of Sexuality, Vol. I: An Introduction.* Translated by R. Hurley, New York: Random House.

Foucault, M. (1980) 'Truth and power' in C. Gordon (ed.) *Power/Knowledge*, New York: Pantheon.

Frazer, N. (1989) *Unruly Practices: Power, Discourse and Gender in Contemporary Social Theory*, Cambridge: Polity Press.

Friedl, E. (1967) 'The position of women: appearance and reality', *Anthropological Quarterly* 40, 3:97–108.

Giddens, A. (1979) *Central Problems in Social Theory: Action, Structure and Contradiction in Social Analysis*, Berkeley: University of California Press.

Gusfield, J. (1987) 'Passage to play: rituals as drinking time in American society' in M. Douglas (ed.) *Constructive Drinking: Perspectives on Drink from Anthropology*, Cambridge: Cambridge University Press.

Handman, M.E. (1981) 'De la soumission a la dependance: le statut de la femme dans un village de Pelion', *The Greek Review of Social Research*, No special: Aspects du changement social dans la campagne grecque: 231–44.

Herzfeld, M. (1985) *The Poetics of Manhood: Contest and Identity in a Cretan Village*, Princeton, N.J.: Princeton University Press.

Hirschon, R. (1978) 'Open body, closed space: the transformation of female sexuality' in S. Ardener (ed.) *Defining Females*, New York: John Wiley and Sons.

Kondo, D.K. (1990) *Crafting Selves: Power, Gender and Discourses of Identity in a Japanese Workplace*, Chicago: University of Chicago Press.

Mars, G. (1987) 'Longshore drinking, economic security and union politics in Newfoundland' in M. Douglas (ed.) *Constructive Drinking: Perspectives on Drink from Anthropology*, Cambridge: Cambridge University Press.

Myerhoff, B. (1986) '"Life not death in Venice": its second life' in V.W. Turner and E.M. Bruner (eds) *The Anthropology of Experience*, Urbana and Chicago: University of Illinois Press.

Ngokwey, N. (1987) 'Varieties of palm wine among the Lele of the Kasai' in M. Douglas (ed.) *Constructive Drinking: Perspectives on Drink from Anthropology*, Cambridge: Cambridge University Press.

Papagaroufali, E. (1990) 'Greek women in politics: gender ideology and practice in neighborhood groups and the family', unpublished Ph.D. thesis, Columbia University.

Papataxiarchis, E. (1991) 'Friends of the heart: male commensal solidarity, gender and kinship in Aegean Greece' in P. Loizos and E. Papataxiarchis (eds) *Contested Identities: Gender and Kinship in Modern Greece*, Princeton, N.J.: Princeton University Press.

4 Drinking on masculinity
Alcohol and gender in Andalusia

Henk Driessen

INTRODUCTION

The study of alcohol and drinking has long been one of the numerous side-tracks of anthropological field work. *Constructive Drinking*, the volume edited by Mary Douglas (1987), made it a focused concern of a contextual analysis that considers drinking a positive and creative activity.[1] In his introductory essay, Dwight Heath (1987:46) presents a list of the most significant generalizations that derive from cross-cultural study. Oddly enough, he does not mention the widespread exclusion of women from taking strong alcohol. This is indeed one of the questions about drinking on the border of culture and biology (cf. Douglas 1987:7). Little substantial research has been devoted to this basic issue. The other contributors to *Constructive Drinking* remain almost silent on the link between gender and drinking. Mars notes in passing that drinking among longshoremen in Newfoundland supports the ideal masculine image. Mars and Altman briefly mention the relationship between drinking and the honour-and-shame complex in Georgia, the former Soviet Union. The exception is Ngokwey who argues that among the Lele of Zaire culturally meaningful differences between the sexes are expressed and reaffirmed in palm-wine drinking.

This article discusses the role of alcohol in the construction of gender by revisiting a case presented elsewhere (Driessen 1983). The setting is rural Andalusia (Spain) in the late 1970s.[2] I will point out recent changes in drinking behaviour and corresponding transformations in gender constructs.

TYPES OF DRINK

The classification of drinks is complex given the recent introduction of several new alcoholic beverages. For our purposes it will suffice to mention the main categories. Wine is the traditional alcoholic drink of the Andalusian plains. People distinguish between red and white, weak and strong (*flojo-fuerte*), fine and crude (*fino-basto*). The local white Montilla (considered a sherry in Western Europe) is the most current male drink in the plains south of Córdoba city and is opposed to red wine (non-local) as strong to weak. Red wine is rarely consumed in bars, though women now frequently drink it diluted with soda water. It was mainly associated with the urban élite. Recently, red Rioja and Valdepeñas wines have become popular drinks accompanying meals in the middle and upper classes. The basic sub-division of white wines is fine and crude. A *fino* is brighter, more expensive, drunk from a sherry glass, and associated with the landed and professional élite. A *medio* is a cheaper, darker and less sophisticated variety of sherry-like wine, the term *medio* referring to the typical wine glass and measure. It is the drink of peasants and workers in taverns and is rarely drunk at home. In the 1970s it was the male drink *par excellence*.

Beer has become important in social drinking over the past three decades, first in bottles, and more recently tapped. A bottle or glass of beer is more expensive than a *medio* and, for this reason, not considered an equivalent of wine in rounds of exchange. Beer has become an acceptable drink for women, partly because it is less strong than Montilla wine. A small glass of *aguardiente*, a regionally produced anise-flavoured liqueur, is the traditional first drink of the early morning among peasants and agricultural labourers, taken to 'kill the little worm'. There is a sweet variety of this male liqueur which is more expensive and sometimes drunk mixed with brandy (*sol y sombra*, literally sun and shade). Liqueur and brandy may be combined with strong black coffee. These are also male drinks. Whisky is a recent innovation in the countryside. During the 1970s it became a popular drink among the élite. It is also a male drink associated with illicit sex. The whisky bar (*whiskeria*) is a place where men congregate with scantily clothed waitresses or hostesses. Strong alcoholic beverages mixed with soft drinks also became popular in the 1970s, first among the élite as a festival drink, and in the 1980s as a more common drink, particularly among young men and women in discothèques. There is a wide variety of these mixed and relatively expensive drinks, among which gin with coca-cola (*cubata* or *cuba libre*) stands out. Due to the increase in the standard of living, the advance of modernization and the incorporation of Spain in the European Economic Community, a broad variety of 'exotic' drinks have spread to the countryside and become available to people of all classes and occupations. Yet wine and beer remain the typical drinks of the working class in agro-towns.

Opposed to alcoholic beverages are water, soft and warm drinks. Water is taken simply to quench thirst. There is always a jug with fresh water in public buildings including taverns. But recently the water-jug is being replaced by bottled water. Milk is considered a children's and a woman's drink. A real man never drinks milk. The same holds for chocolate milk which is a typical drink of the home taken in the late afternoon with biscuits. Milk is thus associated with the domestic domain, while coffee is a drink of the public domain. Tea (*manzanilla*, camomile tea) is rarely taken in rural towns. If consumed, it is in order to ease stomach pain. In the city, however, tea may be an alternative for coffee. As a rule, warm drinks mark the transition from leisure to work, while alcoholic beverages mark the passage from work to leisure and from normal to special time. Men drink far more and stronger alcoholic drinks than women. The distinction between strong and soft (alcoholic) drinks is imbued with the Andalusian notion of masculinity. There is a clear cultural connotation that strong drinks belong to strong bodies. Tensions between the sexes also tend to gravitate towards the consumption of alcohol.

PLACES AND TIMES OF DRINKING

The tavern, bar or café is the focal institution of public life. It is more than a recreational centre where men gather for daily rounds of sociability and exchange. It is a social context for the creation and maintenance of friendship and the celebration of masculinity.[3] Drinking alcohol together creates a temporary ambience of oneness, fraternity and equality that does not exist outside the bar. Drinking in bars is ritualized behaviour, that is, staged, ordered, stylized, evocative, and carrying a message (cf. Moore and Myerhoff 1977:7–8). There is an extensive literature in ethnography on commensality and the integrative functions of drinking (cf. Gibson and Weinberg 1980). Writes Pitt-Rivers (1977:10): 'Food and drink always have ritual value, for the ingestion together of a common substance creates a bond.' Drinking not only creates a bond, but also serves to reinforce existing bonds and express the cultural substance of social relationships.

Andalusian men of all ages and classes spend much of their leisure time away from home in their favourite bar, often located in the barrio where they live. When a man gets up in the morning he immediately leaves his house to have a glass of coffee, anisette, or cognac. If he works in or near town, he will have some glasses of wine or beer between one and two before going home for lunch. After lunch or after the siesta in summer he will have another coffee. The high time of bar attendance is in the evening between seven and ten when the cafés fill up with busily talking and gesticulating men. Alcohol, cigarettes, *tapas* (snacks of olives, cheese, crisps, ham, fish, potato salad, shellfish, and other delicacies often accompany wine and beer), gestures, tall stories, horseplay, discussions of work, politics, football and sex are the recurrent ingredients of bar sociability.

Men usually drink before not after eating a meal. *Tapas* are viewed as a different kind of food closely associated with bars and social drinking. All rites of passage and festivals are occasions for drinking alcohol, more alcohol than usual in terms of quantity and quality. During some of these occasions the home is turned into a public domain where alcoholic beverages are consumed.

DRINKING ETIQUETTE

Bar attendance is a patterned social activity regulated by strict etiquette that hinges on reciprocity, honour, and self-control. Andalusia is a region where men value social drinking highly, where alcohol is an essential ingredient of adult male interaction. Yet a certain ambivalence *vis-à-vis* alcohol is simultaneously expressed not only by women but also by men.[4]

An adult man who withdraws himself too much from the company of bar mates must have very good reasons to do so if he is not to be accused of anti-social and consequently anti-masculine behaviour. On the other hand, too much participation in bar sociability also has its dangers. Masculinity is by definition competitive, won or lost in confrontations with other men. It entails comparison, challenge, defence, and offence and hinges upon honour. Social drinking is thus often competitive. A real man must drink a lot without becoming drunk. Intoxication is considered ugly and socially disapproved of for it indicates a lack of self-control – a focal quality of virility – and also a lack of sharing. Drinking alone is the habit of alcoholics, most solitary drinkers being drunkards. A man who becomes addicted to alcohol cannot control himself and thus loses face. There are, however, a few times when drunkenness is permissible: the festival of the patron saint (cf. Aguilera 1978:30), *romerias* or pilgrimages to shrines in the countryside (cf. Corbin and Corbin 1987:123), and the occasional *juerga*, an extended spree in a neighbouring town or city (cf. Gilmore 1980: 190–1) or *perol*, which takes place in the countryside where a lamb or a billy-goat is killed and prepared for a banquet (cf. Driessen 1983:127–8). Men believe that these bacchanalia are necessary for their well-being. Apart from these special occasions, drunkenness is not tolerated in men. The standards for women are different. Whereas drinking among men is competitive, hard and at times abusive, more than slight drinking (one or two bottles of beer) by women is already condemned. Even on special occasions tipsiness in women is not permissible. A tipsy or drunken woman is classified as a prostitute. Men expect of their wives, daughters and sisters non-conspicuous behaviour, sobriety and restraint.

ALCOHOL AND RELIGION

Some pioneers in the ethnography of drinking have explored the links between religion and alcohol. Most attention has been paid to the drinking patterns of the Irish and Jews in the United States. Snyder (1962) has argued that Judaism acts as a check on heavy drinking. Religious Jews learn to control their drinking through the ritual use of alcohol. Among the Catholic Irish there is no such ritual control of drinking behaviour in a religious context and hence more hard drinking occurs (Bales 1962). Heath (1987) maintains that prohibition of alcohol has never been successful except when couched in sacred terms. But even then it does not seem to be very effective. Think, for instance, of the frequent use and abuse of alcoholic beverages among Muslims in the Maghreb.[5]

The relationship between drinking and religion in Andalusia is complex. The church preaches temperance but lacks the means to exert control on the lower and middle classes. Sobriety on religious grounds is only important to a small minority of men. It is striking that religious festivals are occasions for outbursts of drunkenness. Patron saint festivals and *romerías* are cases in point (cf. Aguilera 1978:88, 96; Corbin and Corbin 1987:121–5). The behaviour of the majority of men who participate in these festivals is a reversal of church prescriptions. Even more revealing is the role of some religious brotherhoods during Lent and Holy Week (Driessen 1984:78, 80–3). *Cofradias* and *hermandades* are all-male societies with their own clubhouses that open up during Lent for congregation and hard drinking at night. If there is a battle between the sexes in Andalusia, it is waged from Carnival till Easter between the members of the confraternities and their wives. The climax of brotherhood sociability is Holy Week with its processions. Members of some of the confraternities engage in heavy drinking to the point of getting drunk before and during the processions. There is outright anti-clericalism and a reversal and parody of some of the official rites and prescriptions in the boisterous cult of the saints in Andalusia. For instance, a widespread mocking of Catholic Communion in bars involves raising a glass of wine while uttering '*el sangre de Jesús*', 'the blood of Christ'. There is a clear anti-authoritarian streak in the Andalusian notion of masculinity.

NOTIONS OF MALE AND FEMALE: CONTRADICTIONS AND CHANGES

Attending bars on a regular basis and engaging in reciprocal and competitive drinking is considered imperative for being a real man just as it is imperative for being a good woman to spend much time at home. The ideal male is strong, tough, formal, independent and the undisputed head of a household. He supports his family, guards the family honour, and spends his leisure time away from home. The ideal woman is virtuous, docile and competent, devoting her life to husband and children. She is the vessel of family shame. The sexual division of labour is rigid, at least in theory. Men hold that their wives should not work outside their home for an income. This construction also corresponds to the Andalusian categorization of social space. The public domain (*calle*, street) is the world of men, while women belong to the private domain of the home (*casa*). Alcohol is a marker of the transition from private to public space. Competitive drinking and joking (*cachondeo*) take place in homosocial settings and are tests of manliness. Both challenge a man's dignity and self-control. Sexual differentiation and domination are thus pervasive themes in social drinking.

Gender constructions did not fit the reality of social class and the division of labour between the sexes in the late 1970s. Since then this lack of fit has increased further. In middle and upper-class families men play an active role in both the private and public spheres. They do not only provide for the family's income, but also control the household budget, make economic decisions and participate in child-rearing. Already in the late 1970s, it was becoming respectable for middle-class women to take white-collar jobs and join their husbands at outdoor activities on summer weekends and festivities. In the lower classes female labour power was and is of paramount importance to the maintenance of a household. It is not exceptional to find women in casual jobs while their father, husband, brother or son are unemployed. The insecurity of the day-labourer's contribution to the household budget and his physical self-removal from the house stress female dominance in the domestic sphere.

Franco's death in 1975, experienced as a *césure*, and the coming of democracy have accelerated changes which began much earlier. In one generation married women radically changed their self-representation. They no longer stay at home every evening, but rather spend weekend evenings with their husbands in restaurant-bars or *pubs* (fancy places for couples) where they sit at tables (they still do not stand at the counter like men) showing off their fashionable clothes and drinking beer (cf. Collier 1986:100). In summer many bars extend their services to the street or *plaza*. Women of all ages sit at these outdoor tables (cf. Uhl 1988:321). On the other hand, neighbourhood bars and taverns (*tabernas*) remain part of the male preserve.

Young adults look down on what they consider to be 'backward' notions of femininity and masculinity. They look to the cities and have their own drinking (and dancing) establishments. Premarital sexual intercourse seems to have increased considerably. Family background has become less important than personal abilities and education more important than property (Collier 1986:103–4). Consumption has increased and become more differentiated. Changes in drinking patterns are a case in point. Men drink more 'alien' drinks. Young adults spend more on a wider gamut of drinks than their parents did when they were young. Alcohol consumption at home seems to be on the rise especially in the cities. Press (1979:143) noted the beginning of this trend in Seville where bar attendance diminished among the condominium-dwelling males:

> Reasons for this include the size of new flats, fewer number and lessened attractiveness of bars in new neighbourhoods, and lack (at least so far) of strong in-group neighbourhood identity. Another reason for decreased bar attendance lies in the isolation of condominium apartments from one another.

CONCLUSION

The pertinent question is not only why Andalusian men in homosocial gatherings often drink in a competitive way but also why they drink more than women. Drinking alcohol is neither a technical act like quenching one's thirst with water nor is it an end in itself. Convivial drinking is a *modus operandi* of culture. Elsewhere I have argued that rites of masculinity staged in bars act to obfuscate the reality of the workers' dependence on the female members of their household and their weak economic and social position in local society. Their vulnerable dominance over women is reinforced by these rites which exclude females (Driessen 1983:131). This argument fits McClelland's power theory: 'Men primarily drink to feel stronger . . . Those for whom personalized power is a particular concern drink more heavily'(1972:334). While power is an important factor in drinking, it is not the prime, cross-culturally valid reason why men drink. There are other factors as well. One of the reasons Andalusian men give to legitimate their heavy drinking is the reduction of anxiety, caused partly by the husband and father role. And they simply like to enjoy a 'time out' period, a loosening of responsibilities and strictures. These folk accounts point to the importance of gender in drinking. Men drink to belong, to create and maintain bonds with other men and to mark their identity as true males. Drinking in homosocial settings dramatizes masculinity. It catches the men who are involved in it to the extent that they believe in what they perform. Like the Lele of Zaire, through drinking Andalusians express and reproduce gender differences which are by implication power differentials.

78 *Alcohol, gender and culture*

NOTES

1 This approach is of course rooted in cultural relativism. While Douglas's claim that this is a specific contribution by anthropology may be justified, it also creates a false contrast with other social sciences, in particular sociology (cf. Marshall 1989: 604). Though not a landmark study such as Pittman and Snyder (1962), McClelland (1972) and Everett, Waddell and Heath (1976), the Douglas volume is none the less an important work of reference.
2 Field work in Andalusia was conducted during the summer of 1974, one year from 1977–78, and visits of some weeks in 1979, 1984, and 1987.
3 For references to bars in Andalusia see the bibliographies in Driessen (1983) and Gilmore (1985).
4 Most members of the traditional élite who held power during the Franco regime strongly disapproved of regular bar attendance and hard drinking. In the first decades of the twentieth century alcoholism aggravated the social malaise among landless workers. It became a major target of anarchist reformers (cf. Mintz 1982:86).
5 On the other hand, prohibition seems to be better observed during the holy month of Ramadan when social control is stricter. Religious sanctions may thus play a role in the social control of drinking, but their impact on behaviour is more modest than Heath assumes.

REFERENCES

Aguilera, F. (1978) *Santa Eulalia's People: Ritual Structure and Process in an Andalucian Multicommunity*, St. Paul: West.
Bales, R.T. (1962) 'Attitudes toward drinking in the Irish culture' in D.J. Pittman and C.R. Snyder (eds) *Society, Culture and Drinking Patterns*, New York: John Wiley and Sons.
Collier, J.F. (1986) 'From Mary to modern woman: the material basis of Marianismo and its transformation in a Spanish village', *American Ethnologist* 13:100–8.
Corbin, J.R. and Corbin, M.P. (1987) *Urbane Thought. Culture and Class in an Andalusian City*, Aldershot: Gower.
Douglas, M. (1987) 'A distinctive anthropological perspective' in M. Douglas (ed.) *Constructive Drinking. Perspectives on Drink from Anthropology*, Cambridge/ Paris: Cambridge University Press/Editions de la Maison des Sciences de l'Homme.
Driessen, H. (1983) 'Male sociability and rituals of masculinity in rural Andalusia', *Anthropological Quarterly* 56:125–34.
Driessen, H. (1984) 'Religious brotherhoods, class and politics in an Andalusian town' in E.R. Wolf (ed.) *Religion, Power and Protest in Local Communities*, Berlin: Mouton.
Everett, M.W., Waddell, J.O. and Heath, D.B. (eds) (1976) *Cross-Cultural Approaches to the Study of Alcohol: An Interdisciplinary Perspective*, The Hague: Mouton.
Gibson, J.A. and Weinberg, D. (1980) 'In vino communitas: Wine and identity in a Swiss alpine village', *Anthropological Quarterly* 52:111–21.
Gilmore, D.D. (1980) *The People of the Plain. Class and Community in Lower Andalusia*, New York: Columbia University Press.

Gilmore, D.D. (1985) 'The role of the bar in Andalusian society: observations on political culture under Franco', *Journal of Anthropological Research* 41: 263–76.

Heath, D.B. (1987) 'A decade of development in the anthropological study of alcohol use: 1970–1980' in M. Douglas (ed.) *Constructive Drinking*, Cambridge: Cambridge University Press.

McClelland, D.E. *et al.* (1972) *The Drinking Man*, New York/London: The Free Press/Collier-MacMillan.

Mars, G. (1987) 'Longshore drinking, economic security and union politics in Newfoundland' in M. Douglas (ed.) *Constructive Drinking*, Cambridge: Cambridge University Press.

Mars, G. and Altman, Y. (1987) 'Alternative mechanism of distribution in a Soviet economy' in M. Douglas (ed.) *Constructive Drinking*, Cambridge: Cambridge University Press.

Marshall, M. (1989) 'Review of Douglas (ed.) Constructive Drinking', *American Ethnologist* 16:603–4.

Mintz, J.R. (1982) *The Anarchists of Casas Viejas*, Chicago: University of Chicago Press.

Moore, S.F. and Myerhoff, B.G. (1977) 'Introduction. Secular ritual: forms and meanings' in S.F. Moore and B.G. Myerhoff (eds) *Secular Ritual*, Assen: Van Gorcum.

Ngokwey, N. (1987) 'Varieties of palm wine among the Lele of the Kasai' in M. Douglas (ed.) *Constructive Drinking*, Cambridge: Cambridge University Press.

Pittman, D.J. and C.R. Snyder (eds) (1962) *Society, Culture and Drinking Patterns*, New York: John Wiley and Sons.

Pitt-Rivers, J.A. (1977) *The Fate of Shechem or the Politics of Sex. Essays in the Anthropology of the Mediterranean*, Cambridge: Cambridge University Press.

Press, I. (1979) *The City as Context. Urbanism and Behavioral Constraint in Sevilla*, Urbana: University of Illinois Press.

Snyder, C.R. (1962) 'Culture and Jewish sobriety: The Ingroup–Outgroup Factor' in D.J. Pittman and Snyder, C.R. (eds) *Society, Culture, and Drinking Patterns*, New York: John Wiley and Sons.

Uhl, S.C. (1988) 'Friendship and fealty in southern Spain', Thesis, Ann Arbor, (MI): UMI.

5 Wine: life's blood and spiritual essence in a Greek Orthodox convent

A. Marina Iossifides

When the pleasure originating from the body enters the mind, it conveys to the latter a corporeal aspect . . . and this is why the whole man is called 'flesh'. . . . Conversely, the spiritual joy which comes from the mind into the body is in no way corrupted by the communion with the body, but transforms the body and makes it spiritual, because it then rejects all evil appetites of the body; it no longer drags the soul downwards, but is elevated together with it.

(Gregory Palamas, quoted from Meyendorff 1983:51)

INTRODUCTION

Christian doctrines are often said to support the separation of the body from the soul. Though this has been shown to be a misconception,[1] it none the less remains a commonly held view. In this chapter I hope to show how, amongst a group of Greek Orthodox nuns, the body is both a symbol of the material, mundane world, contrasting thereby with the spirit, as well as being an aspect of the divine, partaking in the salvation of the soul.

What relationship though does this have with alcohol? The unity between body and soul is achieved most strikingly in the ritual of Holy Communion and central to this ritual is the presence of wine. Without wine there could be no communion, no unity of mind, spirit and body; no communion between divine and human and, thus, no hope of salvation and life after death.

Such a study, of course, does not immediately assist those in organizations seeking to prevent alcohol abuse. It does however begin to offer an insight into the spiritual qualities associated with wine in Greece. And given that the history of Greece is interwoven to a large extent with the history of the Greek Orthodox Church, it is not inconceivable that church ideology has affected secular practices. One need only look at the work of many of the anthropologists researching in Greece.[2] This chapter then seeks to aid the understanding of how wine fits into the complex relationship between secular and religious, between body and soul, and how it contributes towards the creation of community within Greek society.

The research on which this chapter is based was conducted between January 1986 and May 1987. I lived in the village of Peta in Western Greece in the region of Epirus, spending a few days each week in one of the two convents near the village. Peta has a permanent population of approximately 2,000. The convent of R., to which I will be referring, is high in the mountains some forty-five minutes drive from the village and boasted then the presence of fourteen nuns and an abbot. The abbot, a gentle and learned old man, served as priest and father confessor to the nuns and pilgrims who visited the convent.

MATERIAL AND SPIRITUAL WORLDS

There is not the space here to introduce the reader fully to monastic practices, beliefs, and to the convent layout itself. Suffice it to say that what seems of paramount importance to the nuns is the symbolic and physical separation between lay and religious, between the material and the spiritual world. For example, when visitors arrive, only one or two nuns designated to the task are present to welcome them. The nuns prefer to avoid contact with outsiders. In the church, the nuns stand apart from the laity, and their cells and the kitchen are strictly prohibited to the non-initiated. This separation is maintained to the extent that even those lay persons close to the nuns, parents or siblings, do not eat with them.

This should not be surprising. The incorporation of food into the body is a dangerous act, since the body is felt to be 'open' to receive substance from without. Boundaries, as noted by Douglas (1966) and others, are being crossed during the meal. Thus, the nuns cross themselves and a blessing is said before and after each meal to protect one from the dangers, as the nuns say, associated with the 'opening' and 'closing' of the body during the meal; to protect one from the 'long, green fingers of Temptation' who seeks to poison one's food.

Commensality, moreover, as a way of defining who eats what with whom, is one of the most powerful ways of defining and differentiating groups.

> Those who sit at meals together are united for all social effects, those who do not eat together are aliens to one another, without fellowship in religion and without reciprocal social duties.
>
> (Smith 1989:251)

Indicating then, as it does, common membership and communality, commensality cannot and should not be part of the nuns' everyday experience where it concerns their interaction with the laity. The nuns have 'died' to the secular life through the ritual of tonsure. They will not be buried in the family plot; they do not attend family baptisms, weddings or funerals; and they are only allowed to visit an ill parent for a few hours a week, if the parent lives nearby. As nuns, these women have begun a spiritual journey which they hope and pray will lead them to permanent unity with the divine after death. They have renounced all ties associated with the body: kinship ties and ties of marriage and child-bearing, ties which serve to incorporate people within a secular community.

They also deny their individual bodily needs: their sexuality and, during the yearly and weekly fasts as well as before receiving the Holy Sacrament, their hunger. With the long periods of prayer, especially during Lent, the nuns also deny their need for sleep. And in the cold, winter mornings before dawn in the unheated church where they raise their voices in prayer, they could well be said to be denying their body's need for heat, though they insisted that their vestments kept them warm, wrapped as they were in the arms of God.

Their separation from and denial of the material world is as complete as they can make it. They seek to transform their bodies and elevate their souls. As one nun said:

> In heaven we are said to have different bodies from the ones we have on earth. These heavenly bodies are eternally 33 years old. They do not age. Nor do they experience thirst or hunger.

This transformation depends in part on the separation of self from mundane needs and ties. But this is not enough. One must also partake of the Holy Sacrament. It is during this communal meal that a person is united with God; that human and divine become one. And in this unity the person is also united with all of Creation for this Creation is God. Thus, though no secular outsider may eat with the nuns, regardless of their kin or social status, all Orthodox together may partake of the meal of the Sacrament from the same vessel within the convent church. A paradox exists. Although the nuns seek to separate themselves physically from the secular world in order to minimize the temptations that threaten their endeavour for eternal life, the greatest expression of unity with the divine is the partaking of Holy Communion by Laity and monastic alike. With this ritual meal those who have been kept separate and apart are unified through an act of commensality into one community.

LITURGY AND HOLY COMMUNION

Preparation to receive the Holy Sacrament begins the preceding week with designated fasts and ideally with confession. In this manner, the body and soul are cleansed and prepared to receive Christ. In the cold, early hours of morning before dawn the rhythmic sound of the talanto, a wooden board and mallet, is heard throughout the convent. Sometime later the bell summons you to a dark church lit only by the glow of the oil lamps and the two small, dim electric lights which allow the cantors to read the texts. The nuns enter silently. They do not greet you. Only one or two will ask you, out of concern, if you slept well.

You are closed therefore upon your own thoughts. The boundaries of your body are secured through the fast; social interaction is minimized or absent. The divine is the only outside entity upon which you can focus. The incense is strong, overwhelming, aromatic. The lights flicker upon the icons gold and red. The voices of the nuns are raised in glorification of God. All your sentiments are focused on that glory and by contrast also on that which is considered weak and human: the grumbling of your stomach; your thirst; your cold feet and hands. You are made to feel acutely aware of the chasm dividing the divine and the human, the spiritual and the material. The preparation is over. The liturgy has begun.

Like the daily, weekly and yearly cycles of convent life the liturgy is structured on the life of Christ, from his nativity to his resurrection. It is the most solemn and yet joyful ritual of the Church for it is through this ritual that human and divine are united in the sight of God and through His sacrifice. During the ritual, lay and religious stand under one roof in the most central area of the convent, the church. However, this is not a place for social interaction as such interaction is understood in the village: interaction between people. In the church, men and women, religious and lay together, create a community while also interacting personally with God through the mediation of the priest. As Mother Mary and Archimandrite Ware (1969:22) note: 'Christian worship is at once personal and corporate, although these two aspects may be at times in tension'. Thus during the liturgy the nuns avoid all eye contact and do not under any circumstances smile. Concentration should be focused on the divine and not on human interrelations for it is only through the divine that human interrelations can achieve their true significance and dimension, their true nature.

The preparation of the sacrament, of the *prosforo*, leavened bread,[3] and wine opens the service. The bread and wine are referred to as gifts since ideally they are provided by those participating in the service. The rite of preparation takes place in the *prothesis*[4] (preparation), sometimes called the *fatni* (manger). There the bread is cut and placed on the paten and the wine is mixed with water and poured into the chalice. The place, the *fatni*, combined with the yet unconsecrated but pure bread and wine, signal the birth of Christ. The bread is cut by an instrument called 'the lance' in remembrance of the piercing of Christ's side on the cross, and the wine and water mixture represent the water and blood that spilled from Christ's side.

The second part of the liturgy is characterized by a procession in which the Gospels are brought into the nave and placed on the altar. The priest reads a designated passage from the Gospels. The procession and the reading allude to the coming of Christ and the bringing of his teachings into the world (Bashir 1960:103).

The final act of the liturgy begins with the transfer of the chalice with the wine and water, and the bread, to the altar. The priest bearing these 'gifts' is followed by two people (in the convent two nuns, in the village two boys) each bearing *exapterga* (six-wings, representing the six-winged angels). This procession is likened by the nuns to Christ's funeral procession at which both humans and angels are in attendance. As a funeral it occurs on earth; as a funeral of God it is attended by beings of divine origin. The material world is inundated by the divine.

Once the gifts are placed on the altar the door leading from the altar to the nave is closed, signalling the burial of Christ. The Creed of Faith is read and the gates are opened to reveal the priest standing with his back to the congregation wafting the gifts with the *aer*[5] in a gesture symbolizing the breath of the Holy Spirit. A hymn follows which, the nuns say, is sung in the very presence of God seated on his throne surrounded by angels. Humans are slowly being raised to the heights of the celestial divine. No longer is it the angels who attend an event on earth but humans who attend one in heaven. The priest then repeats the words of Christ at the last supper: 'Take, eat; this is my body which is broken for you unto the remission of sins'; and 'Drink ye of it; this is my blood of the New Testament, which is shed for you and for many unto the remission of sins'.

The priest, following Christ's command to do this in his memory, lifts the paten and the chalice, saying as he does so: 'Thine own, from Thine own we offer in behalf of all and for all'. That is to say, 'What is Yours we offer, Your servants in behalf of all humans, and for all Your mercies'. It is now that the bread and wine are transformed into the living body and blood of Christ. The sacrifice is complete.

The bread and wine are now prepared for the communion. The priest breaks the bread into four parts.[6] One portion is placed in the chalice. Warm water which has been prepared is now blessed and poured into the chalice: 'Blessed is the warmth of Thy Saints' (the warmth of the heart); 'The warmth of faith is full of the Holy Spirit' (the warmth of faith is enkindled in the human soul through the action of the Holy Spirit). In these two blessings the spiritual and the material are now, finally, fully combined.

The people approach the priest who holds the chalice containing the blood and body of Christ. The priest places a small spoonful of the bread soaked in the wine into the open mouth of the recipient who with this action is united with Christ. Men receive communion first, followed by women and children. The nuns receive communion only after all those of the laity who are to take communion have done so.

The communion over, the priest places the chalice on the altar, blesses the congregation, and a short Pentecostal hymn is sung. The cycle of Christ's birth, life, death and resurrection has been completed.

Finally, the whole congregation lines up to receive the priest's blessing and a small bite-size piece of bread, the *antidhoro* ('instead of the gift'): bread which has been blessed but is not consecrated. *Antidhoro* is given to the whole congregation whether a person has received the holy sacrament or not. This bread unites those who did not receive the sacrament with those who did while also marking the difference between them. For this bread, though serving as a symbol of commensality and community, can only partially express the unification with Christ. Without wine, the blood, the bread cannot be the true body of Christ; it is not complete. Bread is essential but it is not enough. Alone it is not the sacrament.

With the completion of the ritual there is a marked sense of relaxation. The heightened tension and formality that accompanies the liturgy and the communion is replaced by an ease in relations and movement. The nuns, previously concentrating on the ritual, now chatter happily with one another or with lay acquaintances. This animated interaction with the world contrasts vividly with the very measured actions preceding and during the liturgy. United with Christ, the nuns and laity are united with all creation through Him. They have found their true nature in God. There are no longer any distinctions. All are members of one blessed community.

WINE, WATER AND SPIRIT

It will be evident to the reader that wine is of central importance to the ritual described above. Its significance, for example, is noted within the Roman Catholic Church where, before Vatican II, the consecrated wine was reserved for the priest, the congregation receiving only the wafer, the body of Christ. Though such a separation between lay and cleric never existed in the Eastern Orthodox Church, the contrast between the 'gift' of the Holy Sacrament and the *antidhoro*, the blessed bread given at the end of the liturgy, emphasizes the special place reserved for the wine, the blood of Christ. Its potency is marked.

It is a potency which can lead to intoxication. Citing Acts (5:11) Feeley-Harnick (1981:57–58) notes that the apostles, filled with the Holy Spirit and speaking in tongues, are described as drunk. And so they are, for they are 'filled with the new wine' which is Christ. Wine is the metaphor describing the inspired words of God. Intoxicated by this new wine, by the blood of Christ, one is transformed.

Yet, it seems too that this potency is diluted. The spiritual is combined with something else. Water is added. Jung (1988:105–107) discusses this dilution. He notes (as does Gefou-Madianou, this volume) the ancient custom of not drinking wine unless it was mixed with water. A drunkard was defined as an *akratopotes*, one who was an 'unmixed drinker'. The modern Greek word for wine, *krasi*, means mixture. How does this relate to the symbolic practices of the Church? We gain some insight by noting that the Monophysites, who believed that Christ had but a single divine nature, sought to preserve this divine nature by leaving the wine undiluted.[7] By contrast, the Orthodox Church, which recognized Christ as both human and divine, symbolized this dual nature by the mixing of water with wine. The indivisibility of this duality in Christ is reinforced by the indivisibility of the mixture of water and wine. A similar interpretation is given by St Cyprian, bishop of Carthage (d.258). He notes that the water represents the congregation. Water is an imperfect substance, since it can both cleanse and be contaminated, must be blessed before it is mixed with the wine of the spirit; just as Christ can be united only with a blessed and sanctified congregation,[8] only with a blessed and purified humanity.

Thus, the mixing of water with wine may signify the dual nature of Christ, who is both human and divine, as well as the union of an imperfect human congregation with the divine. Wine symbolizes the divine, the spirit. It is the blood of Christ, intoxicating and unifying.

BLOODLESS SACRIFICE

When reading the religious texts given to me by the nuns and speaking with the nuns themselves, what struck me most concerning the liturgy was the insistence that the sacrifice experienced in the liturgy was indeed bloodless (*anemakti theisia*). Their insistence seemed out of proportion with the fact that there was indeed no blood in the liturgy. Moreover, how is their insistence to be understood when the nuns also speak of the blood that Christ shed for the salvation of humankind and of the pain He suffered upon death? How is it to be understood when the bread and the wine are said to be literally the blood and the body of Christ and the liturgy the actual sacrifice, as the authors and the nuns insist?

Bashir (1960:112ff) notes that while the blood of the Old Testament is the blood of animals given in sacrifice to God, the blood of the New Testament is the blood of Christ shed for humankind's salvation. Because the wine in the liturgy is mystically transformed into Christ's blood, the New Testament sacrifice is a 'bloodless sacrifice'. It does not involve the immolation of living creatures. This serves to distinguish Christians from all other humans. It is a mark of sanctity.

Skiadha (1980:67) offers a slightly different understanding. The wine in the chalice is mixed with warm water in order that it may resemble living blood. We may see it then as a living Christ who is consumed despite the fact that He was killed on the sacrificial altar. The 'bloodless sacrifice' reinforces the miracle of the conquering of death by Christ.

Yet, why this emphasis on blood? Let us examine some of the associations made with blood. The blood of dead animals, for example, is regarded with ambiguity. It is said amongst the laity that when the animal is dead, the dirty and unhealthy elements should come out. Some say that this happens when the animal is hung; others when the flesh is cooked. It remains that slaughtered animals are hung for a few days before they are consumed and the meat is always well cooked. Few people have an appreciation of rare meat. In fact, they find it repulsive – too much blood.

This may be because blood is linked with vitality and life.[9] Passed on from parents to children, it creates kinship ties, basic to concepts of the continuity of life. Blood is further associated with life as exemplified by the epithet: 'a hot-blooded man' (*thermo-emos*). This refers to a man who is full of life and sexuality, and who is quick-tempered. To eat therefore that which is dead, but which still contains blood that has not been cooked and is as yet untransformed, is considered an anathema. This is further reinforced by phrases such as 'blood was spilled' (*chithike ema*), which serves as a vivid metaphor of death or wounding. This may be related to notions of containment. Blood spilled either from wounds or during menses indicates a loss of life, blood uncontained. The life, like the blood, has been drained away.

With the communion, however, it is the living Christ who is consumed. As the bread is soaked in wine, so too is the blood contained by the flesh. The wine and bread have been transformed, 'spiritually cooked' we may say, to become the living body which is consumed. The two together, the co-mingling of living blood and body, combined with the grace of the Holy Spirit, create life; transform the sacrifice, the spilling of blood, into a bloodless act, into a conquering of death and the containment of blood. The Holy Spirit,[10] as the breath of life, symbolized in the wafting of the bread and wine with the *aer*, signals the fulfilment of the resurrection. Body, blood, and spirit have been united after death. Communion then is the only instance when blood as an element, transformed from wine, is consumed for it is part of life, fully and wholly contained.[11]

THE MEAL AND THE MAKING OF A COMMUNITY

We see then that the wine symbolizes the spirit, the blood of Christ, and life. 'When you take communion you take within you the body and the blood and the soul of Christ', say the nuns.

For this reason the nuns avoid kissing those who have received communion for it would show too great a familiarity with Christ who is within. And both laity and nuns insisted that spitting is also prohibited since one would be spitting out Christ. For a brief period one is in union with Christ and should act accordingly. This union however lasts a day at most. As humans we are prone to sin and this sin severs us once again from the divine as it did that first and most dreadful time in the Garden of Eden. As humans, say the nuns, we can only strive continually against our baser, fallen natures to keep God's laws and to receive, whenever possible, the Holy Sacrament which unites us, however briefly, with Christ – a unity which brings us to our true nature as it existed before the Fall.

In the New Testament it is just this incorporation with Christ through his blood which gives the wine its power in the communion. It is evident that the liturgy contains within it the re-enactment of the Last Supper. To understand the power of this meal Feeley-Harnick (1981) asserts that we must understand how bizarre the meal was to those who sat with Jesus at the table to partake in it. It must be remembered that one of the strictest Mosaic laws from which even foreigners were not exempt was the prohibition on consuming blood. Thus historically too, blood had to separated from food. To consume blood was a transgression punishable by death:

> Only be sure that you do not eat the blood; for the blood is the life, and you shall not eat the life with the flesh.
>
> (Deuteronomy 12:23)

The Last Supper in which Jesus asks his disciples to eat of his body and drink of blood in remembrance of him is truly horrifying. But as Feeley-Harnick (1981:67) notes: 'it is merely the last in a long series of culinary disasters'.

In her discussion of the Eucharist and the Passover in early Christianity Feeley-Harnik notes that the Jewish community was divided according to descent and laws of purity. Food was one of the important languages through which Jews sought to express relationships amongst humans and within God. Thus, the sectarianism within the Jewish community was expressed primarily in dietary rules (1981:91). For example, the Essenes (1981:41) were forbidden to intermarry, eat, or have any close contact with other Jews, while for most Jews eating with Gentiles was considered extremely polluting.

The early Christians, as a Jewish sect among many, used the language of food to establish themselves and to make clear the novelty of Christ's interpretations of the law. Christianity sought to be a religion of unification opposed to the separatist nationalism of the Jews. For this reason Christ did not distinguish with whom or what he ate. He is depicted eating and drinking with harlots as well as with Pharisees. He does not obey the Sabbath or follow proper ritual conduct during meals.

His transgressions, however, carry even greater significance. The Last Supper, argues Feeley-Harnick, is focused primarily on the Passover. Passover is in commemoration of the Jewish Exodus from Egypt and describes the killing of the lamb by every family so that the Lord would pass over those families when he struck down the first-born in Egypt. Passover is thus focused on the family (1981:134–135). The lamb is killed by and for the family and the blood is applied to the doorposts and lintel of the house.

With Jesus, the Passover is transformed into a meal that includes all people. He does not celebrate the Passover with his family but with his disciples (1981:144). They represent the relationship of family and kin, being brothers as God's children, and not in the terms of descent.[12] Jew or Gentile, if they partake in the sacrificial meal they become one of the chosen people. The kinship as well as dietary laws are confounded. Blood which should not be consumed is consumed. There are no longer any divisions between humans.

But there is also no division between the divine and the human. The sacrifice made is that of the Son by the Father. The first-born is not spared as in the Passover but presides at the meal in which he, both human and god, is also both victim and priest. As Sykes (1980:72) notes, the 'memorial of Christ's death entails the intimate social fellowship of a common meal' – a fellowship between humans and with the divine in which life, blood, the wine is consumed.

SENSUALITY AND UNITY

In discussing the transubstantiation of the gifts it is sometimes suggested that the bread and wine are 'just symbols'; that they simply stand for the blood and body of Christ but are not really themselves flesh and blood. This is strictly refuted by some Orthodox theologians and by the nuns. This is not to say that the nuns do not recognize the symbolic aspect of the bread and wine, but that beyond this symbolism lie the unknowable ways of God.

The transubstantiation of bread and wine into body and blood is believed to take place despite the lack of perceptible physical transformation.[13] This lack, oddly enough, serves to support the belief that with the Eucharist human and divine, material and spiritual, are combined. The transformation of the elements into the living Christ is a transformation experienced by the nuns on receiving communion. In consuming the transformed bread and wine the nuns told me that they were filled and warmed. They felt no immediate need of food for they were no longer hungry. Filled with the Spirit they were immune to the cold of winter and the summer's heat, to the physical needs of their bodies. The spiritual transformation of the bread and wine had physical effects upon the nuns, which reflect the nuns imperceptible yet miraculous spiritual transformation as well as confirming the imperceptible yet effective transformation of the elements.

The divine is first glimpsed in the hymns; the icons; the incense; the read texts and prayers; the voice of the priest; the glow of the candles and it is ultimately realized with the consumption of the divine itself as made physically present in the transformed elements. What is inchoate is given physical expression; what is unknowable is revealed in the most common products, bread and wine.

This use of bread and wine enhances the emotive power of the communion. First, both laity and nuns will readily tell you that the three elements blessed by God are bread, wine and oil. Wheat, grapes and olives have been for centuries the basic agricultural products of Greece and, one could say, of the Mediterranean. They are the staples of life, the assurance of survival. Thus, the combination of wheat and wine consumed in the communion reinforces the feeling that these are the very elements of life – those elements which sustain and nourish.

Second, the combining of bread and wine symbolizes the unity of categories which are kept strictly separated in all other aspects of convent life: the male and the female. Lay men and women visiting the convent do not eat at the same table unless they are married. And even if married they do not sleep in the same room should they stay the night. In the church, men and women stand apart: the men to the right, the women to the left. And, as already mentioned, men receive the sacrament first followed then by women. Men and women, defined in opposition to one another as sexual beings, must be physically separated in order that their thoughts will not focus on mundane aspects, especially those related to physical human reproduction. Rather they should focus on the higher, more spiritual goal of the eternal life of the soul.

Following a simple binary opposition, we could say that the bread usually associated with the women of the house, who in the past baked bread at least twice weekly, is mixed with wine, usually associated with the men of the house, who in the past made wine for home consumption. However, while wine is also associated with the household which is perceived as continuing through time, it is *prosforo* and not bread which is offered as a ritual gift. It is that 'bread' which is made by women who have

either abstained from sex or are socially and/or physically unable to reproduce: preferably elderly widows. Thus, physical reproduction, associated
more closely with women, is denied while unity and continuity, associated
more closely with the house and in this area with men, are reinforced.[14]

Combined, then, *prosforo* and wine create the eternity-granting, living
flesh of Christ, mirroring possibly the creation of living children by men
and women in the secular world. It seems that it is only through the
combining of categories, the male and the female, the divine and the
material, that life, in whatever form, is created.[15] But, in the communion the
life granted is eternal and marks the end of physical reproduction and the
re-creation of life on earth. With communion no blood is passed on from
one generation to the next. Rather, the blood given is Christ's, assuring
individual eternity and the unity of human and divine, of male and female.
The wine as the more potent, spiritual, male substance encompasses the
more mundane, female substance that is bread. Combined the two become
Christ who is eternal continuity, in opposition to eternal reproduction.

FROM CONVENT TO COFFEEHOUSE

As we have seen, the symbolism of wine within the liturgy is highly
complex, embedded as it is in historic and social contexts. In this section, I
wish to explore some of the themes outlined above in relation to the
consumption of alcohol in secular contexts in Greece.

The wine of the sacrament, of the Last Supper, stresses the creation of
community over and above kinship. Wine is also the spiritual essence of
life, that which grants divine intoxication and a coming into one's true
nature in Christ. The wine, however, also serves to distinguish those who
partake of this communal meal from those who do not. For though the
blessed bread may be given to the whole of the congregation (even, according to Ware (1985:295), to those non-Orthodox present at the liturgy), the
wine is given only to those baptized Orthodox who have prepared themselves to receive the communion. Wine then serves to release the true self,
to create community, as well as to distinguish those outside that community.

Making a rather gross generalization, there are two distinct areas where
alcohol is consumed in the village: the coffeehouse and the home. Though
young people are spending increasing amounts of time in bars, discos, and
bouzouksidhika (cabaret-like night-spots), establishments for the greater
part located outside the village, we shall reserve discussion of these areas
for another paper. For our purposes here, we shall concentrate on the
drinking practices associated with everyday life in the village.

Social life, as in many areas in rural Greece, is characterized by the
spatial segregation of the sexes. While the relationship between men and

houses differs between (again generally speaking) Aegean Basin communities characterized by uxorilocality and mainland communities characterized by patrilocality, it remains that, throughout Greece, domestic kinship is of central significance for women in the attainment of social personhood. Though marriage and the establishment of 'one's own family' is important for men, especially on the mainland, since the continuity of the house and name depends upon their marriage, male bachelorhood does not entail the social loneliness and negation that female spinsterhood does. Married and unmarried men, unlike women, have a place where they can go to spend their leisure hours away from the kin-structured domestic community: the coffeehouse. These coffeehouses which generally ring the central village square, provide informal space for doing business, discussing issues of wider significance, meeting friends, drinking, and playing cards. In the coffeehouses the formal discourses of the village are created and there too outsiders are entertained.

Women are not welcomed in coffeehouses unless accompanied by their husbands or a male relative and even then women avoid entering this male domain. Only during village-wide festivities or during a private family function will women enter the coffeehouse freely, but during these events both the function and the context of the coffeehouse have been transformed.

Women spend most of their time in the home or in the neighbourhoods. They are associated with the domestic arena of the home, with its upkeep, with the children that assure the family's continuity, and with the rituals that serve to maintain the household's spiritual and material well-being. Women's lives are embedded in kinship relations: in the home and in the kin-based neighbourhoods that surround that home.

Alcohol and its consumption in the village takes place primarily in the male-dominated coffeehouse. Alcohol and the relations created through the treating (*kerasma*) and the acceptance of alcoholic drinks, either wine, or ouzo or *tsipouro* (both grape-based drinks high in alcohol content), underlie the very essence of coffeehouse life. Groups of friends (*parees*) gather almost daily to drink together. They treat each other, their group, an incoming friend, the group at the next table, following a standard ritual procedure. The one who is treated raises his glass in acknowledgement of the person who treated him and his salute is returned by the host. He is now indebted to the host. However, it is considered highly improper to return the *kerasma* immediately for that would imply that one does not want to continue relations with one's host or the hosting group. Rather the debt should remain 'open', thereby assuring the continuity of the relations through the return of the *kerasma* at a later time. In these *kerasma* relations there is no distinction in class or background. And, since sons and fathers tend to frequent different coffeehouses, as do brothers, kinship relations are also minimized.[16] Instead, what is stressed is the common bond between men. Through the drink it is felt that men come into their own. They can leave behind the cares of the family, the competitive drive to establish their household and children in the eyes of the community, and relax. In the congenial atmosphere of the coffeehouse surrounded by friends and peers men can dance, sing, speak freely. As one man in Peta put it: 'It is the only truly democratic place in the village. It is the only place where you can speak your mind'.

In the coffeehouse men speak easily about women. In this space they can express their unfettered sexual nature; a nature not bound by house, family and wife. For this reason, possibly, women avoid drinking the wine or the even more potent *tsipouro* or ouzo in public with non-related men. Should they do so it is considered daring and even provocative. They are consuming a substance associated with men, thereby implying the opening of relations between themselves and these unrelated men. These drinks within the context of the coffeehouse are for men only, both substance and place being too potent for women to handle alone.

The egalitarian, unisexual nature of coffeehouse relations created by the relations of *kerasma* differ, as Papataxiarchis (1988, 1991) has noted, from the competitive kin and domestic-based neighbourhood groups.[17] Thus, though friendships may arise between women within neighbourhoods dominated by their presence,[18] it is there too where the expressions of antagonism between domestic groups are most evident. One cannot move one's house or easily avoid a neighbour. But one can change one's coffeehouse or avoid an enemy. More importantly, however, the nature of the relations within the coffeehouse is to seek to avoid antagonisms; relations which stand in opposition to the competitive and hierarchical nature associated with the structure of kinship. This sense of community, unity, and equality, what Papataxiarchis (1991) characterizes as anti-structure, recalls Turner's (1969) term 'communitas' which, in contrast to structure, is a commitment to the values of human similarity, transforming the person from a socially bound entity into someone of self-expression.

Alcohol relations then in the coffeehouse, as within the ritual of Holy Communion, stress the expression, the coming into, of one's true nature as well as creating a sense of community distinct from secular kinship. Yet, there are two very important differences.

The first has to do with the nature of this self-expression, this male spirituality as Loizos and Papataxiarchis (1991) define it. The distinction between the spiritual self-expression in the village coffeehouse and that in the convent may be likened to the distinction made by Gusfield (1987) between play associated with leisure and other types of leisure time. Play, he notes, is:

leisure characterized by spontaneity, by unscheduled action, by a blur-
ring of social boundaries and by activity which is chiefly unproductive
from an economic viewpoint.

(Gusfield 1987: 84)

It may also be expressed through the development of non-hierarchical
relations, an exposure of self, and the solidifying of personal relations. This
type of behaviour is in opposition to work which is characterized by
routine, discipline, and scheduling. Such a description of playful leisure
well depicts the atmosphere created within the coffeehouse. But, Gusfield
notes, there is another type of leisure which may be a time of self-commit-
ment, discipline, and contemplation.

For the deeply religious, the secular world of work may push one to wear
a mask which adjures the sacred world of the spiritual and/or mystical
attainments. Leisure permits the expression of a self for whom the very
term 'play' is an abomination. To be absent from work is to be able to
enter a different world; to be released to God.

(Gusfield 1987: 84)

The nuns do not wear a 'mask' since they are forever within the 'sacred
world'. The sense of time removed, time apart from the secular, material
world, however, is only fully realized with the Holy Communion. It is the
time *par excellence of* self-contemplation, a deeply profound and serious
moment.

The second difference between coffeehouse and convent has to do with
expressions of human nature and sexuality. Relations in the coffeehouse are
unisexual, spiritual, and opposed to the mundane and thus often compared with
monasticism.[19] Yet these unisexual relations which stress the spiritual aspect of
men entail to a large extent aspects of male sexuality unfettered by reproduction. These expressions of sexuality, which do not necessarily lead to
sexual congress,[20] are defined in opposition to the female world of house-
bound sexuality – a sexuality of reproduction. Thus, though coffeehouse and
convent rituals in part express an egalitarian ethos and a sense of community,
coffeehouse commensality remains directly antithetical to notions of reproduction and kinship. In fact it is defined by this antithesis in part because male
identity, which is considered inherently sexual, is defined through its opposition to female sexuality which is socially bound by reproduction.

REPRODUCTION: MATERIAL AND TRANSCENDENT

Gefou-Madianou (this volume) notes that in the wine-growing region of
Koropi, Attica, sweet wine is a product of the home. It is associated

therefore with women, who have domesticated the raw wine, made by men, by 'cooking' it (boiling it) with the addition of sugar, and who serve it in the home mainly to men on special occasions. This wine is also associated with fertility, strength, and warmth and as such is given as a curative on many occasions, most significantly to women after childbirth.

In Peta wine is no longer produced, nor was it ever a major crop. None the less, men did produce wine for home consumption and *tsipouro* for consumption in the coffeehouses or on festive occasions, although, unlike Gefou-Madianou's material, wine in Peta, is associated predominantly with the home. Whereas *tsipouro* drunk in the coffeehouse is consumed either alone or with *mezedhes* (sing. *mezes*), that is olives, nuts, or at best small bite-sized morsels of bread, cheese, or raw vegetables, in Peta wine is served with the meal, a meal ideally cooked and served by women in the home. It is an aspect of household commensality. Moreover, wine, associated with festive household occasions, is also associated with the religious rituals of marriage, baptism, Easter and Christmas, that is any ritual occasion which unites people under one roof in a bond of commensality.

In this manner, just as sweet wine made by women and offered to men serves, as Gefou-Madianou notes, symbolically to unite men and women, so too does wine in Peta (and elsewhere) as part of the meal serve to unite men and women within the household. It is an aspect of commensality which reinforces the unity and continuity of the house through time,[21] a unity and continuity which depends upon the uniting through marriage of two complimentary opposites – a man and a woman – which in turn assures continuity of the birth of children through their sexuality.

This same wine is also used for Holy Communion in Koropi. How is this related, if at all, to household commensality, given that Christ's Passover meal, as noted above, is in defiance of kinship? Are not the nuns 'dead' to the secular world, forgoing ties of kinship in order to dedicate themselves to Christ? Is wine then in the Church simply in opposition to kinship as alcohol in the coffeehouse is?

As there is no space here to discuss fully the relations of the church with the secular world, allow me to restrict the argument to the convent. Briefly, the nuns do feel that they have 'died' to the secular world and in some ways they are regarded as such. For example, they describe how their parents mourned for them when they entered the convent as they would mourn for someone dead. Yet, in practice, ill parents are cared for, kin visit the convent whenever they choose to, and contact is maintained either by phone, through letters or visits.

Despite this contact, the nuns feel that with their tonsure they have joined another, greater family, the family of God. 'The Panayia (Virgin Mary) is the Mother of us all,' they say. 'She cares for us in all things and we have but to obey her wishes.' God is Father: stern, commanding but with infinite love. Care is also granted to the nuns, as to all who seek it, by the saints and guardian angels. Having once been baptized and receiving communion, you are closely bound with, a member of, this celestial family.

Secular kinship therefore is not denied in the sense that it is not recognized, but exists in the sense that it is transcended. There is a greater, more encompassing kinship. And through this kinship one is re-created anew in Christ. One's soul transcends the bounded, imperfect material realm, to achieve eternal continuity in the life beyond.

In this sense, neither is reproduction denied. It too is transcended, making all aspects of sexuality unnecessary and even detrimental since sexuality turns one's attentions away from the spiritual. Reproduction on earth through the joining of man and woman in marriage is but an aspect of the divine after the Fall, a reproduction made faulty by the necessary presence of human sexuality. True 'reproduction' occurs with the joining of the male and female in Christ; in the dissolution of difference through unity; in the combining of the bread and the wine, the female and the male, the human and the divine. True reproduction lies in the realization of what Jung (1988:117) terms the androgynous nature of the mystical Christ.

Communion, then, the partaking of the body and especially the blood of Christ, signifies the rebirth of the soul and body in Christ. The wine, and the meal, of the household are but simple impoverished images of the wine, the meal of the Eucharist.[22] Only in the sacrament is the impoverished image of the divine, the household, transcended. Only in the sacrament is sexuality finally conquered and reproduction fully and truly achieved.

CONCLUSION

This chapter has sought to explicate the relationship between the body and the soul as it is understood by a group of nuns in a convent in western Greece. Central to the discussion has been the symbolic complex surrounding wine and its consumption both in religious and a secular domain.

With the Holy Communion the separation of the material and spiritual, the secular and the religious, is transcended. United with all of creation since one is united with God through the sacrament, these divisions become meaningless. Lay and monastics are unified through Christ's body and even more so through His blood into one community. Even more profoundly, it is held that there is no male or female in Christ. Both exist within Him; they are one.

The overcoming of social divisions, the egalitarian, communal spirit, is also found in the *kerasma* relations in the secular coffeehouses. There men, through the relations of reciprocity that alcohol consumption entails, find their true self-expression in opposition to the female-centred, agonistic world of kinship. However, though similarities exist between convent and coffeehouse, it remains that the opposition to kinship and reproduction and the emphasis on male sexuality stands in direct contrast to monastic ideals.

The consumption of wine within the home, by contrast, reinforces notions of reproduction and kinship, notions found within the convent. However, whereas in the household this reproduction and the continuity it promises are by their nature sexual, in the convent reproduction and continuity centre on the spiritual, on the unity with Christ, are directly opposed to, or rather not dependent upon, sexuality. In both instances it is the unity of opposites that is needed to achieve continuity but in the convent this unity entails the ultimate overcoming of division, of antithesis.

To conclude, though many of the doctrines of the Church stress the separation of the body from the soul, it is ultimately the uniting of these two aspects and what they symbolize which leads to salvation and eternal life after death. It is only with the inclusion, the uniting, of wine – the blood, the spirit, the life – with the bread – the body – that reproduction, salvation, and continuity are achieved, for eternity.

ACKNOWLEDGEMENTS

I am indebted to Dimitra Gefou-Madianou for her constant support and insightful criticism as well as for encouraging me to attend and present a paper at the EASA conference in Coimbra. I benefited both from the presentations and the discussion which ensued. I would also like to thank Akis Papataxiarchis and Maria Phylactou for discussions which stimulated the writing of this chapter and Peter Loizos who inspired me to study monasticism and supported me throughout the project. My thanks also go to the Fulbright Foundation for funding the field work upon which the chapter is based.

NOTES

1 See, for example, Brown (1981), Bynum (1987), Meyendorff (1974), McKevitt (1988), Sherrard (1976), Ware (1985).
2 For example, Danforth (1982), du Boulay (1986), Hirschon (1981), Kenna (1976), Rushton (1983).
3 Much can be said about *prosforo*. However, let me limit myself to noting that *prosforo* is leavened bread used for Holy Communion in contrast with the wafer, unleavened bread, used by the Roman Catholic Church. In the past, *prosforo* was made by the women of the house who had fasted, who were not menstruating, and who had abstained from sex the night before. Because of these stringent precepts, the task was often left to older widows. Today it is the baker who makes the *prosforo*. The nuns often refuse gifts of *prosforo* from the laity since they do not feel that store-bought bread is clean (*katharo*) and cannot be sure of the cleanliness of home-made bread.

4　The prothesis is to the left of the altar and like the altar lies behind the *templo*, a large solid screen, usually of wood and covered with icons, which separates the altar from the nave, the laity from the priest.

5　The *aer*, notes Bashir (1960: 48), is a cloth or veil which protects the gifts from dust and flies and symbolizes the air that covers the earth.

6　Bashir (1960:115). Jung (1988:115) notes that the bread is divided into the four corresponding parts containing the letters I, X, NI, KA ('Iisous Xristos Nika – Jesus Christ is Victorious). The arrangement of the letters represents quaternity, characteristic of wholeness, and thereby refers to Christ glorified, Christ the *Pantokrator* (Holder of the Universe).

7　Monophysites were persecuted by the Orthodox Church who condemned their doctrine, finding in it the possibility to deny Christ's humanity. Christ must be fully God and fully human. Only if he is God can he redeem humanity from sin. But only if he is fully human can humans participate in the sacrifice. Christ, as man-God, serves as a bridge linking humanity with the divine.

8　Though the early Christians celebrated the Eucharist with water, Jung suggests that this simply portrays early Christian concern with the symbolism of the mysteries and not the literal observance of the sacrament.

9　See, for example, Blum and Blum (1970: 131–132); Campbell (1964:193).

10　The importance of the Holy Spirit should not be minimized. As there is no space to elaborate, let me simply note that the distinction between life and death is often portrayed as the presence or absence of the spirit or soul, entities which are sometimes interchanged. The spirit is often associated with the intellect and conscience of the person, guiding the human soul to God. The soul is the divine element of the person. When someone dies it is said by both the nuns and the villagers that the soul leaves the body through the mouth. Sometimes this departure is invisible 'like a breath'; sometimes it is described as a little bird which flies to the skies. The image is of a spiritual, ethereal entity that makes its way effortlessly to the heavens.

11　See also Pina-Cabral (1986:122–123).

12　See also Brown (1981:23–35).

13　My thanks to C. McKevitt for this point. A point also noted by Ware (1985: 290), Zizoulas (1985:81).

14　See Bloch and Parry (1982: Introduction).

15　The association between bread and women, wine and men, and the combining of these categories in order to ensure reproduction is discussed in a more secular context in rural Portugal by Pina-Cabral (1986:41–45).

16　Papataxiarchis has examined the nature of male friendship in Lesbos and its relationship with alcohol consumption in the coffeehouse. Though male friendship seems to be opposed to kinship in Lesbos as well as in Rhodes (Herzfeld 1976:196–7), Euboea (du Boulay 1974:214–220) and in Peta, material from predominantly pastoral communities seems to show that friendship among men who are not agnatically related is often considered problematic (Campbell 1964:205, Herzfeld 1985:51, 59). Though friendship is peripheral to this paper, it does remain important when considering its relationship to the structure of kinship.

17　For example, see du Boulay (1976), Hirschon (1989:176–183).

18　See Kennedy 1986.

19　See, for example, Madianou, this volume, Loizos and Papataxiarchis (1991).

Though monasteries and convents tend to be unisexual in their membership there are monasteries which have mixed membership and in the convent we are discussing here the Abbot resided in the convent. Beyond this, our concern is with the Holy Communion in which both men and women participate.

20 See Papataxiarchis (1988), Loizos and Papataxiarchis (1991), Campbell (1964:280).

21 An example of this is Campbell (1964:117, 134).

22 Many anthropologists have noted the association between the household meal and the divine meal. See, for example, Campbell (1964:341), Dubisch (1986: 207), du Boulay (1974:54–55), Hirschon (1981:81–82).

REFERENCES

Bashir, A. Archbishop (1960) *Studies in the Greek Church* (3rd edn), London: Compiled by Archbishop Bashir.

Bloch, M. and Parry, J. (eds) (1982) *Death and the Regeneration of Life*, Cambridge: Cambridge University Press.

Blum, R. and Blum, E. (1970) *The Dangerous Hour: the Lore of Crisis and Mystery in Rural Greece*, London: Chatto and Windus.

Brown, P. (1981) *The Cult of Saints: its Rise and Function in Latin Christianity*, Chicago: University of Chicago Press.

Bynum, C.W. (1987) *Holy Feast and Holy Fast: the Religious Significance of Food to Medieval Women*, London: University of California Press.

Campbell, J.K (1964) *Honour, Family and Patronage: a Study of Institutions and Moral Values in a Greek Mountain Community*, Oxford: Clarendon Press.

Danforth, L.M. and Tsiaras, A. (1982) *The Death Rituals of Rural Greece*, Princeton, N.J.: Princeton University Press.

Douglas, M. (1966) *Purity and Danger: an Analysis of the Concepts of Pollution and Taboo*, London: Routledge.

du Boulay, J. (1974) *Portrait of a Greek Mountain Village*, Oxford: Clarendon Press.

du Boulay, J. (1976) 'Lies, mockery, and family integrity' in J.G. Peristiany (ed.) *Mediterranean Family Structures*, Cambridge: Cambridge University Press, pp. 389–406.

du Boulay, J. (1986) 'Women – images of their nature and destiny in rural Greece' in J. Dubisch (ed.) *Gender and Power in Rural Greece*, Princeton, N.J.: Princeton University Press, pp.139–68.

Dubisch, J. (1986) 'Culture enters through the kitchen: women, food, and social boundaries in rural Greece' in J. Dubisch (ed.) *Gender and Power in Rural Greece*, Princeton, N.J.: Princeton University Press, pp.195–214.

Feeley-Harnick, G. (1981) *The Lord's Table: Eucharist and Passover in Early Christianity*, Philadelphia: University of Pennsylvania Press.

Gusfield, J. (1987) 'Passage to play: rituals of drinking time in American society' in M. Douglas (ed.) *Constructive Drinking: Perspectives on Drink from Anthropology*, Cambridge: Cambridge University Press, pp.73–90.

Herzfeld, M. (1976) 'Categories of inclusion and exclusion in a Rhodian village', Ph.D. thesis, Oxford: Oxford University.

Herzfeld, M. (1985) *The Poetics of Manhood: Contest and Identity in a Cretan Mountain Village*, Princeton, N.J.: Princeton University Press.

Hirschon, R. (1981) 'Essential objects and the sacred: interior and exterior space in an urban Greek locality' in S. Ardener (ed.) *Women and Space: Ground Rules and Social Maps*, London: Croom Helm, pp.77–88.

Hirschon, R. (1989) *Heirs of the Greek Catastrophe*, Oxford: Clarendon Press.

Jung, C.G. (1988) *Psychology and Western Religion*. Translated by R.F.C Hull, London: Ark Paperbacks.

Kenna, M.E. (1976) 'Houses, fields, and graves: property and ritual obligation on a Greek island', *Ethnology*, 15: 21–34.

Kennedy, R. (1986) 'Women's friendships in Crete: a psychological perspective' in J. Dubisch (ed.) *Gender and Power in Rural Greece*, Princeton, N.J.: Princeton University Press, pp.121–38.

Loizos, P. and Papataxiarchis, E. (1991) 'Gender, sexuality and the person in Greek culture' in P. Loizos and E. Papataxiarchis (eds) *Contested Identities*, Princeton, N.J.: University of Princeton Press.

McKevitt, C. (1988) 'Suffering and sanctity: an anthropological study of a southern Italian saint cult', Ph.D. thesis, London: London School of Economics.

Meyendorff, J. (1974) *Byzantine Theology: Historical Trends and Doctrinal Themes*, London: Mowbray Press.

Meyendorff, J. (ed.) (1983) *Gregory Palamar: The Triads*. Translated by N. Gendle, London: SPCK.

Mother Mary of the Orthodox Monastery of the Veil of the Mother of God, Bussey-en-Othe, France, and Archimandrite Kallistos Ware (trans.) (1969) *The Festal Menaion*, London: Faber and Faber.

Papataxiarchis, E. (1988) 'Worlds apart: women and men in Greek Aegean household and coffeeshop', Ph.D. thesis, London: London School of Economics.

Papataxiarchis, E. (1991) 'Friends of the heart: male commensal solidarity, gender and kinship in Aegean Greece' in P. Loizos and E. Papataxiarchis (eds) *Contested Identities*, Princeton, N.J.: University of Princeton Press, pp.156–179.

de Pina-Cabral, J. (1986) *Sons of Adam, Daughters of Eve: the Peasant Worldview of the Alto Minho*, Oxford, Clarendon Press.

Rushton, L. (1983) 'Doves and magpies: village women in the Greek Orthodox Church', in P. Holden (ed.) *Women's Religious Experience: Cross-Cultural Perspectives*, London: Croom Helm, pp.57–70.

Sherrard, P. (1976) *Christianity and Eros: Essays on the Theme of Sexual Love*, London: SPCK.

Skiadha, V.G. (1980) *Liturgyia ke ketischisi*, Athens: Organisation for the Publication of Educational Books.

Smith, W.R. (1889) *Lectures in the Religion of the Semites: First Series, the Fundamental Institutions*, Edinburgh: A. and C. Black.

Sykes, S.W. (1980) 'Sacrifice in the New Testament and Christian theology' in M.F.C. Bourdillon and M. Fortes (eds) *Sacrifice*, New York: Academic, pp. 61–83.

Turner, V. (1969) *The Ritual Process*, Chicago: Aldine.

Ware, T. (1985 (1964)) *The Orthodox Church*, London: Penguin.

Zizoulas, J. (1985) *Being as Communion: Studies in Personhood and the Church*, London: Darton, Longman and Todd.

6   Wine and men in Alsace, France

Isabelle Bianquis-Gasser

INTRODUCTION

This study is concerned with the production and consumption of wine in the French region of Alsace. Alsace is located in eastern France bordering Germany. Its location has not only entangled the region in border disputes between the two countries but has meant that Alsace, depending on fluctuating political and economic circumstances, has been alternatively under either French or German rule.[1] This in turn has influenced the people and practices of the region lending them distinct characteristics not observable in other regions of France.

What is common, however, throughout France is the almost sacred nature attributed to wine. Wine is associated with immortality, with blood, the vital fluid of life, and with knowledge. And this is not simply a characteristic of the French. All wine-producing countries have drawn, to greater or lesser extents, associations between wine and the knowledge that organizes their world/cosmology. For example, in ancient Egypt wine was associated with blood. The sun was an eye and the iris a grape. When the sun wept, the blood-wine of its tears gave birth to humankind. Gods such as Osiris and Dionysos were gods associated with the phallus and with wine; gods of fertility and life but also gods of the life that exists after death (Goodenough 1965).

Thus it is that wine is associated with two seemingly contradictory aspects of human life. Wine is associated with blood, fertility and human life, but it is also associated with death and the divine.

In Alsace in the vinedresser's daily and yearly activities some aspects of this duality between life and death, the mundane and the divine, will be observed. The research carried out for this chapter followed the yearly phases of the vinedresser's routine, from the vineyards to the cellar; from the work carried out by women and men to the more sensitive work carried out by men alone; from the feasts to the solemn rites that accompany the proper making of wine. The Alsace region produces mainly a white wine and only a small quantity of red. There are approximately nine thousand vinedressers in the region though I limited my acquaintance to forty.

THE AGRICULTURAL CALENDAR

A detailed study of the agricultural calendar presents two very distinct cycles. The first we may call the vine cycle. This cycle seems to be intimately connected with the human cycle of birth. The second cycle, the wine cycle, seems to be associated with death and the underworld. Thus it is as if the Alsatian vinedresser has imposed the human biological cycles of birth and death upon the agricultural cycle. Within the ever-repeating seasonal cycles the vinedresser too year after year repeats the same procedures. With the pruning of the vines he gives birth to a generation of grapes, and with this action repeats a cosmogony which explains and gives meaning to the beginning and object of existence in the world.

The vine cycle: from garden to hill

The vine cycle is the responsibility of the man of the household. He begins a generation of grapevines with the planting of the young shoots in the garden near the house, an area usually associated with women. Like the kitchen, the garden is symbolically a woman's domain. In the garden a woman will plant and tend her vegetables and flowers. Men do not enter this part of the household.

Yet it is in this most female space that men plant the tender young vine shoots. And it is in this act that the human and agricultural cycles first intersect. For the act of sowing is likened to impregnation and just as a wife gives her body to her husband, so too does she give her garden. It is the woman's body, as it is her garden, that will ensure fertility and growth.

After a year the young grapevines are ready to be transplanted, to enter into the proper production cycle which takes place on the hills nearby. They are, in a sense, ready now to move from the enclosed space of the household to join the more public (social) space of the world beyond the household's boundaries.

The vine cycle – from pruning to knotting

Today the pruning of the grapevines takes place in November, but fifty years ago it took place in February. As the Alsatian dictum notes:

> On the second of February, day of the Virgin Mary's Purification we must stop spinning, put away the spinning wheel and get out the pruning knife.
>
> (Barth 1958)

The pruning of the grapevines symbolizes the flow of fertility from the earth into the vine. Only men may prune the vines on this day and in so doing they allow the sap to make its way up the stalks revivifying the plant. The sap is likened to sperm. For these reasons, pruning is typically a man's activity. Women never assume this responsibility.

The association of pruning with the Virgin's Purification on 2 February, forty days after Christmas, links pruning with the re-establishment of the human cycle of fertility. The re-establishment of the menstrual cycle, symbolized by the churching of the Virgin and her full reinstatement into the social world, is conceptually associated with the beginning of the vine cycle.

By contrast, in the more distant past of ancient Rome the second of February marked the commencement of the Festival of the Dead. During this month, the last month of the year, the souls of the dead were said to leave their underground dwellings to roam the earth and mingle with the living. They were identified as flames flickering in and around the towns.

The breakdown of the barriers between the living and the dead, and the links between the end of one cycle of fertility and the birth and commencement of a new one, are also marked in the spring festivals and carnival that were and are held throughout Europe at this time (Gaignebet 1974). The carnival, in which the dead participate and are then sent back to their underground abode, is also linked with winter's death and the birth, or re-birth, of spring. In this revival, however, not only men but women too must take part.

And so it is that, though it is the men who prune, it is the women who must bind the vine shoots to a pole, two shoots to each. It is a task which is called the 'binding in the form of a distaff'.

In Alsace, knots carry symbolic significance for women. Knots are associated with home and family, with nidification. When a woman desires to become pregnant she knots everything she finds in her home. However, when the time of birth approaches, she unties these knots: the knots on her apron, the knots in the lace. The association drawn between women, fertility and knots is further reinforced by the small cakes baked for the carnival. These cakes look as if they have been woven and are said to resemble the female genitalia.

The task of knotting the vines then is symbolically loaded for women. In assisting her husband she assists the vine to bear fruit. In the task of knotting she transposes her own biological role onto the agricultural cycle.

The vine cycle: from knotting to fruition

The second date of importance in the vine cycle is 24 June, the day women officially enter the vineyard for the second time. Yet, like 2 February, this is a symbolic date, for women have been assisting their husbands in the field ever since pruning began. However, 24 June marks the day that women enter the field to bind the shoots once again.

It is said that on this day the vine blossoms and the grapes should appear together. It is on this day that the flower should be pollinated. It is on this day that the grape germ should be visible. If not, the crop will be compromised. This anticipated loss dismays the vinedressers who term the unrealized grapes 'abortions' or 'aborted children'. But if germ has appeared and the weather is good, as it was some years ago, then the Alsatian vinedressers organize a feast.

June 24 is the celebration of St John and the baptism as well as marking the summer solstice and the waning of the days. St John, born to an old woman, is the mirror image of Christ, born to a young woman, six months earlier. And Christ's birth on the winter solstice marks the waxing of the days. Associated with wine, Christ here too stands in antithesis to St John who is associated with water. June 24, then, is associated with water and birth. It announces the appearance of the grape germ which is associated with water (Van Gennep 1953).

Though there are many stages between this second knotting and the final sealing of the grapes in the vats in the cellars on 2 November. Suffice it to say that from 2 February to 2 November nine months ensue, a period of growth similar to the nine months' gestation period of humans. Throughout this period men and women work at complimentary tasks in the vineyards; never at the same task and never at random.

The wine cycle: birth and fermentation

Yet, while women may, and in fact should, assist in the fields knotting the plants, they are strictly prohibited from entering the cellars where the wine is kept. For them to do so would risk the wine being transformed into vinegar. Thus, this second cycle, the wine cycle, which takes place in the cellars, is strictly a man's domain.

The wine cycle begins just after 1 November, All Saints' Day, on All Souls' Day (2 November) on which day prayers are said for the souls of the departed. It begins in the dark silent cellars far from the sun, from water and sounds, and from people, all of which characterize life in the vineyards. The vintagers have gathered their grapes. They have pressed the grapes; they have killed them. To be born again one must first die. To realize the regeneration of life it is necessary to suffer change, to suffer a transformation (Eliade 1977); a transformation well depicted by the Christian iconographic symbol of the mystic wine press.

Fermentation, the chemical changes, occur in the tun's belly. And round and wet as the tun is, compared as it is by the vinedressers to a womb, the tun truly is a belly. The tun is decorated with aquatic animals: fish, dolphins, sirens, a play once again on the symbolism of water. Aside from comments made by art historians who see these forms as a revival of Graeco-Roman art, we may note a few points concerning the symbolic complexes associating water and birth and juxtaposing water to wine.

The wine is formed in the tun's belly from grapes associated in this instance with water. Water here symbolizes fecundity but also initiation, the commencement and the transformation into another form.[2] And as with baptism this water symbolizes the uniting of human with the divine.

In a similar vein we might interpret the cooper's emblem carved on the porch of the cellar. This emblem depicts a ham with two hooks or a six-pointed star.[3] This emblem is always carved on the northern side of the porch since a good cellar should always look north. In this light could this emblem be identified with the star which announced the birth of Christ? The six-pointed star is also identified as a symbol of long life, or with those who have knowledge of their existence after death.

These, however, are all speculations since the vinedressers cannot explain the symbolism of this star carved on their cellars. None the less, the link between fecundity and knowledge and their association with the cellars is interesting given that it is precisely in the cellars that men prepare an unusual birth. They assist in the birthing of alcohol, a substance which allows them, through their consumption of it, to associate with the divine. Only men make wine and only men drink wine. Never do women go down into the cellars during the fermentation process. If they do so they will impede the birth, particularly if they are menstruating.

On 11 November, St Martin's Day, the fermentation has been completed. On 24 December the wine is ideally first drawn off. It is, so to speak, born into the world as Christ is. Forty days after Christmas, on 2 February, the day of the Virgin's Purification, the wine is for the first time publicly consumed. On this day when the vines are first pruned and the new cycle begins, the wine first makes its social appearance. It is socially born as Christ and the Virgin are now fully socialized. There then follows one last forty-day cycle before the second drawing off of the wine at Easter. Thus, these alcoholic births are perfectly linked with the religious calendar – three forty-day periods (approximately) from physical birth to full regeneration in the resurrection.

WINE AND THE WORLD BEYOND

Wine is also associated with death and the link between this world and the world beyond death. For example, when men drink in their cellars, the glasses are thrown under the tuns in memory of their dead. Similarly, those who are dying are offered 'straw wine', a high quality wine, because it is believed that this wine will ease the flow of the dying in his/her journey to the other world. Wine establishes a connection with the other world; it serves as a vector easing and leading the way to another existence. Finally, when a child dies before it has been baptized, it is buried in the graveyard beside the church where the water of the baptismal font and the wine of the mass are thrown. The vinedressers say that the child is in this way three times baptized: by the rain, by the water of the baptismal font, and by the wine of the mass.

Wine thus originates from the earth and to the earth it returns. The Alsatian word '*beweinen*' means to weep, or to water with wine. And if Alsatians are noted to drink heavily after funerals this is because wine honours the dead person's memory and assists in the circulation of souls. Wine symbolizes the bond between the divine and the human, the living and the dead.

CONCLUSION

In this chapter I have sought to highlight the manner by which wine in the Alsace region is associated with the people's world conception. Here by way of concluding we might speculate as to why wine is considered a men's affair. Two possibilities come to mind. The first is given by the vinedressers themselves. They say that drinking wine with other men is a sacrament. The cellar is likened to a chapel: cool, vaulted, silent, and dark. The cycle of life and death that the wine follows speaks of a regeneration and thus of immortality. To achieve this immortal state men must drink deeply of this potent substance. They must lose their everyday conscious state, their mundane awareness. Only in this manner can they join, be united with, the divine.

Women on the other hand find their immortality, their continuity, through the bearing of children. Children represent, more for women than for men, a continuity after death. Thus, as women bear children, men give birth to wine.

We could also perhaps see the association between wine and men arising from a completely different source; give a historical or rather mythological interpretation. It could possibly be said that women like Pandora of mythic times are a bane, sent to men by the avenging gods (Bonnefoy 1981). In this light it is understandable why women, inferior beings, do not drink this most divine substance. Though the myth of Pandora is never referred to by the vinedressers, yet they do consider that wine is a noble substance, a product of stature. Women, they believe, are simply incapable of appreciating its grandeur, its qualities.

Yet now, even these most sacred acts of producing and consuming wine are slowly undergoing transformation. For today, more and more women are both producers and consumers of wine. They, more and more like men, both give birth to and lose consciousness in wine. They too participate in the divine cycle of birth and rebirth, in the regeneration of vine and wine.

NOTES

1 Alsace was part of Germany from the tenth until the seventeenth century. It then passed into French hands until 1871 when it was once again annexed to Germany until 1918. From this time until the present Alsace has remained part of French national territory.
2 Aquatic animals are used in many parts of Africa and South America as representations of a new birth, a birth which brings together man and divinity.
3 One's first impression of this carving is that it is the Greek holy rood with the TAU or RHO which were carved on the first Christian sarcophagus.

REFERENCES

Barth, M. (1958) *Der Rebbau des Elsass und die Absatzgebiete seisser Weine*, Strasbourg, Paris: ed. Fx Le Roux.
Bonnefoy, Y. (1981) *Dictionnaire des mythologies*, Paris: Flammarion.
Cahen, M. (1921) *La libation*, Paris: Champion.
Dion, R. (1930) *Le vin*, Lib: F. Alcan.
Dumezil, G. (1975) *Fêtes romaines d'été et d'automne*, Paris: Gallimard.
Eliade, M. (1964) *Traité d'histoire des religions*, Paris: Payot.
Gaignebet, C. (1974) *Le Carnaval*, Paris: Payot.
Goodenough, E. (1965) *Jewish Symbols in the Greco-Roman Period*, Bollinger series XXXVII, Kingsport USA: Pantheon Books.
Jeanmaire, H. (1951) *Dionysos*, Paris: Payot.
Juillard, E. (1953) *La vie rurale dans la plaine de Basse, Alsace*, Strasbourg, Paris: ed. Fx Le Roux.
Pâques, V. (1964) *L'arbre cosmique dans la pensée populaire et la vie quotidienne du nord-ouest africain*, Paris: Musée de l'Homme.
Perrin, A. (1938) *La civilisation de la vigne*, Paris: Gallimard.
Pline L'Ancien (1971) *Histoire naturelle*, Paris, Les Belles Lettres, Livre 14, 1958, Livre 23.
Reau, L. (1955) *Iconographie de l'art chrétien*, Paris: PUF.
Reuss, R. (1898) *L'Alsace au XVIIè siècle*, Paris: Bouillon.
Rolland, E. (1967) *Flore populaire ou histoire naturelle des plantes*, Paris: Maisonneuve.
Roubin, L. (1970) *Les chambrettes des Provençaux*, Paris: Plon.
Sittler, L. (1974) *L'agriculture et la viticulture en Alsace à travers les siècles*, Colmar, Ingersheim: ed. SAEP.
Van Gennep, A. (1953) *Manuel de folklore français contemporain*, Paris: Picard.
Voragine, J de (1967) *La légende dorée*, Paris: Garnier Flammarion.

7 Exclusion and unity, retsina and sweet wine

Commensality and gender in a Greek agrotown

Dimitra Gefou-Madianou

INTRODUCTION

I was sitting at the *parakouzino*[1] of Mr Yiannis's house working on my field notes and waiting for his wife, Mrs Sophia, to return from the market. First I heard her shrill voice describing to her *kouniadhos* (her husband's brother) who lived next door what she had been doing – what she had bought and how much she had paid. I then heard her slippers shuffling quickly in the yard. She paused briefly to put on her apron which she had hung from a branch of the gib lemon tree on her way out and entered the *parakouzino* holding a plastic bag with fish in one hand and two loaves of bread in the other, still struggling to tie her apron strings around her waist. Her face was red and sweaty from the warm early August wind. She was wearing her everyday robe, not having bothered to change for the trip to the market – who bothers to change for things like that anyway? – although she had to pass through the main street and the square of the village where most of the coffeehouses are situated and where the men pass the time of day. Now, in the backyard, cleaning the fish and feeding the entrails to the cats, Mrs Sophia excitedly told me whom she had met in the market. Mrs Sophia loved going to the market, but she could only do it when Mr Yiannis was away for he was the one who did most of the household shopping.[2]

Half an hour later the whine of the front gate and Mr Yiannis's characteristic cough made Mrs Sophia, who was frying the fish, jump. Moving quickly from the *parakouzino* she placed the cooked fish and a big bowl of boiled herbs on the *parakouzino* table while I put away my notebooks and maps. She knew someone else was with him. A quick look from the window had informed her that Yiorgos, the 19-year-old son of Mr Yiannis's elder brother, had come for a visit. He had been serving in the army over the past year but had taken leave these last few days to help his father with the cleaning of the barrels and the grape harvest. Though he lived next door he tended to spend much of his time in Mr Yiannis's household for Mr

Yiannis did not have any sons and Yiorgos was carrying Mr Yiannis's father's and grandfather's names – Yiorgos Niko Lekas. He was the heir and representative through his names of the continuity of the Lekas family. Mrs Sophia had started cutting the bread when we heard Mr Yiannis's heavy steps moving towards the *katoy*.[3] With that Mrs Sophia relaxed. She knew she had time now.

Yiannis loved visiting the barrels. Every time he entered the *katoy* he would inspect them, checking to make sure that everything was in order. This was his special place in the household. He took care of it, cleaned it, painted it with whitewash every year. He was proud of it because it was deep and warm and kept his retsina good all year round, making him a respected producer in the community. Mrs Sophia knew that he would bring some retsina wine for lunch from his *chroniariko* barrel – the barrel in which the good retsina was kept all year round; the barrel that Mr Yiannis called the family barrel because he did not sell wine from this one. Mr Yiannis would often go down to the *katoy* to bring fresh retsina for lunch and dinner, and especially so when a friend was visiting.

This visit to the barrels gave Mrs Sophia another 5–10 minutes. Without talking – she rarely talked when Mr Yiannis was around – Mrs Sophia continued setting the table, bustling to and from *parakouzino* to the *kellari* to fetch olive oil and *feta* cheese, going to the main house to get the clean towel we would use to dry our hands before sitting down to eat. Lunch should be and was always served when Mr Yiannis came home (usually around 12 o'clock). That day Mr Yiannis had gone to Athens to buy some straw for his barrels (and had unexpectedly come back a little early, thus explaining Mrs Sophia's agitation) as the barrel season would start in a few days and he had to be prepared.[4]

Everything was set when Mr Yiannis entered the kitchen, greeting us with a loud voice. He stood there at the entrance bending his head a little for he was taller than the *parakouzino* door, holding up his washed hands, with a helpless look in his eyes, water dripping on to the floor. He had washed his hands at the tap outside the kitchen. Despina, his 22-year-old daughter, rushed to hand him the towel. Next to him stood his nephew holding the *mastrapa*[5] filled with the retsina brought from the *katoy*, not doing anything with it, until Despina took it from his hands, carefully emptied the retsina into a glass jar and put the copper jug in its place on the window frame outside the kitchen. The *mastrapa* is a *katoy* item. Its place is not in the kitchen. Mr Yiannis watched the scene with satisfaction. He often told me with pride that he did not know where Sophia kept things in the house. He did not even know how much oil, a household product, was left in the *kellari*. Mr Yiannis moved to take his seat at his usual place at the table. We all sat except for Mrs Sophia who was still going back and forth serving big portions of food on to individual plates, always serving her husband first. It was a task she both enjoyed and one which she guarded jealously. It is a ritual Mrs Sophia inherited when her mother-in-law died. Mr Yiannis started distributing the bread: two pieces to each one of us just next to our plates. Silently we waited for Mr Yiannis to begin. He welcomes his nephew first, wishes good luck to my children and my family, and to his daughter he wishes success in her exams. He then begins eating. Mrs Sophia reinforces her husband's wishes with one word, 'Amen'. After a while he distributes the wine, filling everyone's glass a little more than half from the kitchen jar.

Before long Mr Yiannis asked Sophia whom she had met on her 'trip' to the market. Mrs Sophia began to give a detailed account of her market trip, an account that was repeatedly interrupted by Mr Yiannis who obviously knew her movements and was simply quizzing her in a stern voice and before everyone to make sure she would tell him her movements in full. It was an interaction that did not disturb Mrs Sophia in the least though I was amazed by the amount and detail of the information Mr Yiannis had acquired concerning his wife's movements in the market in so little time. As he explained to me later, 'It is a duty of all friends and male relatives to notice what the women of the house are doing when out in public and to inform one another'.

Scenes like this one are an everyday occurrence in the Messogia community (a pseudonym), a community in Attica, where I have conducted field work for the past three years.[6] In many Greek ethnographies a marked separation between the world of women and the world of men is noted.[7] This separation has often gone under the analytic distinction of private versus public domains – an analytic distinction which rightly has been questioned as too confining in relation to what people believe and how they act (Dubisch 1983, 1986; Hirschon 1978, 1983; and Danforth 1983; also Hoffman *et al.* 1974).

In Messogia, the people do indeed distinguish between male and female domains, distinctions which often parallel the private/public distinctions noted in other works. Yet although Messogia is a virilocal[8] community where agnatic ties play a very important role in social life and in which men are the owners of the households and the vineyards – possessions, particularly the vineyards, which are basic to male identity – it is women who control the household; keep the money; lock and unlock doors; cook and distribute food and who ensure that their men appear properly clothed and polished in the public world of the coffeehouse. They, too, are the makers and distributors of the powerful, mystic and sacred sweet wine: a wine which is offered to the church and through the blessing of the priest becomes an element within the Holy Communion. This same wine, when not blessed by a priest in church, is given to men in small quantities to strengthen them, thereby increasing the likelihood of the proper and successful sowing of male seed, which ensures the birth of children and more especially male offspring (see also Herzfeld 1985).

In order to understand the particular social construction of gender via alcohol among the people in Messogia the present analysis will have to investigate aspects of Messogia culture that at first sight seem not directly related to alcohol. First, the people of Messogia must be seen in a broader context in order to understand the conditions which have led to their social isolation despite their proximity to Athens. Second, having sketched the social organization of the community and the central role of land and especially of the vineyards (*ambeli*) and their by-product wine to the community's identity, attention will be focused on the relationship between retsina and sweet wine in the social construction of gender in this community. It will be shown that the processes of production, distribution and commensal uses of retsina and sweet wine play out the paradoxical distinctions and re-unification or integration of the sexes in everyday life, as well as the distinction and unification of household and community. Retsina and sweet wine, though associated with men and women respectively, ensure through their transformative properties both male identity and fertility; they ensure the regenerating power of fertility both within the household and vineyards, securing thereby the continuity of people, households and community.

Social and ritual life in Messogia all year round and especially during the *moustia* period[9] is characterized and dominated by wine. A marked separation of the genders is also reflected in the retsina and sweet wine production and consumption; a separation associated with notions and beliefs of pollution and purity which in the local perception are associated with female and male natures respectively.

The production, distribution and consumption of retsina in all-male and in mixed gatherings provide alternative types of commensal drinking, one suited to relations in the coffeehouse and the *katoy* and the other to household relations. On the other hand the production, distribution and consumption of sweet wine provides modes of commensal gatherings through which broader communal relations are constructed and which transcend individuals (men or women), drinking groups in the coffeehouse or in the *katoy*, as well as family and kinship relations. It is in this context that the marked separation of male and female worlds may be understood and the complex, fluid, yet exciting and mystic world of transformations approached.

In the Messogia region two distinct gender domains are indeed discernible. It will be shown that gender identities are constructed through the production, distribution and consumption of retsina and sweet wine, associated with men and women respectively. However, though these two domains are from one viewpoint distinct and separate, it is also evident that not only are they complementary, but in constant interaction with one another. In short, gender domains and discourses are not clear cut. For example, women, though denied participation in the strictly defined male gatherings of the coffeehouses and *katoy*, are nevertheless present in that they are frequently referred to and signficantly influence the construction of male discourse and identity.

THE MESSOGIA PEOPLE AND THEIR LAND (VINEYARDS)

Messogia is a small agrotown numbering 12,800 inhabitants (1981 census).[10] It is one of seven communities constituting a distinct region, the Messogia,[11] in south-east Attica some 30–40 km from Athens. The indigenous people of the area, *Arvanites*, trace their origin back to the thirteenth century A.D. to Albania and the Dalmatian Coasts, areas which they insist on calling 'Northern Epiros' (*Vorios Epiros*) in order to emphasize their Greek ethnicity. These Christian ancestors had originally moved to Attica either to work as mercenaries or as farmers and shepherds for the Dukes of Athens (Lambros 1905, Keramopoulos 1945, Koumaris 1943, Biris 1960, Hatzisotiriou 1973, Gerontas 1984). In return many were given permission to cultivate land in the sparsely inhabited regions of Attica during the thirteenth and early fourteenth centuries (Gerontas 1984; Papanikolaou 1947). It is because of this historic past that the Messogites speak of themselves as being truly Greek, despite their 'Albanian' origins.

The people of the whole area nowadays number about 50,000 and are best known for their retsina production and their local dialect *Arvanitika* – a mixture of Greek, Albanian, Slavic and Turkish (ibid.).[12]

Social life in Messogia is experienced predominently in households, neighbourhoods, *kafenia* (coffeehouses) and vineyards. Households are grouped within neighbourhoods in large conglomerations of male kinsmen. It is an endogamous virilocal community. Women move out from their family home into that of their husband. For this reason women are considered divisive since their entry into the spousal home marks the division of the parental household and land and especially vineyards. By bringing a dowry, however, women enable their husbands to create their own household and more importantly to become producers of their own wine. Moreover, though men own the family house and vineyards, it is women who are the true 'mistresses of the house'[13] and through their production of sweet wine link past and future generations.

Until 1965 when the main coastal and mainland roads connecting Athens with Sounion were constructed, the region was a relatively poor agricultural area comprising small endogamous, 'closed' communities. These local communities were often antagonistic, but considered themselves 'brothers' and acted accordingly when facing individuals or groups coming from outside their region. This was particularly evident in relation to Athenians whom they called *skliades* (*sklias* = bourgeois), a highly insulting appellation.

With the construction of the coastal and mainland roads connecting Athens and Sounion in the 1960s, greater access to Athens was afforded to the Messogites. Moreover, over the past 15 years the area has undergone dramatic transformations. The urbanization of the 1960s and 1970s witnessed the rapid growth of Athens and the greater Attica region as well as the industrialization of the Messogia area, challenging the strictly endogamous and agricultural nature of the community. Today people practise a dual economy, still working as agriculturalists but also as clerks and/or skilled workers.[14] Yet, despite these changes, Messogites, probably because of their endogamous practices and their language, still exhibit unique characteristics which differentiate them from other communities in Attica, particularly Athenian urbanites (Hatzisotiriou 1980, 1985, Tsovaridou 1981).

The main crops of the area comprise the typical 'Mediterranean triad' (Braudel 1985), grapes, wheat and olives, from which derives the Messogites' basic diet – wine, bread and olive oil – as well as the community's economic base. Grapevines in particular have, for centuries, practically constituted a mono-crop, and even today vineyards occupy almost half of the cultivated land in Messogia (Markou 1988). The vineyards' by-products, wine and must, show in fact an increase[15] over the past 10 years despite the dramatic industrialization and economic development of the area (C.P.E.R. (K.E.P.E.) 1988, Statistical Yearbooks – Ministry of Agriculture 1980, 1986). Thirty-seven million litres of wine are produced yearly in the whole area of Messogia (ibid.).

Despite this, or because of this, Messogites are economically dependent on the Athenian market, selling their vineyard products, especially must and retsina wine, and in more recent times vegetables and wage-labour. Strong, often tense, patron–client relations[16] have been constructed therefore over the years between Messogites peasants and important and influential Athenian merchants and politicians. This may result in part from the Messogites' illiteracy and their difficulty in handling the Greek language, rendering them unable to bargain and protect themselves from middlemen. For all these reasons Messogites tend to regard the Athenians with suspicion, viewing them as exploiters who take but give little in return.[17]

On the other hand, government officials[18] and Athenians have always regarded the Messogites way of life as being based on an anti-progressive ethic (*Kathisterimenoi*). They regard the Messogites as fraudulent peasants (*poniri choriates*), lazy, and uneducated; a backward people who have not taken 'advantage' of their proximity to Athens and its civilization. The Messogites often refer to the prominent Athenian historian who once, when standing at the top of Hymettus mountain – the mountain separating Athens from the Messogia region – said looking towards Athens: '*I chora tou pnevmatos*' (the city of spirit), and then turning towards Messogia: '*I chora tou oinopnevmatos*' (the country of spirits–alcohol; also implying imbecility) (Kambouroglou 1959).

In part, this may be due to the close relationship Messogites have with their land, a relationship which discourages the selling of land and especially vineyards. People here tend to buy and create rather than sell or uproot vines in favour of more profitable crops. The close ties between people and the land, and more particularly vineyards, should be and is very strong. Social identity is symbolically expressed through vines. Messogites hold that their ancestors lived and were buried on this land. Vine plants (*koutsoura*) were planted by their ancestors and in this sense they mark the community's continuity. In fact, Messogites often describe themselves as descendants of their ancestors' vineyards rather than as descendants of their ancestors as people.

> People are born and die; *koutsoura* are eternal; for even if an *ambeli* [vineyard] is replanted it is from the same *koutsoura* that we take the young shoots; in that way the *ambeli* is reborn; and so it goes; these *koutsoura* have been in this land for always.

Koutsoura (vine plants), in other words, are the symbols of permanence and continuity, of the community's history and culture. For until recently vineyards constituted not only the source of subsistence for Messogites but, as today, the mode through which, social stratification occurs and social identity is constructed. A *veros Messogitis* (true Messogite) is a man who ownes vineyards, a landowner as opposed to a land labourer[19] and, more to the point, a household wine producer as opposed to a non-producer in the community.[20]

Vineyards in principle belonged and belong to men, as do houses. They are usually transmitted from one generation to the next patrilineally. Very rarely, and only in special cases, are they given as dowry. This was the principle until thirty to forty years ago, but things are changing today. The phenomenon is complex and cannot be fully analysed in this chapter. What is suggested here is the signification of the fundamental rules.[21] Thus ideally, like households which are grouped in neighbourhoods comprised of male kin, vineyards are grouped by male lineage, particular plots belonging to particular households within the same lineage. The Douneika *ambelia* are comprised of the *ambelia* of Petro Dounis, Spyro Dounis, etc.

Men moreover have personalized their relationships with their vineyards. Vineyards are given names indicating who in the family first created the vineyard. This vineyard family name carries such social weight that it is often maintained even if the vineyard changes owner.[22]

The close identity between men and their vines is further characterized by the fact that there are no clearly visible boundaries from one vineyard to the next. Everyone knows to whom a particular vineyard belongs and disputes over vineyards or even plants are non-existent in the region. It would be similar to arguing over whether one's finger belongs to the owner or to someone else. It is for this reason that Messogites have never bothered to acquire titles (written documents) to their land. They become very agitated when asked for titles: 'Even the rocks know that these *koutsoura* belong to my family'. As a consequence, they are faced with major obstacles when they wish to sell land, or when they have to pay taxes.

Vineyard owners and especially retsina producers[23] visit their vineyards often, thereby expressing their close ties with the plants and the land. Especially during the period before grape harvest men may visit the vineyard three or four times a day. The vineyard, they say, 'tells' them when it is the right time for the harvest; it is for this reason that they must visit, in order to 'hear' the *ambeli*: 'It's not only the ripeness and colour of the grape; the humidity has to be right; the leaves have to be turned in a certain way, upside down; the moon will give certain signs; and it should not have rained the night before'. Then they know it is the right time; the vineyard calls then; it's time for them to go. Thus, they never know when the harvest will occur; each vineyard has its own time: 'Do all women give birth at the same time? No; each one has her own time; only (God) knows these things.' (The informant did not actually say the word God but pointed upwards.) The vineyard owners will not only visit their vineyard during the harvest season but will often go for walks in the vineyards even during winter when there is no work to be done. They care for the vineyards a lot. They walk up and down, stopping every now and again for a cigarette; they may even talk to the vine plants. They know how old each vineyard is, who planted each vine and the special care different kinds of vines need. They are very proud when they succeed in creating a vineyard within their own lifetime. To do so will assure them a kind of eternity. Their name will be remembered and will live on through the vines.

Thus men make all major decisions concerning the vineyards. There is great competition among wine-producers concerning the health of their vineyards, their productivity and the retsina these vineyards produce. Their reputation as 'successful producers' is not only judged by the final product – the must or the retsina sold to the merchants during the *mustia* period – but is constantly evaluated throughout the various stages of the agricultural cycle. The final and most important judgement takes place in the *katoy*, when the retsina is first tasted by fellow producers and friends.

THE *KAFENIO*

The pervasive nature of alcohol in Messogia society is witnessed by the numerous *kafenia* and *tavernas*[24] concentrated in the village square and on both sides of the main village street. Drinking, an important everyday activity, is practised by men in groups in *kafenia* (coffeehouses) and tavernas. It is in these places that social relations are constructed; social status expressed; antagonisms and disputes manifested and resolved; reputations gained and male identity expressed. *Kafenia* also constitute the institutions where the rites of passage transforming male adolescents into men take place. There are approximately fifty-two coffeehouses and tavernas in the village including those scattered along the road leading to the small tourist site near the sea, also considered part of the town. In the Messogia region the ratio of public drinking institutions per capita is 1:160 male inhabitants, a very high ratio when compared to other districts of Greece (see also Herzfeld 1985, Papataxiarchis 1988).

The central role played by alcohol in the construction of male identity and in the building of community relations has been noted by other Greek and Mediterranean ethnographers.[25] In particular, in the early 1980s anthropologists working in the Mediterranean associated the construction of male identity with a coffeehouse or bar discourse.[26] An anti-household, anti-productive ethos has also been noted in the construction of male identity, an identity which can only be created in the absence of women, it seems. Yet ethnographic evidence from Messogia suggests that, despite their absence from the *kafenia* (coffeehouses) and tavernas, women may be indirectly 'present' and influence male discussions concerning domestic and family issues. I have seen, for example, Sophia – known to us from the story above – asking her husband's friend Thanassis to advise Yiannis (her husband) not to 'give' his vineyard to his nephew Yiorgos. Yiannis considers this option in light of the fact that he has no sons to inherit the land from him. A few days later this matter came up in a discussion Yiannis had with Thanassis both in the *kafenio* and again in Thanassis's *katoy* in the presence of Tasso (another producer, and member of the *parea*). Both men advised Yiannis not to make a hasty decision on the matter. He should give it some more thought. Though Sophia's name was not mentioned in these discussions, her presence was evident in that she had asked Thanassis to speak with her husband and in that her husband was fully aware that she had done so.[27] Important household matters, such as marriage arrangements, personal problems with wives, or more recently the buying and selling of vineyards, are often discussed among friends in the *kafenio* and *katoy* despite their often delicate and private nature. It is, in fact, amazing how much 'privacy' is achieved especially in the loud, lively, noisy, bright, yet intimate world of the *kafenio*.

Women avoid entering the *kafenio*. However, they will insist that their husbands visit the *kafenio*, assisting them to dress and depart from the female-run, almost matrifocally oriented, household to find refuge in the *kafenio*, a male refuge *par excellence*.[28] As an educated, married woman studying their community, I was occasionally 'allowed' to visit some *kafenia*[29] in the square during the evenings but always in the company of either my husband or one of my older adult male friends in the village.[30]

Messogites men spend a large part of their day and evening in the *kafenio*. Though it is not possible here to deal with all aspects of *kafenio* life in Messogia, it should be noted that the organization of the everyday life of the *kafenio* is structured in part by the social status of its clientele,[31] and this was especially so in the past. Today the distinctions between landowners and labourers, wine producers and non-producers, are less clear-cut than they seem to have been twenty-five to thirty years ago.[32] Yet, despite the fact that these distinctions are blurred, there are differences, the most striking being that though large, wine-producing landowners will visit the coffeehouses they will also spend many evenings drinking in the *katoy* with male friends of similar social background and status. None the less, the fact remains that life in the coffeehouse follows much the same rhythm for both large landowners and labourers.

A typical man's day begins with a visit to the *kafenio* for his morning coffee. Later, he may stop in for a snack and a drink, usually beer or ouzo. It is in the afternoon and evening, however, that *kafenia* fill with men playing cards, discussing politics, conducting business and later drinking beer (mostly) or wine with their *pareas* (group of male friends who regularly drink together).[33] And it is late in the evening that the atmosphere in the *kafenion* may become highly convivial. Men sit with their *pareas*, drinking and eating, discussing among themselves as well as with others in the *kafenio*. Not only do they treat other men within their *parea*, but they will exchange *kerasmata* (treating someone in this instance to beer or wine) between *pareas*. Thus, despite status differences, an egalitarian ethos is created through the *kerasmata* and the talk, an ethos which transcends individuals and social categories. Rich landowners even today do not stay in *kafenio* until late. They prefer to meet their *parea* in the *katoy* or outside the village.

Moreover, it is through these male gatherings in the *kafenia* that one apsect of male identity is created. And it is from within this collectivity that individuals are able to confront those who are more powerful than they. For example, men may confront a landlord through a spokesman to demand a wage increase. Or they may, in a similar manner, confront an Athenian merchant concerning the price of must and retsina. Everyone knows the story of Vangelis Dimas who, back in the 1960s, stood up in the *kafenio* and addressed the Prime Minister, Georgios Papandreou, who was at the time visiting the village with some of his deputies from the area. Dimas pointed out to the group of politicians that the price of an *oka* (1,300 grams) of grape must was less than a cup of Greek coffee. This act was and still is widely discussed because Papandreou nearly doubled the price of must that same day. In these instances then men not only assert themselves as men and as spokesmen of their *parea* or social group, but as spokesmen of their community's identity in the face of those deemed outsiders.

RETSINA AND KATOY: MEN'S WORLD IN THE HOUSEHOLD

As noted above men are not only the main consumers but also the sole producers of retsina. After the grape harvest and must production, and for the following forty days (called *krassoma* or *ginoma*[34]) men – as producers of retsina – spend most of their time in the *katoy*.[35] They practically live there.

Again, in the limited space of this chapter, only those aspects of retsina production deemed essential to our discussion will be noted. To begin with, cleanliness is vital in retsina production. First the *katoy* and the barrels are thoroughly cleaned.[36] Then the freshly harvested grapes are pressed. From the time the grapes are collected to the time the must and resin (for the retsina flavour) are put into the barrels is usually only three days at most. Activities must be done very quickly which means that this period is one of great tension. All activities have to be coordinated with true mastery.

Must is quickly put from the must tank (sterna) into the barrels. Fermentation should occur only in the barrel. Then freshly collected resin (i.e. retsina – from Hymettus or Pendeli mountain pinetrees), which is the only ingredient added, is put into each barrel. For each barrel a small piece of resin is diluted in the *mastrapas* with lukewarm water and then placed very carefully and with great attention, first into the family barrel, and then into the other barrels. Water must be the right temperature: neither too cold, nor too hot. It should have the temperature of must. While other men may help in most of the other activities, this act of putting the first resin into the barrel has to be done by the *nikokiris* (the owner of the household and the *katoy*).

After the resin is placed in the barrels the festive atmosphere which existed during the grape harvest and pressing ceases. A curtain is drawn separating the barrels from the rest of the *katoy*. The *katoy* door closes. Barrels have to be left alone in the warm *katoy*. Everything is quiet. The *nikokiris*, however, is not relaxed at all. He stays in the *katoy* to take care of the barrels; he coaxes them and blows into them with a cane in order to stir the must and assist the fermentation. Every now and then he puts his ear to each barrel and listens carefully. The fermentation process has started; he is happy. One barrel has overflowed. He has to take some must out. Another barrel needs some more must. He does not sleep at nights; he must be close to his barrels. In fact, the barrels are an extension of his body; he has become one with them. He gives them names, heroic names, like the one he calls *Averof* – the famous battleship. He keeps visiting the barrels, touching them, still listening to them even when they are finally firmly closed. He will only truly relax in December, with the end of the first and most important fermentation period.

After he had done all this for his barrels and his wine, and after I, myself, had experienced this excitement in the household of Yianni Lekas, I was amazed to hear from him that he had not actually done anything: 'Retsina is a natural thing (*fisiko prama*). It is made by itself (*yinete mono tou*). It is clean and pure (*katharo ke aghno*), a living organism (*zondano prama*); it has living bodies in it. It is from nature (*ine apo ti fisi*); I haven't done anything to it; I was simply there.'[37]

It is in December then, when the first fermentation has ceased, that together with his friends – people of the same age group and fellow retsina producers – a producer will be judged. One of the barrels kept for the household will be opened and the wine drunk from the barrel tap first (*tapa* or *stoupi*) and then from the *mastrapa*, passed from one man to the other. His friends will praise him; and it is then he feels justified. His destiny as a successful retsina producer has been fulfilled, for this year at least.

These all-male gatherings in the *katoy* take place all year long but especially from December to May (Saint Nicolas to the village saint's day). After May, most of the wine is usually finished. The best *katoya* (plural) are those in the basement of the house or the basement of the storeroom, outside the house. They have to be deep, warm and, most importantly, clean, both symbolically and literally. For this reason women and especially still fertile women are not allowed in the *katoy*, particularly during fermentation. They are considered unclean. Similarly, in contrast with the *kafenio* where men enter easily with mud on their boots, where they feel free to stamp out their cigarettes on the floor or even occasionally to spit, and where the dingy walls do not seem to insult the eye, the *katoy* shines with cleanliness. Its walls are whitewashed, by the men, its floors are swept clean, smoking is prohibited and great care is taken when entering so as not to bring in dirt. In this all-male realm, time seems to stop: 'When in there one does not understand if it is day or night, winter or summer. It's always dark and the temperature there always the same.'

Contrasted with the *kafenio* all-male gatherings where mainly beer-drinking occurs, the *katoy* wine-drinking and meat-eating gatherings[38] are of a more private and intimate character. While drinking and eating, the men may discuss household affairs as noted above or their *vassana* (personal worries which may also concern the household). Later on, they may sing and sometimes dance. Men express their *merakia* (desires) when drinking in the *katoy*. They also call the 'steam' of the fermenting must *merakia* (see also Herzfeld 1986). To these all-male *katoy* gatherings, they often invite the village barber – a good singer and guitar player whose father was a retsina producer and also a rhyme maker. Sometimes, under the influence of wine, men get into the big empty barrels and sleep off the retsina. In these wine drinking gatherings men transcend or go beyond the confines and constraints of the everyday world.[39] Their talk becomes sentimental, their bodies more expressive; they laugh, cry, tell jokes, and most importantly 'open their souls'[40] (*anigoun tin psychi tous*) to their close friends.[41]

In these *katoy* gatherings only the owners of vineyards, the ones who know the 'secrets' of retsina, are invited. In the dark, humid, and warm world of the *katoy* where must is transformed into retsina, these male 'peasants' through the drinking of retsina, sometimes to the point of *methy* (drunkenness),[42] are transformed, achieving their true identity both as people (true *nikokirides*) and as community members (*veri Messogites*). For they are the ones who, through vineyard cultivation and retsina production, are securing the community's continuity as well as their own. Firstly, a man cannot become a *nikokiris*[43] unless he has barrels in his household (*nikokiris dichos varellia den ginete*). Secondly, the community's unique identity is secured (saved) either in comparison to neighbouring communities, who have rented their vineyards to big wine companies, or as compared to Athenians whom they say they have taught – through retsina – what the true 'spirit' of life is (referring to the saying of the prominent historian; see p.144).[44] In fact, not too many years ago, they used to engage in competitive drinking bouts with Athenians who would eventually drop to the floor drunk. It was a 'game' they thoroughly enjoyed. For it is a rule among Messogites that men should be able to drink quantities of alcohol; they should always maintain their self-control. On the one hand, this spiritual intoxication which comes through the sharing of the family wine and *kerasma* codes – they drink always from the family barrels, the barrels they never sell – stresses the group and community solidarity, and the symbolic continuity found in this extreme type of collectivism. This is more dramatically expressed by the fact that when a wine producer dies his *parea* members have to drink all the remaining wine in the deceased's family barrel. On the other hand, it contrasts the anti-community and thus destructive drinking of the sole drinker.[45]

SWEET WINE AND *KELLARI*: WOMEN'S WORLD IN THE HOUSEHOLD

However, it is not only retsina wine that is made but also sweet wine. The processes of production of each type of wine, though both take place in the household, are vastly different, as are their modes of consumption. Retsina is made from the best of the white grapes, the *Savatiana* variety, grown in the area. While it is not important from which vineyard the grapes are taken for the retsina,[46] sweet wine must be made from grapes taken from all the vineyards of the household and then, ideally, mixed with black grapes (Messogites call the red grapes black), specially cultivated for sweet wine.[47]

Sweet wine is made exclusively by the women of the household. Men are completely excluded from the process. The women harvest white grapes from all the vineyards during harvest time[48] and keep them for a few days until the big rush of must production for the retsina is over.[49] The black grapes (if the household has a black grape vineyard) are picked from the vineyards by women and kept in the basket(s) for a few days (usually three) so that their must becomes thick and dark.[50] After this three-day period, barefoot women press the grapes, separately, white grapes first then the black ones. The women who do this have to be clean, that is, either older women past the menopause, or young women who are not menstruating. Nor should the women be *lechones* (have recently given birth), or have had conjugal relations the night before or during the cooking of sweet wine.

The grapes are pressed in baskets which have been placed into large copper pots.[51] Before mixing the two types of must, they are drained using a clean white cloth. The must is then mixed and cooked in one of the copper pots over a strong fire in the yard. When it starts boiling they 'cut' it with soil (a handful of soil is thrown into the pot to settle the frothy wine) taken from the household vineyards.[52] They dampen the fire and allow the wine to settle. Women continue doing this until all the froth has been removed.

The production of sweet wine takes three days and nights and it is cooked in a festive, yet serious, atmosphere. During this period women have to watch over the fire especially during the night. The must has to boil down to approximately half its original volume. Women constantly stir the wine removing the froth. All these boiling and draining procedures aim at mixing the two ingredients, soil and must, thoroughly. Boiling is followed by periods of cooling down so that the mixing of the soil with the must is secured and so that the final product will be a red (rosé) sparkling liquid, sweet and thick (thicker than retsina).

Though the women of individual household may produce the sweet wine for their own particular household, it is the preferred practice to produce the wine in the company of one's mother-in-law and one's husband's brothers' wives. This is contrasted with the production of retsina which is made by a single male householder, and seems to parallel the Messogites' insistence that sweet wine be made from a mixture of grapes gathered from all the vineyards.

Sweet wine is strong, stronger than retsina (usually around 15–20 per cent vol.). It is thought to keep for years without going bad. If it becomes very thick due to its high sugar content, the women water it down with retsina wine. It is kept by each *nikokira* in her *kellari*.[53]

A *kellari* is a small, windowless room, attached to the *parakouzino*. It may be said that what the *katoy* is to men, the *kellari* is to women. There is a major difference, however: while men use the *katoy* to socialize and transcend their mundane selves with their male *parea*, the *kellari* is used primarily to store comestible products of the household: olive oil, flour, bread, but most importantly sweet wine. Some women keep the money of the household there. In fact women 'hide' things there from the rest of the family. They often lock the *kellari* especially when they leave the house. Only the mistress of the house (*nikokira*) has access to the *kellari*. Not many years ago a newly married bride who lived with her mother-in-law did not have access to the *kellari* right away. She was only slowly 'initiated' into the world of the kellari; using household products for cooking, serving food, etc. She was allowed to use the *kellari* freely and had access to its key only when she became the mistress of the house in her own right. In recent times, some women also put the refrigerator in the *kellari*. In this way they control food consumption in the household. Men need women to serve them food at any time of the day. They excuse themselves by saying they don't know where things are in the house.

Sweet wine is used for two purposes. First, it is taken to church together with home-made bread (see Iossifides 1990, 1991) to be used as one of the elements in the Holy Communion. Through this sweet wine and bread, made and offered to the church by women, consecrated by the priest and partaken of ideally at least by all members of the community, women serve as unifying forces, linking the household with the divine and with the community. It may be said then that women hold pivotal roles since, through the sweet wine and food which they cook, they create a discourse which allows them to unite different categories.

Sweet wine is also given in small quantities to men by their wives to ensure the procreation of male offspring and thus the continuation of the household. It is given to men by their wives in private, either in the evening when men come home to spend the night or early in the morning before they go to the fields to work together.[54] The knowledge of how sweet wine is made, when and in what doses it should be given to men (unlike retsina it should not make them 'dizzy', it should simply 'warm' them) is a knowledge passed down from mothers to daughters, but more particularly from mothers-in-law to daughters-in-law. Thus, despite the virilocal residence pattern which might lead one to assume the existence of strong antagonisms between mothers-in-law and daughters-in-law (see Dimen 1986, du Boulay 1974, Campbell 1964), it seems that a bond between these two groups of women is created through the sweet wine. Mothers-in-law are the holders of the knowledge concerning sweet wine while their daughters-in-law, since they know the days when they can conceive, determine the days when their husbands should receive the sweet wine. Together, the two women form a pact. They have a common goal: the continuity of the household via sweet wine. They need one another: the brides (daughters-in-law) in order to learn the secrets of the sweet wine; the mothers-in-law in order, through the young women, to ensure the household's continuity through the birth of sons to their sons.

In this sense, it may be said that mothers-in-law not only legitimate their position through the brides but also maintain a hold on their sons through them. Women as mothers and wives are responsible for making and keeping their sons/husbands healthy and strong. This strong bond between mothers and sons is evident also in that women are directly and solely responsible for the birth of male offspring, thus reinforcing the production of sweet wine. Moreover, it should be noted that sweet wine is given to mothers who have just given birth to strengthen them, and even more so to those who are breast feeding male infants (*agoromanes*).

CONCLUSION: TRANSFORMATIONS AND UNIFICATIONS

The social construction of gender in Messogia is constituted through the reflections and refractions between genders in a constant interplay between the world of men and the world of women via wine: retsina and sweet wine. Drinking captures and reflects the relations between the separation of genders and the construction of same-sex identities (men to men, women to women) separated and reunited and mirroring one another.

Vineyards and retsina are natural and pure and belong to men, who are the stable figures of the community, those who secure its continuation. Retsina production and consumption, especially in *katoy* all-male gatherings, provide a type of commensality through which individual identities and communal relations (real or symbolic) are constructed. Women on the other hand are thought to be the carriers of uncleanliness; they are refused places where retsina is fermented and consumed by male *pareas* (drinking groups). The reunion of the two – men and women – is also accomplished via sweet wine, as a fertilizing substance in conjugal relations, thus securing the reproduction of the household through offspring, particularly male. It is through the production (cooking) of sweet wine and by offering small quantities of it to men (husbands) that women transform their negative sexuality into productive (positive) fertility and through male offspring they also contribute to the continuation of the household. More importantly, by offering sweet wine to church (which through the blessing of the priest is transformed into Holy Communion), they are transforming themselves from agents of division and thus of communal life discontinuation into mediators of the community's symbolic re-unification. For sweet wine unites men and women as human beings in a community transcending the household and kinship relations. Thus, community also transcends the coffeehouse and the retsina *katoy* gatherings. Wine then creates boundaries between genders, separating them from one another, and defines the nexus between the mundane and spiritual worlds. It also dictates the unification of the genders. In Messogia this constant movement of exclusion and unity of the genders via wine can be captured as a jigsaw line.

It is against this background that interactions and transformations of substances (commodities)[55] and persons can be understood and analysed both on a practical and a symbolic level.

Despite the seemingly marked separation between the worlds of men and women, there are some arenas central to the comunity's social life, where men and women work or celebrate together. These arenas are centred around the vineyards, the household and the community's religious/social ceremonies and festivities. Though the vineyards belong to men, and women are refused participation in the retsina-production process, women do work alongside their husbands in the vineyards all year round, even during the grape harvest. Occasionally, women may also bring vineyards to their husband's household in the form of dowry, thereby allowing their husbands to start their own wine production earlier than expected, that is, before the inheritance of the parental vineyards between brothers.[56]

Yet, though women help men in the vineyards and in gathering the grapes,[57] men are excluded from harvesting the black grapes used for the sweet wine. Despite the fact that men may carry the grapes from the vineyards to the household they do not assist in the pressing of the grapes; neither do they assist in the cooking of the must, nor in the wine's bottling and storage in the *kellari*.

During household rituals like name days, baptisms and weddings, and for everyday meals, women cook food while men are responsible for retsina. And in these household gatherings both men and women eat and drink together. It is expected however that women, especially young ones, as well as children, would drink much less than men. Eating should always be accompanied by wine-drinking and vice versa. In fact, women are not simply *allowed* to drink, they are expected to do so. The discourse constructed during rituals which are household oriented emphasizes the unity of men and women.[58] Similarly, men and women will drink and eat together when working in the fields. Women also accompany their husbands, fathers, or brothers to the *kafenia* (taverns) during the village saint's festivity or other important religious celebrations (approximately five times a year) or when baptisms and weddings are celebrated there.

Men through their association with the vineyards and through their production and consumption of retsina (in all-male gatherings) tap into a natural and pure world. In this world – the *katoy* – men may assist in the birth of a natural entity, retsina, through which they can truly express themselves as men and transcend the everyday world. The process of retsina production may also possibly allow for a conceptual parallel with pregnancy or the birth of children, natural entities which women carry and produce. Men care for the retsina, following its progress in the belly of the barrel with great intensity, caring for it and coaxing it to grow well. In the *katoy*, significantly, women are prohibited entry, as unclean. In this sense men, though defined in antithesis to women, also mirror them in the 'pregnancy' and 'birth' of retsina. Retsina in the *katoy* is not a drink but something given by nature through the mediation of men, as children are through the mediation of women.

Moreover, this 'birth' (retsina) assures the 'fertility' of the community and household not only in economic terms but also in terms of their regeneration and continuity. For the fertility of the fields and especially the vineyards is harnessed in men's 'agony' and anticipation for a good grape harvest. Two more instances stress this association between vineyards and fertility. Babies in Messogia 'come' from *ambelia* (vineyards). They are not brought by a stork as in other areas of Greece. The association of vineyards and fertility is also expressed in the Messogites' belief – yet not openly expressed – that it is 'blessed' (they use the word *evlogia* which also means prosperity) and 'good' for the household's prosperity when married couples, especially newly married ones, have conjugal relations in the vineyards; a belief which is often put to practice.

Therefore, we see that both men and women are considered necessary to and take part in the reproduction of human beings, and thus of the social world, the household and the community. They both bring the natural reproductive power of the vineyards into the cycle of human fertility and reproduction. It is not only the male-associated vineyards which ideally take part in the human reproductive cycle, but also the female-associated sweet wine.

Women's position in Messogia is more insecure than men's. First they have to cope with their 'unclean' nature depending on their physiology (menstruating and giving birth). This uncleanness is expressed by the fact that they are prohibited entry to the *katoy* – a male place *par excellence* – especially during retsina fermentation; by the fact that menstruating women cannot assist in the pressing of grapes, neither for retsina nor for sweet wine. This 'unclean' nature of women is also linked with their sexuality which, if uncontrolled, may lead to illegitimate children and thus the dishonour and disruption of the household. Second, they have to deal with their instability (moving upon marriage) and their negative reputation as divisive of land (vineyards) and household when they get married. Sweet wine production and distribution offers women the means to negotiate their insecure and negative position in the household and the community. There is little space in this chapter to expand on this but the associations which could be drawn are evident.

Women, we may say, mirror men, but men of a different category. Women's unclean nature is not only simply negatively perceived but also provides women the means of constituting themselves positively. Women give birth to natural beings, i.e. children. They acknowledge the power of the official church, attending services and receiving the bread and sweet wine of Holy Communion from the hands of the priest. They are the mediators between the family and community. They are the creators of the congregation of the church and, in their turn, offer a type of communion. The precious sweet wine is offered to men in small quantities to ensure fertility and spiritual cleanliness. Women, therefore, are responsible for their men's fertility, for the production of male offspring, and in this sense they control male productive sexuality, via sweet wine, dictating when and where conjugal relations are to occur.

Thus, just as men take greater responsibility, if not all responsibility, for the production of retsina, women carry the greater burden in the production of children, especially male children, through the preparation and distribution of sweet wine.

Women, through the preparation and distribution of sweet wine, fulfil their social role, being mothers-in-law and obtaining brides – bearers of male children. They, like priests, offer sweet wine with sacred powers to men, thus securing the reunion of separated genders in the realm of the household. They also become responsible agents and powerful actors in making good the mundane world, both in the household arena and the broader community.

Thus, women come in contact with the transcendent through the official church and harness this power to ensure both their position in society and their correct continuity. Men come in contact with the transcendent through the all-male relations in the coffeehouse and especially of the *katoy* gatherings.

Thus, though there are places and contexts in which men and women are strictly separated, there are also contexts in which men and women are united. What is clearly distinct is that men seek transcendence via wine in their homosocial gatherings while women do not, or may not need to seek this type of transcendence.[59]

Retsina and sweet wine have offered us suitable examples and the means for the discussion and analysis of the limited value of this extreme separation of the worlds of genders. For, as has been shown, these two worlds are not as separate as one's first impression may be. Why, then, is separation and exclusion so markedly expressed? Why, as we have noticed in the story presented at the beginning of this chapter, are the worlds of men and women kept so distinct even during rituals (a meal) which are believed to express and symbolize the unity of the family?

It may be that, as Bloch (1982) has suggested in his revealing article on death, women and power among the Merina: 'in order to deny that aspect of things [death] emphatically and thereby "create" the victory [life over death], the enemy must be first set up in order to be knocked down'. In Messogia, men by definition, as owners of the vineyards, the house, and the family name, do secure the household and community's continuation, except for one thing: male (and female) offspring. Women, as carriers of the negative role of being 'unclean' and divisive, are excluded from the men's world. However, through sweet wine and its (re-)creative qualities, women negotiate and finally gain an integrative role. In this manner they secure their household's and community's continuation. Their role in society is thus pivotal. For this reason I would agree with Dubisch (1986:207–8) that women, on both practical and symbolic levels, are providers of the 'glue' that helps bind distinct social units.

ACKNOWLEDGEMENTS

I would like to thank Henk Driessen, Nia Georges, Dwight Heath, Michael Herzfeld, A. Marina Iossifides, Akis Papataxiarchis and Dimitris Tsaoussis for their stimulating and helpful comments on earlier drafts of this chapter. I am especially indebted to A. Marina Iossifides for both her insightful comments and her encouragement throughout this project. To Michael Madianos I am particularly thankful for participating with such zest and sensitivity in the all-male gatherings from which I was excluded, and for offering me his critical insights from the man's point of view. He also asked all those simple, straightforward questions from which I learned so much.

This chapter is based on fieldwork carried out during 1988–91 in a Messogia agrotown. At a certain point during this period a team of graduate students from Panteion University worked in the community under my supervision, participating in the WHO/Euro Collaborative Study on Community Response to Alcohol-Related Problems'. I would like to thank all of them and especially Rania Astrinaki, Stella Galani, Marina Makri and Mania Padouva, who offered insightful comments and suggestions about my work. The research was partially supported by CEC DG-5 and WHO/Euro and I am grateful to these organizations. I am, of course, eternally grateful to the people of Messogia.

NOTES

1 The *parakouzino* is a separate construction attached to the main house where most families in Messogia spend their days and in many cases their winter nights as well. It is usually a one-room construction with a smaller windowless room attached to one side, called the *kellari*. Though newly built houses have modern kitchens people still tend to use the old *parakouzino* or create a new one, leaving the house with its new kitchen as a place where guests are welcomed and entertained.

2 He would go to the grocer's, the butcher's, and the fishmonger's. Mr Yiannis would only ask his wife to go with him to the *laiki*, an open-air weekly market, and this especially when Mrs Sophia was in need of household goods. In fact, he even preferred his wife to go to Athens with him to shop rather than to the village market, for people in the village could not help but gossip.

3 *Katoy* literally means the basement of the house. In this context it is a place where the wine barrels are kept. It can also be a separate construction next to the house.

4 Barrel season: the period just before the *trygos* – the grape harvest – when barrels in the *katoy* had to be cleaned and fixed for the production of new wine; usually August through to the beginning of September.

5 The *mastrapa* is a copper wine-jug. It is also called *matara* (wineskin), because it was in the past covered by leather.

6 My first contact with the area was in 1977–78 when I was working on my MA thesis, 'Winery Cooperatives in Messogia' – Attica, Columbia University, New York, 1978. Prior to this ethnographic study a research team from Panteion University had worked in the area in order to collect data for the WHO Collaborative Study on 'Community Response to Alcohol-Related Problems', the outcome of which was the Country Report of this study. I would like to thank all members of the team: R. Astrinaki, S. Galani, M. Makri, M. Padouva, G. Roussopoulos and Ch. Ziouvas.

7 See for example: Campbell (1964), Friedl (1965, 1967), du Boulay (1974, 1976, 1986), Dubisch (1983, 1986, 1991), Hirschon (1978, 1983, 1989), Danforth (1983), Handman (1983), Dimitriou-Kotsoni (1988). See also Giovannini (1981).

8 See also Herzfeld (1983, 1985) where he discusses 'residual patriliny' in Crete.

9 Time period form August until early December which includes the barrel period (see above), *trygos* (the grape harvest) and *patima* (the pressing of the grapes), *retsinoma* (putting resin into the barrels filled with must) and finally the opening of the first barrel.

10 It is estimated that the population is about 17,000 including the non-permanent population of internal migrants who have moved into the community since 1965 – a result of the urbanization of Athens. Despite the fact that its size corresponds to a town, Messogites still call it a village and I myself call it that way.

11 I have borrowed the same name for my community.

12 It is not a written language. It was spoken by the community people almost exclusively before the Second World War. It has been suggested that this was one of the basic reasons why the Messogia people remained illiterate (Michael-Dede 1986, Hatzisotiriou 1973). Many people over 40–50 years of age are bilingual; some very old people of the community, especially women, still speak almost exclusively Arvanitica. (For the origin of Arvanitica see also Kollias 1990.)

13 See Loizos and Papataxiarchis (1991).

14 This dualism is found in other Mediterranean societies, for example in Southern Italy, Spain, and Portugal (Gilmore 1987, de Pina-Cabral 1989, Boissevain 1979).

15 According to the five-year plan of the Ministry of Agriculture, the Greek Government has shown an interest in promoting vineyard cultivation in the region, with the assistance of EEC funding. Wine in the area has become an increasingly viable competitive commodity in the European Common Market.

16 Patron–client relations have developed in more recent years between influential Messogites who have moved to Athens and the local Messogites; or between Messogites who act as 'intermediaries' between peasants and Athenians, a phenomenon noted in other Mediterranean societies (P. Schneider and J. Schneider 1972, 1976, Silverman 1965, 1970, Gellner 1977, Davis 1977).

17 See Wolf's (1966) discussion on the peasant dilemma and the role of the city.

18 Many governments and especially the Junta of 1967–74 adopted a hostile attitude towards the Arvanitica dialect. Official policy from 1967 onwards, as organized by the Ministry of Education, stressed the imperative of not talking Arvanitica at school. Also, teachers advised grand-parents not to speak Arvanitica at home. Teachers in Messogia still believe that the low percentage of students who go to university is a result of Arvanitika and the consumption of retsina by children at home.

19 Landlords (*archondes*) trace their origin back to the first families who settled in the area. They number five to eight households in the community nowadays. They are still holders of large plots of land, especially vineyards. Other families have also moved up the social ladder by buying land and cultivating vines. For example, land labourers (*ergates*, also called *trayiaskades* from the characteristic hat they still wear) used to work exclusively on the land of the large landholders. In recent times, due to the opening of the market and increased wages, they are able to buy vineyards and produce the highly esteemed retsina themselves.

20 The non-producer of retsina may still be a vineyard owner and producer (*paragogos*) of grapes or must, properties which still link him to the community, but do not secure his reputation as a household retsina producer, '*spitiko*', and thus may exclude him from participation in the *katoy* all-male gatherings. On the other hand, by buying retsina from a village producer and keeping it in the family barrel, he may renegotiate his reputation among the retsina household producers.

21 When vineyards are given as dowry, a strategy through endogamy rules is applied aiming at returning the vineyard back to the same family name. This strategy was more frequently applied in the past when rules of endogamy and marriage arrangements (even between children who were still very young) were more strictly exercised. See also Kenna (1976).

22 Vineyard names also indicate location, sometimes in conjunction with the family name. In this form the vineyard may often be referred to in the diminutive. In this case people will refer to the vineyard as the vineyard of household A who is now owned by household B.

23 Some landowners sell their grapes to the merchant and buy retsina from village producers. This wine is stored in the family barrel, and used throughout the year.

24 In fact, alcohol may even be drunk in almost all village shops where men do the household shopping, i.e. the grocer's, or the butcher's. It is important to note that in recent times these shops, concentrated in what is called the *agora* (market), were 'transformed' every evening into regular tavernas. They still are, but now only during village celebrations. These drinking places used to have names which reflected what the owner served with the wine, for example *kreatadiko* ('meat place'), *bakaliaradiko* ('fish place').

25 See, for example, Campbell (1964), Photiadis (1965), Driessen (1983), Gilmore (1985), Herzfeld (1985), Allen (1985), Beck (1985), Loizos and Papataxiarchis (1991), Cowan (1990). See also Barrows and Room (1991).

26 See Brandes (1978, 1979, 1980), Gilmore and Gilmore (1979, 1985), Herzfeld (1985), Loizos and Papataxiarchis (1991), Papataxiarchis (1991).

27 This issue has been a topic of discussion between husband and wife for months now. Yiannis's older brother is trying to persuade Yiannis to sell his vineyards cheaply to his son, Yiorgos, the natural heir of their households since he carries the brothers' father's and grandfather's names. Sophia in response notes: 'We have a daughter, so what? Our future son-in-law may like vineyards and retsina.'

28 It has been noted that this behaviour arises within uxorilocal, matrifocal communities (Papataxiarchis 1991). In Messogia the same practice is exhibited though it is a virilocal community. Might it therefore be suggested that we have to look also at other sociocultural variables to explicate these sharp gender distinctions?

29 Only those *kafenia* that in recent times have been transformed into *kafeteries* and restaurants during the day and are thus less explicitly male domains.

30 Much of the material in the men's talk while drinking either in the *kafenio* or the *katoy* male gatherings was taken/recorded by my husband and a young man – now studying to become an anthropologist – who worked under my supervision.

31 Age, kinship and marital status may also differentiate men's behaviour in the *kafenio*. Older people, for example, spend most of their day in *kafenia*, but go home early in the evening. Close relatives like father and son never frequent the same *kafenio*. During the first years of their married life men tend to spend less time in *kafenio* and drink less. Children of poor families start their 'careers' in *kafenio* earlier than children of important landowners.

32 In the past *archondes* (large landowners) had their own *kafenio* in the village square, but this practice is less evident nowadays. There are, however, still two *kafenia* – one in the central square and one on the main street very close to the square – which are called *kafenia ton archondon* (coffeehouses of the important landholders), which lesser wine producers and the successful skilled workers (*technites*) frequent. Also, there is still one *kafenio*, called *to ergatiko*

(of the labourers) where only labourers and people of left-wing orientation go. This *kafenio* is known for the card-playing that goes on there.

33 In older times (20–30 years ago) *archondes* would drink only coffee in the *kafenio*. They would occasionally drink beer or retsina in taverns. Retsina was drunk by them mainly in the *katoy*. This contrasted with the labourers who would only drink wine and in later years beer in taverns and coffeehouses.

34 Sometimes Messogites use the same word (*yinoma*) to denote the rising of the dough for bread. See also Pina-Cabral (1986) for a link between male fertility and the making of bread.

35 They also called the place *sta varelia* (in the barrels), *patitiri* (grape-pressing place) or sometimes, when joking between themselves, men call it *boutia* (from the Arvanitiki word *di bute* = barrels) but also connoting the Greek colloquial word for thighs (*boutia*).

36 They have to be washed with warm water three times. No soap or detergent should be used. In recent years because fixing the barrels has become very expensive – coopers are few and barrels are imported – many people use caustic potash to clean the barrels, though never the family barrel(s). These have to be cleaned and fixed every year, an activity they call *foundoma*, in which barrels are opened and the insides scraped. Barrels are then reassembled and made to fit by putting straw between the barrel spars, and finally washed with warm water.

37 Messogites are very annoyed when wine chemists suggest they put sugar or preservatives in the must. When some of them have to do it they do it secretly. In any case, they would never do it for the barrels kept for their own consumption. Messogites are very suspicious of wine chemists. There is a story about a wine chemist who was seriously beaten by Niko Bassis some years ago because not only did he insist that Nikos should put sugar in his wine, but also told others in the village that he should do so, thereby suggesting that Bassis's wine was no good.

38 Men will either bring some grilled meat (*mezedes*) from the *kafenio* or will themselves grill some meat bought from the market (usually lamb chops) on charcoal, which is always kept near the *katoy*. They cook it outside the *katoy*.

39 These gatherings resemble the homosocial gatherings of men – members of the Bechtassi Orders who would also transcend their everyday selves either by smoking hashish or sometimes by drinking wine (Myrmiroglou 1940, Gefou-Madianou 1985).

40 For a discussion of body/soul see Scheper-Hughes (1978).

41 Men usually express their fear and anxiety that in a few years big wine-producing companies will buy their land and vine plants; they also fear that Athens will expand towards their place; Athenians will then uproot their vineyards and build houses and multi-storey buildings.

42 See Introduction, this volume.

43 For a thorough discussion of *nikokyris* and *nikokira*, see J. Salamone and S.D. Salamone (1980).

44 Their village wine, they say, is the best because of the mild, sunny and dry climate of their village and lack of water in their fields; they produce smaller quantities compared with neighbouring communities, but a better quality retsina.

45 It is believed in Messogia that those having problems with alcohol are the ones who failed to construct and maintain their male *parea*, and are thus obliged to drink alone. For it is not only the quantity one drinks, but also the mode of

consumption as well as its social meaning that matter (see also Papageorgis 1987, Papataxiarchis 1988).

46 Of all vineyards owned by a retsina producer, and after the division of the vineyards to his sons, one vineyard would be reserved for the retsina of the family barrel. Usually the retsina for household consumption was not made from a particular vineyard. A household retsina producer would take care each year that the best grapes – which may come from a different vineyard each year – were kept for his household retsina production. Special care was taken always to fill the family barrel first with the must of freshly pressed grapes.

47 Black grapes, and especially a variety called in Arvanitica *herthe-geli* (the cock's testicles) that was widely used for the preparation of sweet wine before the phylloxera years, are rarely cultivated in the area now. Sweet-wine production has not been reduced by the lack of these black grapes after the phylloxera years. Before the phylloxera of the 1950s more varieties of mostly white, but also black vine grapes were cultivated. The vine plants of the black grapes were and still are highly valued by Messogites. It was important and necessary for each household to have at least some vine plants of this type. These black vine grapes were more delicate than the white Savatiana ones but were severely damaged by phylloxera in the 1950s. Sweet wine nowadays is produced mainly from white grapes taken from all the household vineyards and mixed when possible with black grapes.

48 Sometimes they select grapes from all vineyards after all the grapes have been harvested. Ideally, men do not harvest grapes; they carry the baskets to the tractors and empty them into the carriage. In this way grapes for the sweet-wine production have not been touched by male hands.

49 Now that many producers have their grapes pressed outside the household, women take must from the same tank that is used for retsina and then mix it with the must of the black grapes. They consider the retsina must is untouched by male hands since a machine has pressed it.

50 The rest of the red grapes are consumed as fruit or are put in the sun and dried to make raisins.

51 These big pots are kept in the house and are used again in cooking the food for marriage celebrations. It may be so because of the number of guests invited and the size of the pots, but an association with household fertility may also be suggested.

52 Women do not specify from which vineyard; what they are clear about is the quality (colour) of the soil. It has to be white (*asprochoma*). Many places in Messogia have this type of soil.

53 *I kellari*, a female noun in Greek.

54 I have never seen a woman offering sweet wine to her husband. I have seen women talking and trying to calculate their fertile days quite accurately. A woman offers sweet wine to her husband during her fertile days of the month. It is believed that sweet wine is 'active' for 48 hours, but the best results are achieved when conjugal relations take place within a few hours after sweet wine has been given to men.

55 See Kopytoff (1986) for approaching the issue of commoditization as a process in the cultural biography of things.

56 Up until 15–20 years ago land other than vineyards, far away from the village near the sea, would be given as a dowry to daughters. After the construction of the coastal road, however, these far-away pieces of usually infertile land have become very expensive building plots bought by rich Athenians. Sons quarrel

with their fathers nowadays insisting that they should have a share of this land instead of vineyards. Vineyards have been given as dowrys more often during recent years. A father ideally never distributes his land or barrels. It is inherited by his sons after his death. In reality, however, and in recent years, he distributes part of the land upon his sons' marriages and the rest after his death. Wine cellars (*katoya*) and barrels are usually inherited by the younger son of the family after his father's death. Some barrels, however, would be given to older sons when they were creating their own wine cellar after their marriage. New barrels were also made or bought when a new *katoy* was constructed as part of each household.

57 When sweet wine is bottled it seems to be of little consequence. Thus, it may be kept in a barrel, in bottles, or in demijohns. By contrast, real retsina wine, they say, can only be made in barrels and within the household. Messogites view the production of retsina by large wine companies with hostility since there it is left to ferment in large metal containers and bottled for selling.

58 Retsina in this context, always accompanied by food cooked by the women, seems to be transformed from a male product *par excellence* and acts as a unifying medium. This transformation of retsina can be achieved only in contexts where family/household or the community's highly commensal gatherings are involved. Food cooked by women and retsina brought by men together symbolize the household unity.

59 Women's same-sex gatherings are mainly work-oriented, household or neighbourhood bound. At these gatherings women do not drink alcohol. It is only on name days or even ordinary (everyday) occasions when they are having guests in the house that they will treat them to store-bought liqueurs along with home-made fruit preserves.

REFERENCES

Allen, P. (1985) 'Apollo and Dionysus: alcohol use in modern Greece', *East European Quarterly*, Vol. XVIII, No 4, pp.461–480.

Barrows, S. and Room, R. (eds) (1991) *Drinking: Behavior and Belief in Modern History*, Berkeley: University of California Press.

Beck, S. (1985) 'Changing styles of drinking: alcohol use in the Balkans', *East European Quarterly*, XVII, No 4, pp.395–413.

Biris, C. (1960) *Arvanites, oi Doriis tou neoterou Hellinismou* (in Greek) (*Albanians, the Dorians of Modern Hellinism*), Athens.

Bloch, M. and Parry, J. (eds) (1982) *Death and the Regeneration of Life*, Cambridge: Cambridge University Press.

Boissevain, J. (1979) 'Toward a social anthropology of the Mediterranean', *Current Anthropology* 20, pp.81–85.

Brandes, S.H. (1978) 'Like wounded stags: male sexual ideology in an Andalusian town' in S.B. Ortner and H. Whitehead (eds) *Sexual Meanings: The Cultural Construction of Gender and Sexuality*, Cambridge: Cambridge University Press.

Brandes, S.H. (1979) 'Drinking patterns and alcohol control in a Castilian mountain village', *Anthropology* 3:1–16.

Brandes, S.H. (1980) *Metaphors of Masculinity: Sex and Status in Andalusian Folklore*, University of Pennsylvania Press.

Braudel, F. (1985) *La Méditerranée, l'espace et l'histoire*, Paris: Flammarion.

Campbell, J. (1964) *Honour, Family and Patronage: A Study of Institutions and Moral Values in a Greek Mountain Community*, Oxford: Clarendon Press.

134   *Alcohol, gender and culture*

Center of Planning and Economic Research (1988–92) *Report of the Five-Year Programme of Economic and Social Development in East Attica 1988–1992.*

Cowan, J. (1990) *Dance and the Body Politic in Northern Greece.* Princeton, N.J.: Princeton University Press.

Danforth, L.M. (1983) 'Power through submission in the Anastenaria', *Journal of Modern Greek Studies*, 1(1):203–223.

Davis, J. (1977) *People of the Mediterranean: An Essay in Comparative Social Anthropology*, London: Routledge & Kegan Paul.

Dimen, M. (1986) 'Servants and sentries: women, power and social production in Kriovrisi' in J. Dubisch (ed.) *Gender and Power in Rural Greece*, Princeton, N.J.: Princeton University Press.

Dimitriou-Kotsoni, S. (1988) 'Gender roles and symbolic systems on an Aegean island', Ph.D. thesis, Department of Anthropology and Sociology, School of Oriental and African Studies, University of London.

Driessen, H. (1983) 'Male sociability and rituals of masculinity in rural Andalusia', *Anthropological Quarterly*, 56:116–24.

Drower, E.S. (1956) *Water into Wine*, London: John Murray.

du Boulay, J. (1974) *Portrait of a Greek Mountain Village*, Oxford: Clarendon Press.

du Boulay, J. (1976) 'Lies, mockery and family integrity' in J.G. Peristiany (ed.) *Mediterranean Family Structures*, Cambridge: Cambridge University Press, pp. 389–406.

du Boulay, J. (1986) 'Women – images of their nature and destiny in rural Greece' in J. Dubisch (ed.) *Gender and Power in Rural Greece*, Princeton, N.J.: Princeton University Press.

Dubisch, J. (1983) 'Greek women: sacred and profane', *Journal of Modern Greek Studies* 1 (1):185–202.

Dubisch, J. (ed.) (1986) *Gender and Power in Rural Greece*, Princeton, N.J.: Princeton University Press.

Dubisch, J. (1991) 'Gender, kinship and religion: "reconstructing" the anthropology of Greece' in P. Loizos and E. Papataxiarchis (eds) *Contested Identities*, Princeton, N.J.: Princeton University Press.

Friedl, E. (1965) *Vassilika: A Village in Modern Greece*, New York: Holt, Rinehart & Winston.

Friedl, E. (1967) 'The position of women: appearance and reality', *Anthropological Quarterly* 40(3):97–108.

Gefou-Madianou, D. (1985) 'Hashish culture and family in a Turkish-speaking Athenian community', Ph.D. thesis, Panteion University, Athens.

Gellner, E. (1977) 'Patrons and clients' in E. Gellner and J. Waterburg (eds) *Patrons and Clients*, London: Gerald Duckworth and Co.

Gerontas, A. (1984) *Oi Arvanites tis Attikis* (in Greek) (*The Albanians of Attica*), Athens.

Gilmore, D. (1985) 'The role of the bar in Andalusian rural society: observations on political culture under Franco', *Journal of Anthropological Research*, Vol. 41, pp.263–277.

Gilmore, D. (ed.) (1987) *Honour and Shame and the Unity of the Mediterranean*, A special publication of the A.A.A. No 22, Washington, D.C.: American Anthropological Association.

Gilmore, M. and Gilmore, D. (1979) 'Machismo: a psychodynamic approach', *Journal of Psychological Anthropology*, 2:3, pp.281–299.

Giovannini, M. (1981) 'Woman: a dominant symbol within the cultural system of a Sicilian town', *Man*, Vol. 16(3), pp.408–426.

Handman, M.E. (1983) *La violence et la ruse: hommes et femmes dans un village Grec*, Aix-en-Provence: Edisud.

Hatzisoteriou, G. (1985) *Konta ston chthesino Messogiti* (*Close to the Messogiti of the Past*), Athens: Asklipios.

Hatzisotiriou, G. (1973) *Istoria tis Peanias ke ton Anatolika tou Hymettou Periohon* (in Greek) (*History of Peania and the Regions East of Hymettus*), Athens: Asklipios.

Hatzisotiriou, G. (1980) *Ta laografika tis Messogeas Attikis* (in Greek) (*Folklore of Messogia – Attica*), Athens: Asklipios.

Herzfeld, M. (1983) 'Interpreting kinship terminology: the problem of patriliny in Rural Greece', *Anthropological Quarterly* 56:157–166.

Herzfeld, M. (1985) *The Poetics of Manhood: Contest and Identity in a Cretan Mountain Village*, Princeton, N.J.: Princeton University Press.

Herzfeld, M. (1986) 'Closure as curse: tropes in the exploration of bodily and social disorder', *Current Anthropology* 2:107–121.

Herzfeld, M. (1987) *Anthropology through the Looking Glass: Critical Ethnography in the Margins of Europe*, Cambridge: Cambridge University Press.

Hirschon, R. (1978) 'Open body/closed space: the transformation of female sexuality' in Shirley Andener (ed.) *Defining Females*, New York: John Wiley & Sons, pp.66–88.

Hirschon, R. (1983) 'Women, the aged and religious activity: oppositions and complementarity in an urban locality', *Journal of Modern Greek Studies* 1(1): 113–130.

Hirschon, R. (1989) *Heirs of the Greek Catastrophe: The Social Life of Asia Minor Refugees in Piraeus*, Oxford: Clarendon Press.

Hoffman, S., Cowan, R. and Aralow, P. (1974) *Kypseli: Women and Men Apart – A Divided Reality* (film). Distributed by the Univ. Extension Media Center, Berkeley: University of California.

Iossifides, A.M. (1990) 'Earthly lives and life everlasting: secular and religious values in two convents and a village in western Greece', Ph.D. thesis, Department of Anthropology, London School of Economics and Political Sciences, University of London.

Iossifides, A.M. (1991) 'Sisters in Christ: metaphors of kinship among Greek nuns' in P. Loizos and E. Papataxiarchis (eds) *Contested Identities*, Princeton, NJ.: Princeton UniversityPress.

Kambouroglou, D. (1959) *Istoria ton Athinon* (in Greek) (*The history of Athens*), Athens: Papademitriou.

Kenna, M. (1976) 'House, Fields and Graves: Property and Ritual Obligation on a Greek Island', *Ethnology* 15:21–34.

Keramopoulos, A. (1945) *Oi Ellines ke oi vorii gitones* (in Greek) (*The Greeks and their Neighbours to the North*), Athens.

Kollias, A. (1990) *Arvanites, Ke ei Katagogi ton Ellinon* (*Arvanites, and the origin of the Greeks*), Athens.

Kopytoff, I. (1986) 'The cultural biography of things: commoditization as process' in A. Appadurai (ed.) *The Social Life of Things: Commodities in Cultural Perspective*, Cambridge: Cambridge University Press.

Koumaris, I. (1943) *Albani ke Ellines* (in Greek) (*Albanians and Greeks*) Proceedings of the Greek Anthropological Association, Athens, pp.30–42.

Lambros, S. (1905) *Ei Onomatologia tis Attikis ke e is tin horan epikisis ton*

Albanon (in Greek) (*Attica Onomatology and the settlement of Albanians*), Athens.

Loizos, P. and Papataxiarchis, E. (eds) (1991) *Contested Identities: Gender and Kinship in Modern Greece*, Princeton, N.J.: Princeton University Press.

McKinlay, Arthur P. (1949) 'Ancient experience with intoxicating drinks: non-classical peoples; non-Attic Greek states II', *Quarterly Journal of Studies on Alcohol* 10: 289–315.

Markou, C. (1988) 'To ambelooiniko provlima sta Mesogiea simera' (The economic problem of vineyards in Messogia today), *Proceedings of the 3rd scientific meeting in S.E. Attica*, Kalyvia.

Michael-Dede, M. (1986) *Apo ti Zoi sta Messogia tis Attikis* (*From Life in Messogia – Attica*), Athens.

Ministry of Agriculture (1980, 1986) East Attica Division, *Statistical Yearbooks*.

Myrmiroglou, V. (1940) *The Dervisses*, Athens: Ekati.

Papageorgis, C. (1987) *Peri Methys* (*About Drunkenness*), Athens: Roes.

Papanikolaou, S. (1947) *To Koropi* (in Greek) (*Koropi*), Athens.

Papataxiarchis, E. (1988) 'Kinship, friendship and gender relations in two East Aegean village communities (Lesbos, Greece)', Ph.D. thesis, Department of Anthropology, London School of Economics and Political Science, University of London.

Papataxiarchis, E. (1991) 'Friends of the heart: male commensal solidarity, gender, and kinship in Aegean Greece' in P. Loizos and E. Papataxiarchis (eds) *Contested Identities: Gender and Kinship in Modern Greece*, Princeton, N.J.: Princeton University Press.

Photiadis, J. (1965) 'The position of the coffeehouse in the social life of the Greek village', *Sociologia Ruralis*, No 5, 45–46.

de Pina-Cabral, J. (1986) *Sons of Adam, Daughters of Eve: The peasant world-view of the Alto Minho*, Oxford: Clarendon Press.

de Pina-Cabral, J. (1989) 'The Mediterranean as a category of regional comparison: a critical view', *Current Anthropology*, No 3, 399–406.

Salamone, J. (Stanton), and Salamone, S.D. (1980) 'The Noikokyris and the Noikokyra: complementary sex roles in a changing socio-economic system'. Paper delivered at the 1980 Symposium of the Modern Greek Studies Association, Philadelphia.

Scheper-Hughes, N. and Lock, M. (1978) 'The mindful body: a prolegomenon to future work in medical anthropology', *Medical Anthrop. Quarterly* 1(1):6–41.

Schneider, J. and Schneider, P. (1976) *Culture and Political Economy in Western Sicily*, New York: Academic Press.

Schneider, P., Schneider, J. and Hansen, E. (1972) 'Modernisation and development: The role of regional elites and noncorporate groups in the European Mediterranean', *Comparative Studies in Society and History*, No 14, 328–350.

Silverman, S. (1965) 'Patronage and community-nation relationships in Central Italy', *Ethnology*, No 4, ii, 172–189.

Silverman, S. (1970) 'Exploitation in rural central Italy. Structure and ideology in stratification study', *Comparative Studies in Society and History*, 327–329.

Tapper, N. (1983) 'Gender and religion in a Turkish town: a comparison of two types of formal women's gatherings' in P. Holden (ed.) *Women's Religious Experience*, London and Canberra: Croom Helm.

Tsovaridou, Th. (1981) *Ei exelixi tis domis tis albanikis ikogenias* (in Greek) (*The development in structure of the Albanic family*), Balkanika, Athens: Symikta.

Wolf, E. (1966) *Peasants*, New Jersey: Prentice-Hall.

8 'I can't drink beer, I've just drunk water'

Alcohol, bodily substance and commensality among Hungarian Rom

Michael Stewart

In the middle of the afternoon on a cold Saturday in January a group of Gypsy men have gathered in the road outside the brightly painted, single-storey house of Mokus and his wife Terez. For a while the talk is listless, the men chat to pass the time, almost as if seeking an excuse to sit around together, to avoid going back alone to their own houses and yards. After a while a couple of the men set off to attend to their own business and it seems the group might break up entirely. Instead Mokus invites those who remain into his house to share a beer. One man excuses himself: 'I can't drink beer, I've just drunk water' (*Naśtig pav bere, paji pilem*), and goes home. But the other seven men gratefully take up the invitation and join Mokus on the floor in his kitchen. The only furniture in the room apart from the iron stove and a flimsy wall cupboard is a bed on which the family sleep. Right now Mokus's three-year-old son is curled up on it.

Terez, who has been inside all along, is greeted politely by the men but otherwise ignored. She knows the men will stay for an hour or more and takes the opportunity to go out into the town to scavenge bread for the pigs she keeps. From outside the front door she picks up her sack and her metal stick with which she'll dig through the Hungarians' rubbish bins and then calls her younger daughter, Rebus, to join her. Meanwhile the men throw together small coins and the odd 50-forint note – enough for a bottle or two of beer each. Moni, the eldest daughter of the house, is sent off on the family bicycle to the local bar to bring back the beer. She goes off with her cousin who lives next door and they return a quarter of an hour later with bags of Köbanyai lager swinging precariously from the handlebars of their bikes.

Köbanyai was the cheapest and weakest beer that the Hungarian socialist state produced. In fact this beer was so insipid (2 per cent or so) that I used to believe nobody could ever put enough inside himself at one time to get properly drunk on it. Nevertheless it was the preferred Gypsy drink – to be exact, in 1985 no other beer would do.

When the beer arrives two or three of the men, using their (capped) teeth, prise the caps off the bottles – each man receives his own bottle. Jozi gets a green one – everyone knows that he's fussy (*kenjeso*) and won't drink from a brown one. And then, together, the men toast each other: 'Be lucky! 'Be lucky, boys! Luck and health to the Gypsies!' (*T'aven baxtale/le śavale; Baxt, Sastipe, le ŕomen!*) They raise their bottles, click them one against another and drink together.

An hour later most of the bottles have been opened – several abandoned half-finished in favour of a fresher bottle. I am no medical expert but it seems a physiological impossibility that the alcohol should have gone to these men's heads – no question, though, the atmosphere is transformed. A certain restraint has gone. Talk and gestures come more easily and with more emphasis. Voices are raised and the conversation has an intensity and purpose it previously lacked. One man raises the sore topic of a *gaźo* (non-Gypsy) who had frustrated some of the men recently in a deal over fodder. Then talk turns to praise for a mutual relative who recently spent several days at the settlement. The images used to describe this man's fine qualities are the stock in trade of Gypsy rhetoric. The tone is sentimental, approaching maudlin. These eight well-built men, well used to drinking many litres of beer but this afternoon having drunk less than a litre each, are now, incredible though it sounds, drunk. It cannot, of course, have been the strictly physical effects of the alcohol, but rather the social construction of sharing a drink together which enabled these men to entertain themselves that afternoon. As the Gypsies themselves put it: 'they made their good mood' (*kerdine lenge voja*). Once the *voja* of the men is made they may be willing to sing to one another. As it happened, two of the men that afternoon were obliged to participate at a gathering in honour of a deceased Gypsy (*pomana*), and the host had a problem with one of his horses to which he needed to attend. The party split up, each man returning to his own household.

A scene such as this was a weekly occurrence on the Gypsy settlement where I lived in northern Hungary. Gypsies put the consumption of alcohol at the heart of their social life. If there is any content in the descriptive term 'a drinking culture', Hungarian Gypsy society must be one such. In order to understand the particular social construction of drinking among these people I delve in this paper into aspects of Gypsy culture that at first sight may seem tangential to the issue at hand. Firstly, I set these Gypsies in the context of the Hungarian socialist state and the political as well as economic pressures they lived under. Secondly, having described the contexts of drinking and the use of different types of alcohol, I discuss some of the bodily effects of alcohol. Alcohol (and most especially brandy) appears to act as a kind of fortifier which enables the body to remain in a pure, healthy state. In order to explain this I will discuss some Gypsy representations of the body, arguing that the bodily effects of alcohol enable it to provide a particularly suitable mode of commensality for male Gypsies when they wish to give symbolic expression to their communal life. Gypsy food provides the essential daily nourishment needed by everyone, but alcohol offers an alternative form of sustenance. Indeed I have begun to think that alcohol provides an alternative image of the sharing of bodily substance in a Gypsy community.

Gypsy social life is dominated by a desire to balance a tendency to individuation and differentiation of Gypsies with an alternative tendency to make all Gypsies identical and undifferentiated. To some extent this opposition is linked to another, between households and brothers. The consumption of alcohol and water provides images of alternative modes of commensality, one suited to relations in the household, the other to communal relations.

THE VLACH GYPSIES OF GYÖNGYÖS

The character of Hungarian Gypsy life can only be partially described in the relatively short term of the socialist period which lasted from 1947 to 1989. The Vlach Gypsies of northern Hungary, or *Rom* as they call themselves, probably settled in this part of the country some time between 1930 and 1945. They have not since then travelled as a way of life. Their ancestors seem most likely to have been part of the large westward migration of Gypsies from the Romanian principalities (Moldavia and Walachia) in the second half of the nineteenth century (see Panaitescu 1941). This whole population of Gypsies (most commonly referred to by the derogatory Hungarian term *oláh* (Vlach) by their Magyar compatriots) has remained distinct from two other groups of Gypsies, the Hungarian Gypsies (*Romungro*-s, also known as 'musician Gypsies') and the Romanian *Beaś* (Boyash) Gypsies who were traditionally foresters and pig-trough makers, both of which groups were resident in Hungary prior to the arrival of the 'Vlachs'.

The Vlach Gypsies lived in the pre-socialist period from a combination of metal-work, mud-brick making and horse trading alongside waged daily labour for peasants and larger landowners. Like other Gypsies in Europe their preferred mode of life involved trading and working as self-employed skilled labourers, but avoiding if possible waged-labour (see for example Okely 1983:49–65). There is some evidence that even prior to the last world war Gypsies were crucially dependent on wages from peasants and other landholders. Collectivization of the land after 1947 by the socialist government largely removed this major source of income. The Gypsies, like their peasant counterparts, have since then found themselves drawn deeper and deeper into dependence on wage-labour in factories (see Stewart 1990).

Despite this change in the Gypsies' occupational role, their structural position within Hungarian society did not change fundamentally – they remained socially peripheral (they lived in ghettos, or isolated settlements on the edge of conurbations), poor (they provided cheap labour to the state) and disproportionately unhealthy (child-death rates are significantly higher among Gypsies than Magyars, for example).

The socialist regime of 1947–1989 took a hostile attitude to the Gypsy population. Official policy from 1960 onwards was organized around the imperative of assimilating the Gypsy populations into the Magyar working class. As elsewhere in Eastern Europe (see Guy 1975) Gypsies were denied the rights of a national minority since it was believed that their way of life was a bizarre survival of pre-socialist social conditions and not a 'culture in its own right'. This way of life was understood to rest on an anti-work ethic which was directly opposed to the socialist ideology of self-realization through disciplined, collective labour. Gypsies were a primary 'social other' of the socialist regime of Hungary and as such were subject to massive social and political pressures to give up their way of life and become proletarians (see Stewart forthcoming a).

Despite the best efforts of the socialist state to bring Gypsy social life to an end, communities of Vlach Gypsies survived and even flourished in many corners of the country. The social morphology of these communities is very diverse (see, for example, Havas 1982). Thus 'my' community can in no sense be said to be characteristic of the living arrangements of most Vlach Gypsies in Hungary. However, the mores ('*morales*') of the Vlach Gypsies appear at first blush to be rather more homogenous.[1] Ideas about what makes one a Gypsy seem widely shared among many Vlach Gypsies almost irrespective of living conditions and economic niche. Being a Gypsy according to this ethical code (*Romanes*, or 'the Gypsy way', as the Gypsies call it) implies a fierce and publicly asserted commitment to maintaining strong social relations with one's own kin, with fellow residents in a settlement and most generally with other Vlach or Romany-speaking Gypsies. The settlements are in part maintained as communities through the daily practice of sharing hay, clothes, food, domestic labour, etc. (see Stewart 1991). This communal ethic also involves a homogenization of activities such as eating, dressing and drinking so that all Gypsies appear to be behaving in a similar fashion.

The ethic of communal life runs against two opposing pressures. Firstly, Gypsy life is not only organized in communities but also through households. In their day-to-day lives men and women first and foremost focus their activities on the reproduction of their household and relations within it, not on reproducing communal relations. This focus is associated with a profoundly competitive and often antagonistic relationship between members of different households which runs in direct conflict to the ethic of sharing and cooperation between putatively identical Gypsies. Secondly, the socialist state's assimilationist programme attempted to play on and foster social differences in Gypsy communities, in particular by encouraging integration of the more 'desirable' Gypsies into Magyar communities. Differences in work-records of family heads as well as differences in standard and mode of living were to be used as a wedge to divide Gypsy communities between those who wished to 'improve' and assimilate and those who were willing to remain shipwrecked at the bottom of Hungarian society.

In a world where the Gypsies were under great pressure to assimilate and integrate themselves into the majority non-Gypsy population, to give up their 'Gypsyness', the question of remaining Gypsy was continually posed. Indeed, as Luc de Heusch perceptively put it (writing about Gypsies elsewhere in Europe), the Gypsies live in a 'state of siege' (1966:34–49). For these men and women, remaining true Gypsies involved a constant struggle. Gypsy identity is not fixed in public institutions or other stable organizational forms rooted, for instance, in shared productive property. While it is true that one's Gypsy identity is fixed, ascribed at birth, it is also and more saliently true that one's identity as a Gypsy is established by practical commitment to the Gypsy way of doing things in a community. This is Gypsy ideology and not just a matter of etic observation. To remain a Gypsy requires constant assertion of one's commitment, frequent proofs of one's good intentions. Sharing a drink together, relaxing the conventions and boundaries which normally pit man against man, household against household, is a peculiarly persuasive way of showing one's willingness to go on being a Gypsy.

This is related to the fact that the key idiom through which the communal ethic is given rhetorical expression and elaboration is one of 'brotherhood'. This gender bias in the representation of activities oriented to a notion of a 'social whole' is related to the tendency in Gypsy discourse to speak of male Gypsies (*Rom*) as if they were the whole society of Gypsies. The term *Rom* ambiguously, but significantly, refers both to male Gypsies and to Gypsies in general. It is thus possible to suggest in formal rhetoric at least that communal relations are male, 'brotherly' ones.

THE SOCIAL REGULATION OF DRINKING

If I recounted my tale of a Saturday afternoon's drinking to most Hungarians I know the only surprise occasioned would concern my reasons for dwelling on the well-known drunkenness of Gypsies. Every self-respecting Magyar 'knows' that if you give work to Gypsies you mustn't pay them till the job is completed or you'll lose your helpers at least until they've drunk away the proceeds of their labour. 'Drunkenness' among Gypsies is as unremarkable as among young men – Gypsies have no sense of the value of accumulation, of delayed gratification, or so it is said. Gypsies live for the present and are incapable of the kind of application and effort shown by normal citizens. At best a patronizing tolerance may be displayed towards their willingness to throw up everything and celebrate over a drink. So Gypsies appear to the Magyar worker-peasants amongst whom they live and work.

Gypsy attitudes to drinking and celebrating are rather more complex than the Magyar outsiders' views. On the Gypsy settlements where I spent most time during my research there were two kinds of alcoholics: members of poor Magyar families who lived there; and single, male Magyars ('dossers') who were cared for, and thus kept out of the appalling state-run detoxification centres, by wealthy Gypsy families in return for their labour. These men though kindly handled were not treated as fully adult and autonomous individuals, and were often the butt of ridicule. On occasion when they succumbed thoroughly to their need they were subject to a comic sexual innuendo in which the Gypsy women teased the men about their sexual prowess and mockingly invited them to meet later in the night to have sex.

So far is Gypsy drinking practice from Magyar fantasy that for the Gypsies the very idea of drunkenness as a total loss of physical self-control is thought to be demeaning and in a certain sense 'un-Gypsy-like'. At one stage during my research there was a young *gaźo* (non-Gypsy) couple on the settlement who used to get drunk at home and then bring their music system out into their garden where they would dance together clinging tightly to one another. Crowds of Gypsies, at first children and then adults, would gather as if at the zoo to stare and laugh at the antics of this couple and egg them on. When Gypsies (both men and women) do get drunk on their own it is normally in despair at not making ends meet or in the midst of a family crisis. In this state a person may wander from house to house on the settlement singing and crying, but would never engage in the public debauchery of this *gaźo* couple.

In fact, in contrast to the Magyar stereotype, far from drinking as much as they can at random, Gypsy drinking is as much a socially based activity as eating. Offering someone a drink is perhaps the most commonly prac- tised form of 'paying respect' (literally giving, *del patjiv*). At home on the settlement neither men nor women normally drink alone. If they have alcohol at home one or two others will be invited to share. Nor do people drink in public (at home, on the settlement, in a public bar) without toasting. When, for instance, a glass of wine is begun the drinker will toast his companions to be lucky and then when he finishes the glass someone is sure to return the toast with a wish for good health (*'Sastipe láse!'*). This is only one particularly stressed aspect of the general mode of appropriate communal behaviour discussed above. To drink alone when there are other Gypsies around would be a particularly poignant denial of commitment to links with significant others. Out in the town, away from the settlement both men and women may drop into a bar for a solitary drink, but even there if they see a Gypsy they are more or less bound to try and treat their fellow Gypsy.

What people drink, when and where is to some degree regulated by custom. The early morning between 6 a.m. and 8 a.m., after a quick wash of the face and hands, is the time to drink fruit brandy (*ratija*). These brandies can either be bought in bottles (two decilitres is the smallest size) in a state shop or privately by the glass from local peasants who distill and sell more potent varieties. From the shops, the pungent mixed fruit (Hungarian, *Vegyes*) variety was in fashion during the time of my research – though cherry brandy was an acceptable substitute. My own tipple, apricot brandy, the drink of the Budapest intelligentsia, is deemed too strong and too sweet by most Gypsies. If the brandy is bought from a shop it will be drunk within the home with early morning visitors, or outside around one of the small fires that are lit each morning in various corners of the settlement. If men do set off to a peasant's still, either in the early morning or at the end of the day, they normally pick up fellow drinkers on the way and stay there as a group until all are satisfied. Brandy is drunk in the morning from a small half-decilitre glass which is commonly thrown back in one swig after wishing one's fellow Gypsies a lucky day. The glass is then passed around to the next person.

Many if not most mornings start with a drink (for men perhaps more so than for women). Some older men with little to do may be in the happy position of being able to stay at a still for long enough to be treated by other Gypsies who turn up until they are pleasantly intoxicated. But this is thought of as a sign of irresponsibility in a young man and to a lesser extent in these old men too.[2] In this case, unlike us who rise sober and, when we do drink, retire at night less than sober, Gypsies start the day mildly pickled and spend the morning at least returning to sobriety.

If people imbibe later on in the day it is to wine or beer that they turn. Wine may be drunk in the evening most commonly at a peasant's house outside the settlement. It is drunk in glasses of one or two decilitres, each man holding his own glass. Beer is more likely to be drunk in a bar in the town or at home at the weekend. In both these cases the drinking is somehow more sociably oriented than the drinking of brandy in the morning. Then brandy is drunk in turns and thrown back. When drinking wine or beer the men drink with one another, often simultaneously, pausing to talk between sips.

On a non-festive day, whether people drink later on in the day depends on chance circumstance. If one goes off the settlement either for business or to visit a relative some beer or wine will undoubtedly be taken. When men set out to do business with a peasant, or couples visit relatives in a nearby village they will stop at least once on the outward and on the homebound journey to have drinks in a bar. In the relatively informal circumstances of a *gaźo* bar men and women will drink whatever pleases them without regard to the others' choices.

When a man or family is paid a formal visit by Gypsies from another settlement or village the choice of beverage is determined by the person who is owed respect in the given situation. If such a gathering takes place in a house and not a bar and involves more than a handful of men then they all tend to drink the same type of alcohol. The more formal the celebration (*mulatśago*) the more firmly this practice is adhered to. For one christening we took dry white wine (though some of the party would have preferred beer) because the father of the child was known to like white wine. 'Today, we drink white wine!' the men chorused (*Ad'es parni mol pas*). At another rather disorganized christening one man insisted on drinking beer while all the others drank red wine and these latter repeatedly teased and mocked the non-conformist who was, as everybody was aware, effectively insulting the youthful co-godfathers. At all these occasions, whatever is drunk, the consumption of large quantities of alcohol should not result in blind drunkenness. Rather the men aim for a kind of benign, mild and long-lasting intoxication.

Women as well as men are allowed, indeed expected, to drink when others are drinking. Nor is anything said of a woman and her daughter going into a bar in town and having a glass or two of sweet brandy on the way back from the morning market. In this sense there is a marked difference from the surrounding *gaźo* population among whom only so-called 'lumpen' women may be found alone in the bars. While Gypsy women's behaviour appears to the stricter peasants to illustrate the depths of a licentious Gypsy freedom, this is not how Gypsies of either sex construe women's drinking. Whereas men drink for the sake of drinking, of being sociable, and rhetorically stress that they make their *voja* in this way, it seemed to me that women often 'excused' having a drink in terms of some extenuating circumstance (relieving an ache, warming up on a cold morning or before scavenging). Gypsy women do not join in the men's drinking sessions at the peasants' stills when they sit around for an hour or so drinking and talking. Nor at markets where women are doing business (selling material to peasants) do they stand around at the bar as their menfolk do. At such times when accompanied by her husband a woman may drink at the bar but when alone a woman will tend to take her brandy back to her pitch and drink it there with her fellow traders – to stand around at the bar would be to invite jealous recriminations from an angry spouse.

These gendered differences in Gypsy drinking are reflected in the celeb-rations (*mulatšago*) which punctuate communal life and which are primarily male affairs. The type of drink chosen is determined by the men: the women, who tend to remain in a separate room, are at best sent out a crate of beer 'so they can celebrate a little too' (*te mulatin ekhtserra, vi len*) as it was once put.[3]

Moreover, whereas it is really perfectly acceptable (if not desirable) for a man to get drunk to the point at which people can say that he knows not what he is saying, this would be extremely inappropriate and shameful for a woman. The logic governing this derives from a profound and widespread association of femininity with dangerously uncontrolled sexuality – a threat that is most sharply (but not exclusively) felt in relation to a still-fertile woman. A woman, at least until she is a grandparent, is thought to be permanently on the verge of loss of control, or at least must make constant and public affirmation of her control for such looseness not to be imputed. For a woman to surrender herself completely to the effects of alcohol would be interpreted as indicative of a more general lack of control.[4] For a woman to drop her guard and enjoy her drink too openly for its sociable qualities could be taken as evidence that she might also relax her sexual restraint with other men. Alcohol loosens men up in socially desirable ways. If a woman is not careful it might loosen up her behaviour in socially unwanted ways. Attitudes to two women illustrate this. An elderly great-grandmother is well known to enjoy her drink but this is simply treated as her, not particularly respectable, foible. A youngish mother of two young children who is thought to drink too much is severely criticized for her lax standards – indeed her house is said by some to be polluted.

Finally, I should mention two contexts in which alcohol may not be taken, indeed in which it is imperative to refuse the offer of a drink. The most important such context is after a burial when the close relatives of the deceased should not let alcohol touch their lips for at least six weeks, but more normally for six months or a year. Many people will commit them-selves publicly to renouncing alcohol for a full year of mourning. Apart from this prohibition there is also the more aleatory phenomenon illustrated in the scene which introduced this chapter when men refuse to drink beer or wine because they've drunk water. Gypsies told me that these drinks on top of water induce stomach pains and vomiting. This belief is held with some conviction and though Gypsies tend to be persistent hosts, rarely taking a simple 'no' as a final refusal of hospitality, I soon discovered that adopting the line that I had drunk water was a safe way to refuse a drink.

DRINKING FOR *VOJA* AND FOR HEALTH

Offering a drink to a fellow Gypsy is a common form of being polite. To treat a fellow Gypsy is to say that one would in principle be willing to engage in making one's *voja* with that person. *Voja* is the state in which men are *laše* (good, light, easy), when men are 'boys' (*šave*) and when they open up to one another through the medium of formal speech modes (Stewart 1989). In daily life men tend to be reticent in their speech, shrouding their actions and plans in secrecy and lies. Through drinking together men transcend this kind of chat (*duma*) and offer 'true speech' (*čači vorba*) to one another, the quintessential form of which is song.[5]

After drinking together men are willing to perform for one another, willing to engage in the complex process of listening to one another and being listened to in turn. *Voja* is the state in which Gypsy men achieve an ideal mode of social existence and become *čače phrala*, 'true brothers' (as 'boys') to one another. Liberated by the effect of sharing a drink together, Gypsy men, who normally adopt a kind of antagonistic, competitive relation with one another, can achieve moments of mutual respect and admiration.

Why should alcohol be so particularly appropriate for this job of creating *voja*? One reason is the representation of alcohol among the non-Gypsy peasant population against whom these Gypsies define themselves. In the peasant culture the 'non-productiveness', the superfluousness of alcohol is a common theme. In the traditional 'proper peasant' morality it was the young unmarried men who frequented the pub, and it was said that they would even steal their fathers' grain to fund their immoral activity (see Fél and Hofer 1969:197–199). The proper way to live as a peasant was to spend one's time and resources producing food with one's own hard, physical labour. Gypsies, by contrast, construct their identity around the idea of avoiding labour, living by their wits and their luck instead. It is understandable then that Gypsies who have lived surrounded by such peasants should be able to feel themselves most Gypsy-like when under the influence of the anti-productive spirit of an alcoholic drink.

But this is unlikely to be a wholly satisfactory explanation of the importance Gypsies attribute to sharing alcohol since it says nothing about the Gypsy construction of drinking. Unfortunately, most of my thoughts about the Gypsy construction of alcohol came after my research ended and so in the following pages I adopt a self-consciously speculative approach, starting out from solid ethnographic evidence and moving gradually on to ever thinner ice.

Rather as beer in England has been thought by some to be a source of good health (see, for example, Orwell 1970:62), Gypsy representations of alcohol assert that its bodily effects include improving one's health (*sastipo*) and strength (*zor*), as well as encouraging one's 'luck' (*baxt*). Because of these associations small children are allowed to sip from beer bottles and from sweeter liqueur-type drinks. Without in any sense encouraging serious drinking among children, mild tipsiness in a child is occasion for amusement not reprimand. Wine, when fortified with spices like dried paprika or, if one is poorer, black pepper, is thought to be particularly good for sorting out stomach disorders. It is also said to strengthen the blood and thus be potent against infection and disease. Rather to my surprise male friends who were feeling queasy might drop in for a glass of wine or brandy to calm their stomachs. Wine or spirits are also smuggled in to hospitalized Gypsies during visits by relatives – much to the frustration of the medical staff. As far as the Gypsies are concerned, a short drink is as likely to help clear the disease from the bodily organs as a course of medication. In a similar spirit great efforts are made to ensure that those unfortunate enough to be imprisoned or doing military service may occasionally receive a small drink of spirits – sometimes, I was told, smuggled inside citrus fruit. Beliefs in the curative powers of alcohol are extended to those metaphorical humans, horses, which when suffering certain stomach complaints may be force-fed a purgative brew of brandy and herbs.

Different drinks are more or less potent in this respect. Wine is talked of as health-giving especially when mixed with the spices like paprika or pepper which are otherwise thought to be enhancing of the body (see also Sutherland 1975:273–5). In this form especially wine is said to heat (*tatjarel*) the mouth and body. But more than either beer or wine, it is *ratija* (brandy/spirits) which is seen as a warming remedy which preserves or restores health – brandy may be said to burn (*phabarel*) the mouth or insides. It seems that it is this kind of difference between drinks which explains their association among the Gypsies with some and not other social moments or occasions. Beer and wine are drunk when Gypsies (primarily men) gather together to talk or celebrate. Brandy, on the other hand, is consumed almost exclusively first thing in the morning, during the middle of the night at a wake, or by women prior to going scavenging through the rubbish of the *gaźo*-s. To understand this better some knowledge of Gypsy concepts of the body is necessary.

ELEMENTS OF A GYPSY SOCIOPHYSIOLOGY

Thanks primarily to the work of two ethnographers (Sutherland 1975 and Okely 1983), the Gypsy body has almost become a feature of the landscape in modern anthropology. Building on insights by earlier students of Gypsy life (notably Miller 1975) and, as importantly, integrating the theoretical perspectives of Mary Douglas (1966) and Frederick Barth (1969), these authors showed how the Gypsy body is treated as a symbol of Gypsy society. Taboos concerning the boundaries of the Gypsy body (its external boundaries in Okely's English case, its vertical above/below waist boundary in Sutherland's Californian Romany case) are symbolically expressive of a separation of the Gypsy ethnic group from its host *gaźo* population. Both authors showed how Gypsy cleanliness beliefs are primarily concerned with the incorporation of people into (and their exclusion from) the ethnic group. To say that someone is clean is to say one can have unrestricted dealings with them, and vice versa.[6]

Purity is the normal state of self-respecting Gypsies in which the threat of pollution is controlled. The *gaźo*-s, unaware of the need to separate upper and lower, are therefore in principle polluted (*marimo*). This means in effect that they are contaminated, the tangible evidence of which is their bad odour or smell (*khan*). Polluted places or persons should be avoided for fear of contamination, or at least contact with them must be regulated.

Not separating lower from upper does not just lead to bad odours but also to dishonour, stupid behaviour, a loss of mental balance and various sickly bodily conditions. For instance, unchristened children, who are polluted by birth, are said to be weak, pale and especially susceptible to infection.[7] For adults, as well as causing skin rashes, strong polluting smells produce nausea and other stomach complaints.[8]

For Californian, English and Hungarian Gypsies alike pollution is a constant possibility. The threat is contained in part, as Miller, Okely and others have shown by attention to the boundaries of the body. In California and Hungary, at least, such attention focuses on the female body. Hungarian Gypsy women are especially careful in their dress, maintaining a clear distinction of their clothing at the waist. Washing habits and sexual habits are also influenced by this concern with boundaries (see Stewart 1988:298–317). When the separation of upper and lower becomes impossible to sustain, as in the final stages of pregnancy, women will tend to keep away from public gatherings of Gypsies out of 'shame' (*laźipe*).

Having been invited to think about the social construction of drinking among the Hungarian Gypsies by the editor of this volume, I have begun to realize that there may be other aspects of Gypsy bodily symbolism which have as yet remained unexplored in the literature. Gypsies, I now believe, are concerned not only with preserving the boundaries of their bodies, they are also concerned with fortifying the substance of these bodies. Alcohol, I suggest, provides one means for doing just that and in doing so it offers a defence against the threat of pollution. The opposition, instanced at the outset of this paper, between water and alcohol provides a clue to the overall picture that I discern.

Listing some of the symbolic associations of water enables one to see the symbolic rationale involved here. For Hungarian as much as for other Gypsies, water is a potential conductor of pollution, because it transmits bodily substance.[9] But in my case – and this may be a Hungarian peculiarity – water may not only conduct pollution but it also, when drunk, cools the body and dilutes the blood. Certainly, this seems to explain the marked Gypsy ambivalence towards using water in cooking. The standard Gypsy food, a meat stew, is cooked in fat, one might almost say boiled in fat and for this water is never an appropriate ingredient. Food, which is always cooked in quantities to enable unexpected guests to be fed and provides one of the key modes of community via commensality, must strengthen and not weaken the body. For formal meals soup may well be cooked and occasionally eaten by the men of the house – but at larger gatherings I was often struck how a few men would politely pick at a wing of chicken or sip a couple of spoons of the soup while others would simply skip the soup – a practice of which the women providers were well aware, often complaining that they didn't know why they bothered making soup since no one ate it!

Apart from the use of water in cooking, both drinking too much water and drinking very cold water are said to be dangerous and conducive to stomach pains.[10] If water cools and thus makes the body susceptible to the threat of contamination by pollution, wine, beer and brandy operate to varying degrees in exactly the opposite way. These drinks differentially heat the body and fortify the blood. Indeed, just as too much water can be damaging, drinking too much brandy in the morning led to more than one man complaining of burning pains in his stomach (*phabol*, or Hungarian *ég a gyómrom*). One cure for this is to drink water.

If one imagines that it is by heating the body that fruit brandy gives its strength (*zor*) and health (*sastipe*) and thus the means to resist polluting dissolution of boundaries, then the contexts in which brandy is drunk fall into a pattern. It is, firstly, drunk on an empty stomach as the (potentially polluting) activities of the night are separated from those of the day during which men and women go their largely separate ways.[11] This function of drinking brandy is particularly marked early in the morning at horse-markets since a man's luck in trade depends on a symbolic separation of himself from his wife whose presence during a deal would spoil his luck – because of her association with polluting menstrual blood (see Stewart forthcoming c). Brandy appears in some way to strengthen the pure Gypsy body against polluting influences at this time. Brandy is also drunk during a wake after midnight. This is a time of considerable uncertainty and fear, and for the close relatives of the deceased a period when the proximity of the deceased is most keenly felt. At any time after midnight the dead person is likely to enter the room (all the windows and doors are left open until burial in order to allow for this). One feels his/her presence as a cold air on the body. Brandy, I suggest, plays a role in keeping this potentially life-threatening contact with the deceased at bay. Thirdly, Gypsy women explained their brandy drinking before scavenging as a means of coping with the smell of the rubbish bins. The pollution of the *gaźo*-s is typically apparent in their smell, or rather stench (*khan*), and so again I would argue that brandy acts here to strengthen the Gypsy women against the potential pollution of breathing in *gaźo* stench.[12] Finally, since ill-health is often attributed to pollution it seems logical that here too *ratija* should be a suitable remedy.

Whereas the use of brandy appears in all these contexts to be almost medicinal, beer and wine offer a medium of commensality in which men can share a form of (bodily) sustenance without risk of pollution, without boundaries between them being eliminated altogether. Beer and wine are never drunk alone at home. Cold water, drunk from a flagon in the house, symbolizes domestic isolation, sitting at home with one's family. So, to mix beer and water would be to confuse two modes of commensality, that of the household and that of the 'brothers', and suffer the consequences of all types of polluting confusion of boundaries. Though it may be thought that I now move off fragile ethnographic ice into plain air, might it not be that soup, which anyway is always covered in a thick layer of body-enhancing, bubbling fat and is liberally laced with hot, red peppers, is offered by women to male guests at a *mulatśago* as a symbol of the domestic unit in a socially appropriable form? Out of politeness the men acknowledge this by picking at the soup but refrain from going further.

Sutherland, Okely and others showed that it was by continuing to respect the boundaries of the body according to the local Gypsy custom that Gypsies marked and maintained their identity. Following from my argument here it would be logical to ask whether Hungarian Gypsies, at least, are also concerned with the sharing of joint substance through the sharing of alcohol. Does 'feeding' one's brothers with drink lead to a sharing of substance with them? Certainly, the concern with the uniformity of drink at *mulatśago* might be connected with such an ideology.

This possibility, that beer and wine provide a mode of sharing not just pleasure but also substance with other Gypsies, is given some support by the way consumption of alcohol is forbidden after the burial of a close

Gypsy relative. An obvious explanation of the taboo would be that drinking is associated with pleasure and celebration and is therefore inappropriate during mourning. This is plausible and Gypsies did in these terms criticize other Gypsies who were felt to have broken mourning restrictions too early. However this explanation remains secondary and *ad hoc* since it fails to explain the massive and conspicuous consumption of alcohol of several sorts during the wake by all close relatives of the deceased right up to the interment of the body.[13]

An alternative and more satisfactory explanation can be found by looking at the processes enacted by the consecutive stages of the rites. Immediately after death, until the burial, the Gypsies' concern is to begin to sever the connection of the living with the recently deceased while at the same time acknowledging this connection. During the wake, and after midnight in particular, the persons attending are obliged to adopt the formal speech modes most characteristic of the deceased (songs, riddles, folk-stories, etc.) in order to pay him or her respect. At this stage of the evening beer is drunk and then at midnight, as I have said, bottles of brandy are opened and passed around.

The burial initiates a new stage in the process of death. After the handing over of the body to the *gaźo* grave-diggers, the rites seem aimed at a final separation, the prevention of a return by the deceased and depositing the death pollution on the *gaźo* priest.[14] It is as the body is interred that I have seen relatives formally renounce alcohol in front of the assembled Gypsies whilst pouring their remaining alcohol on to the grave itself. From this moment until the final *pomana* (feast for the deceased), when it is said that the departed is firmly placed in the other world, close relatives should refrain from drinking.

After this *pomana* all drinking (but especially of brandy first thing in the morning) by those touched by the loss should be preceded by pouring a small drink on the ground for the deceased. Now that the dead person is safely consigned to another world it becomes possible once again to share one's drink with them. This is most explicit on the evening of All Souls' Day when families gather around significant graves, often lying on or beside them as if a guest in someone's home, and share drinks with their dead while recalling their lives in their talk.

The symbolism of these rites implies that drinking is a means not just of sharing experience in a particularly fine form but also to a greater or lesser degree bodily substance with other Gypsies. More than that, alcohol seems to allow 'just the right amount' of commensality, neither too much nor too little. In particular it avoids the kind of commensality represented by consuming food together. During the wake, though (cold, white) food is put out, no Gypsy partakes – when I was present at wakes I was urged to eat as much as I could, since it is said that the food consumed by the stranger reaches the dead man. A stranger, lacking any ties to the dead person and so untouched by death pollution, may without danger be fully commensal with the deceased – not so the Gypsies, who restrict their commensality to their drinking.

The behaviour of a woman whose husband had died unexpectedly in tragic circumstances illustrates this representation of alcohol. On the day of the funeral, before the priest arrived with his own entourage, this woman spent an hour or two accompanied by her daughters at the chapel of rest beside her husband's body. After a period of apparently uncontrolled wailing outside the chapel she approached the open coffin and opened two bottles of beer to 'share' with her husband, whom she addressed in an intermittent, beseeching song-like speech. Just as the sharing of beer among men allows the breaking down of certain barriers and the establishing of a form of community through commensality, so this woman, I believe, also used the act of drinking beer to bridge a separation. Alcohol appears then to be a means of linking people in a form of identity that is life-enhancing. It is only when connections must be denied, when a separation must be maintained between Gypsies, that drinking is forbidden.

ALCOHOL AND THE NATURE OF GYPSY IDENTITY

Emile Durkheim located the sacred at the centre of society (1976). For him it was the social core, that which makes a society what it is which was sacralized. Mary Douglas (1966) and Edmund Leach (1972) relocated the sacred to the edge of society. That which lay betwixt and between social groups and categories was the object of awe and veneration since it symbolized the limits of a particular form of society. With hindsight we can see that there is no real opposition between these complementary perspectives. And so recent work on the concept of the person and the construction of the body (for example, Martin 1987) has led me away from the well-established concern with Gypsy ritual boundaries to reconsider the ritual representation of the substance of the Gypsy body.

However, in shifting the analytical focus I hope to have brought an important if little considered aspect of Gypsy identity to the fore. Previous concern with boundaries may have led to the practice of treating Gypsies as just one special case of modern/industrial 'ethnicity'. They are of course an instance of just that, but there is also something more remarkable going on here than the preservation of ethnic distinctiveness. The very notion of identity for the Hungarian Gypsies seems to differ from ours, they do not construct their identity in the manner that we tend to. These Gypsies are fairly explicit that the identity gained at birth forms only one part of one's person. Equally, indeed more, important is the identity acquired through joint action with one's fellows (see Stewart forthcoming b, and 1991). In the most extreme case, one can be born a *gaźo* but if one lives with Gypsies and adopts their way of life one can become a full and respected member of the community, and people I know have done this.[15]

Though Gypsies have a remarkably 'sociological' ideology of identity, they none the less imagine the physical embodiment of identity in various ways. Unlike peasants they do not have the means to link their identity to a circumscribed tract of land, and they are not disposed to pay much attention to inherited, ascribed characteristics. Metaphors of inherited substance carry relatively little weight here. Given this focus on the achieved nature of identity it fits very well that shared food and alcohol should provide the medium for the construction of wholesome, Gypsy bodily substance. At times these forms of sustenance can be thought of as complementary.[16] At other times, however, they are opposed. Gypsy food (*romano xaben*) is essential to life, but it comes from the household. Gypsy social identity is based on a transcendence of the divisive interests of particular families through the construction of a communal brotherhood. This sense of brotherhood is above all generated by the sharing of drink and speech (especially song) in the *mulatśago*. It is striking that at these occasions many Gypsy men will refuse to mix not just water but food too with the elixir of their brotherliness.

ACKNOWLEDGEMENTS

Research was funded by the British Economic and Social Research Council. The London School of Economics and the Radcliffe-Brown Memorial Fund of the Royal Anthropological Institute kindly helped with the completion of my doctoral thesis. The film producer John Blake produced the fertile observation which gave birth to this chapter. Fenella Cannell helped to keep the beast alive, as did Janet Carsten, whose influence will be apparent to anyone who knows her work.

NOTES

1 My research among these Vlach Gypsies – carried out between October 1984 and January 1986 in the town of Gyöngyös in northern Hungary – was the first field work-based study carried out since the late nineteenth century when L. Wlislocki spent time living with tent-Gypsies in what was then the Transylvanian region of Hungary. My assertion of uniformity should be taken as more of a hypothesis based upon brief encounters with other Gypsies in Hungary than a statement of proven fact.

2 Such early morning drinking is in no sense comparable with the alcoholic's need for the hand-steadying drink.

3 At New Year when men and women celebrate together there will normally however be a bottle of sweet brandy for those who can't take the harsher fruit brandy.

4 A non-Gypsy woman friend of mine once became extremely drunk while visiting me and in this state collapsed semi-conscious. My Gypsy hosts made it quite clear that they had told me for too long that *gaźo* women from Budapest were all 'licensed whores' (*lubnuj*) and here was my proof.

5 I remember first visiting Gypsies with a musicologist collecting ballads and being told that no one could sing because they had no *voja*. The solution, my musicologist friend told me, was to bring some beer. With a bottle or two of beer *voja* was more easily found. This turns out not to have been a ruse to wangle a free drink off the unsuspecting *gaźo*-s. Gypsies themselves when they celebrate aim to create their *voja* and the prime means of doing this is sharing alcohol.

6 The term in California, as in Hungary, is *vuźipe* (Sutherland 1975:258). The Hungarian and Californian Gypsies both speak dialects of Romany, unlike most English Gypsies.

7 The Gypsy christening (*bolimo*) in the *gaźo*-s' church is thus primarily concerned with the bodily condition of the child, with removing the pollution of birth from it. At the same time as the priest performs this purely carnal operation, the Gypsy men drink and sing at home for the sake of the child's spiritual well-being.

8 I have, for instance, seen men retch as they come out of a bar in the early morning, claiming that the place 'stank' (*khandel*) in a polluting way.

9 When washing the human body it is important that water which has cleaned the lower body should not be used for the upper regions. Washing in a bath is thus polluting because the water effectively amalgamates that which ought to be kept distinct. Because water carries bodily substance people tend to wash before darkness falls in order to dispose of the dirty water before nightfall – to throw it out at night would put one at the mercy of spirits such as *bivuźo* (the unclean) who bring illness. Equally, the water with which the dead person was washed had to be disposed of out of sight on pain of causing sickness to anyone who chanced on it accidentally. After childbirth, until the christening (that is, for as long as birth pollution is held to last) it is in principle wrong for a woman to draw water from a well for fear that she will pollute it and all after her. Incidentally, it is also said that staring into standing water can cause soul-loss and death.

10 I was often warned not to drink ice-cold water in case it caused stomach pains but I took no notice of this at the time. I noticed too that men would often object to the frosty temperature at which I served them beer and would leave it to warm up before touching it.

11 Though reproductive sexuality is a source of pollution I can't say whether sexual activity overheats the body or causes it to lose heat. Pregnancy, however, can lead women to complain regularly of a burning stomach.

12 After buying a house from *gaźo* owners Gypsies will typically make ostentatious noises to other Gypsies about the smell inside the house and how they bleached and sterilized the place inside out.

13 Indeed, I saw families virtually beggared by the cost of maintaining a wake and keeping up a sufficient flow of alcohol each night.

14 Okely suggested that the process of dying among English Gypsies is in effect

a process of assimilation into the non-Gypsy world (1983: 228). In this case it seems to me that, while the body of the Vlach Gypsy is given in the end to the *gaźo*-s and buried in *gaźo* soil, her/his soul is in some sense kept by the Gypsies.

15 Kelderaś Gypsies in Paris are similarly 'sociological' in their attribution of identity (Patrick William, personal communication).

16 Just before sending proofs of this chapter to press I discovered a stray note from the first weeks of my research recording a conversation among informants about the edibility of hedgehogs. Everyone was agreed that traditionally hedgehogs were a favoured food of the Gypsies and that after eating hedgehog one should drink wine and especially not water. Now hedgehogs, I later discovered, are represented as quasi clan animals by these Gypsies, the consumption of whose flesh is one of the marks of true Gypsiness – though one informant had originally claimed that since seeing a television programme which revealed that hedgehogs were in fact cursed souls of dead Gypsies he had refused to eat them (cf Okely, 1983:94–5). Having no framework to understand the prohibition on mixing water with hedgehog I, of course, immediately forgot it.

REFERENCES

Barth, F. (1969) 'Introduction' in Barth (ed.) *Ethnic Groups and Boundaries*, London: George Allen and Unwin.

Douglas, M. (1966) *Purity and Danger*, London: Routledge & Kegan Paul.

Durkheim, E. (1976) 1912 *The Elementary Forms of Religious Life*, London: George Allen and Unwin.

Fél, E. and Hofer, T. (1969) *Proper Peasants: Traditional Life in a Hungarian Village*, Viking Fund Publication in Anthropology 46.

Gropper, R. (1975) *Gypsies in the City*, New Jersey: Darwin Press.

Guy, W. (1975) 'Ways of looking at Rom: the case of Czechoslovakia' in F. Rehfisch (ed.) *Gypsies, Tinkers and other Travellers*, London: Academic.

Havas, G. (1982) 'Foglalkozásváltási stratégiák különbözö cigány közösségekben' ('Strategies for changing occupations in differing Gypsy Communities') in Andor (ed.) *Cigany Vizsgálatok*: 181–202, Budapest, Müvelödési Kutató Intézet.

de Heusch, L. (1966) *A la découverte des Tsiganes: une expedition de réconnaissance*, Bruxelles: Ed. de L'Institut de Sociologie. de L'Université Libre.

Leach, E. (1972) 'Anthropological aspects of language: animal categories and verbal abuse' in P. Maranda (ed.) *Mythology*, Harmondsworth: Penguin.

Martin, E. (1987) *The Woman in the Body: A Cultural Analysis of Reproduction*, Boston: Beacon.

Miller, C. (1975) 'American Rom and the ideology of defilement' in F. Rehfisch (ed.) *Gypsies, Tinkers and other Travellers*, London: Academic.

Panaitescu, P. (1941) 'The Gypsies in Wallachia and Moldavia: a chapter of economic history', *J.G.L.S.* 20, part 2 pp.58–72.

Okely, J. (1983) *The Traveller-Gypsies*, Cambridge: Cambridge University Press.

Orwell, G. (1970) *Collected Essays*, Vol. 3, Harmondsworth: Penguin.

Stewart, M. (1988) 'Brothers in song: the persistence of Gypsy identity and community in socialist Hungary', unpublished Ph.D. thesis, University of London.

Stewart, M. (1989) '"True Speech": song and the moral order of a Vlach Gypsy community in Hungary', *Man*, NS Vol. 24 (1) pp.79–102.

Stewart, M. (1990) 'Gypsies, work and civil society' in C. Hann (ed.) *Market Economy and Civil Society in Hungary*, London: Frank Cass.

Stewart, M. (1991) 'Un peuple sans patrie', *Terrain* 17, Octobre 1991, pp.39–52.

Stewart, M. (forthcoming a) 'Gypsies, the work ethic and Hungarian socialism' in C. Hann (ed.) *The Social Anthropology of Socialism*, London: Routledge & Kegan Paul.

Stewart, M. (forthcoming b) 'Substantial and relational identity: are Gypsies an ethnic group?', *Ricerca Folklorica*.

Stewart, M. (forthcoming c) 'Gypsies at the horse fair: a non-market model of trade' in R. Dilley (ed.) *Contesting Markets*, Edinburgh: University Press.

Sutherland, A. (1975) *Gypsies: The Hidden Americans*, London: Tavistock.

9 Drinking and masculinity in everyday Swedish culture

Gunilla Bjerén

Writing about a phenomenon that is common in many societies, including those of the intended readership, presents particular problems. Unless one carries out explicitly comparative studies, the reader cannot assess what is particular and what is general to the phenomenon you are describing. The ethnographic description encompasses all: aspects common to many different societies, aspects peculiar to the one you are describing and aspects idiosyncratic to the context in which the reported material was collected. The phenomenon described in the following pages is thus one that is not particular to Sweden, nor to the forest town where the observations were made. It captures the Swedish version of the 'sub-arctic vodka belt', one that prevails in many cultures where beer and distilled 'white spirits' are the traditional media for social drinking and intoxication. The question of what is unique and what is general cannot be resolved without a comparative context.

The topic of this chapter is not a comparison between drinking patterns. Some of the observations will therefore appear well known and maybe trivial to colleagues familiar with other cultures within the 'vodka belt' or more distant beer cultures. In conversation with colleagues from other areas I have learned that the fundamental social and cultural dynamics of beer/ vodka drinking appear at least superficially similar cross-culturally. A description of the minutiae of drinking is required to bring out the particulars.

THE CONTEXT

Historical background

Swedes take their drinking seriously. The Swedish state takes their drinking seriously as well. Swedish drinking patterns and the meaning of alcohol in Swedish society are construed in an atmosphere of tension between the aspiration to drink as much as individuals feel is appropriate and the ambitions of a paternalistic state apparatus to limit the medical and social effects of indulgence.

Legal restrictions on the production and sale of spirits have a long history in Sweden, dating back to the late eighteenth century when the Crown put all production of distilled beverages under its monopoly (1776). The reason for this was entirely fiscal; the measure was extremely unpopular and in 1787 farmers were again allowed to distill alcohol for their own use.[1] In 1809 the restrictions on the production and sale of *brännvin* were further alleviated. (Brännvin is the Swedish name for alcohol distilled from a base of potatoes or cereals. It corresponds to the Russian vodka.) The social and economic consequences of unrestricted availability of *brännvin* led to an abstentionist movement which won over representatives of the Crown and finally induced parliament[2] to restrict the production and sale of alcohol again in 1853. The restrictions this time were motivated by social reasons as well as fiscal.

In 1916 rationing of alcohol was introduced and remained in force until 1955. Since then, government attempts to control the consumption of alcohol have been made via a high-price policy, with retention of the state monopoly of production and sales. All kinds of wines and spirits, as well as beer of the strongest grades, can be bought only in government outlets. An individual has to be 20 years of age to purchase anything in the alcohol shops; young people must be prepared to show an identity card indicating their age. Notorious alcoholics are blacklisted; obviously intoxicated people will not be served.

As a consequence of its alcohol policies, Sweden today has among the highest prices on alcohol in Europe, one of the strictest laws on alcohol and driving, and one of the lowest per capita consumption rates, and one of the lowest rate of death from cirrhosis of the liver.[3]

Restrictions on alcohol have always been unpopular among the general (male) population but also a question on which opinion has been highly divided. In 1922, for instance, in a national referendum, 49 per cent voted for a total ban on alcoholic beverages while 51 per cent were for continued sales.

The self-image of Swedes is splintered in many directions; one is of a hard-working population suffering under intolerable paternalism from a few dogmatic teetotallers ruling parliament; another is of a culture of males totally unable to control their own use of alcohol and therefore in need of stern restrictions to limit the bad effects of their hedonism. Whatever the facts, Swedes consider themselves the heaviest drinkers in the world (apart from the Finns, and possibly the Russians), and return from travels abroad astounded at the fact that people living under more liberal regimes have not killed themselves drinking a long time ago.

The setting

The material reported in this chapter was collected during a long-term study (1976–1991) of a small forest town, called Torsby, in western Sweden. The town itself has a population of about 4,000; it is the administrative, educational, and commercial cente of a large and sparsely populated forest region with a total population numbering about 16,000 (Bjerén 1981).

The section of the town population born in the area is dominated by what in the English-speaking literature would be termed 'working class': men working at the saw mill, at the post and roads administration, in transportation or in lower-ranking clerical posts and women working in the hospital as nursing assistants, in teaching or in office work. It is among such people that my field work and later field visits have taken place.

Part of official alcohol policy has been to restrict the number of public places where you can buy alcohol. Permission to sell stronger beer, wine and spirits is granted by the *socialnämnd*, the politically appointed committee on social affairs that is part of municipal administration. In most municipalities (and Torsby and all of its vast hinterland together make up one municipality) permission is rarely given, and always to establishments serving food as well as drinks. Consequently, in a place like Torsby, there are no pubs and no bars. One or two eating places open at night[4] will have *full-ständiga rättigheter*, 'total rights' (to sell alcoholic beverages) – their prices alone ensure that no serious drinking can take place on the premises. One glass of medium-strong beer will cost around 35SEK (about £3.50). Most drinking, consequently, is done away from commercial establishments – for the young at home before they go out – or literally outside the place you intend to visit, or on the sly inside the place by topping up your soft drink under the table from a bottle brought in pocket or bag, or during visits to the toilet . . . all according to the principle 'if there is a will there is a way'.

Drinking situations

For adults who have developed a *modus vivendi* with alcohol there are several distinct drinking situations. In addition, each social circle develops its own habits, and each new cohort modifies patterns as its members arrive at their *modus vivendi*.

What I say below pertains to the *brännvin* drinkers. Wine-drinking is considered more refined and the untutored are bashful in the face of the, to them, unknown rituals of wine-drinking. Wine-drinking is also thought to lead to a worse hangover than drinking *brännvin*, and the drunkenness itself not to be as pleasurable. Wine-drinking is a habit acquired primarily in local high society or in big-city circles. The life of university students is closely linked to wine-drinking. The radical student movement of the 1960s is nowadays at times scornfully brushed off as the 'red wine left' (*rödvinsvänstern*).

As I mention below, however, wine-drinking is making inroads through the new drinking patterns of women.

MEN DRINKING TOGETHER

First, there is all-male drinking, although there is little spatial segregation of sexes in Swedish society and for men living with women there are few arenas for all-male drinking in everyday life. In most younger and middle-aged households both husband and wife work outside the home; young children spend their day in municipal day-care centres, with *dagmammor* ('day mothers', nowadays municipally employed and promoted to 'family day-care homes') or with relatives and friends. Older children go to school. Most women work part-time, 50–75 per cent, and are thus able to combine work with picking up children and preparing the family dinner. Men go straight home from work and have dinner some time between 4.30 p.m. and 6.30 p.m. after having had lunch between 11 a.m. and 12 noon, either at a lunch restaurant or brought with them from home. Small-town Swedes expect to eat prepared food twice a day. During winter weekdays, adults might leave home again to go to meetings or attend evening classes, but rarely to go visiting. Summer changes this as official Sweden more or less closes for two months, many work places shut down for a month, people work shorter hours and take most of their five-week holiday.

Some occupations and work places have long traditions of male drinking. In this region, forestry is an example of this. Now that forestry is mechanized and no longer entails camp-living away from home this has changed. But other activities played out in and around forestry are bound up with all-male drinking. Hunting, particularly moose-hunting, and fishing on the many lakes in the forest are such activities, as are all the meetings that men must have to organize the hunt and administer the care of the lakes and fishing waters. Among some men, drinking itself is an activity of the forest, as they retreat to forest cabins for the sole purpose of drinking to get drunk. Sports and the organization of sports is another arena for male drinking – motor sport, ice-hockey, and football all provide arenas for male socializing and drinking.

Drinking in Sweden is an activity heavily loaded with emotions and meaning. In yesterday's Sweden it was also purely male. 'You gossip like a woman, but you drink like a man.' It is shameful and joyful; it brings you together and sets you apart. If you don't learn the rules, drinking might place you outside society. If you don't partake, you might never enter society.

Drinking is never neutral. It is reward and celebration – for something you have done for me, for something we have done together, something we will be doing together, and in celebration of being together. When men drink, they 'show what kind of men they are', both through their relation to the drink itself and through what they reveal about themselves while they are drinking. There are many, many jokes and sayings about drinking in Swedish. One of the most telling is the one that says that 'all joy without spirits is artificial joy'. *Ta en sup och va'som en människa!* ('Take a schnapps and be like a human being!')

MEN DRINKING WHILE WOMEN WATCH

When older men and women drink together in company with others one is reminded of the play of the *capercaillie* and other large forest fowl. Pretending indifference, the women watch, perhaps secretly worried that one or other of the brave cocks will come to harm, destroy his reputation by drinking himself under the table or by a too-open display of emotion, be it sorrow or anger. The men show off with considerable bravado, or withdraw by themselves with their '*grogg*' to talk business. (A Swedish grogg is a drink consisting of neat spirits diluted with water or soft drinks of different kinds.) A pleasant evening is when everybody has had as much to drink as they can handle, nobody has become 'derailed' (*spårat ur*), and there is a taxi to take you home.

Domestic drinking is a fairly quiet affair. Weekdays are not for drinking; the working day begins early (7 a.m. or 8 a.m.) and people retire early. Friday and Saturday evenings can be celebrated with extra special food, drink, beer and *brännvin*, and tall drinks made with soft drink mixed with vodka, *brännvin* or whisky to end the evening.

WOMEN DRINKING

Lately, women have taken to drinking together. This is a recent development. The social drink *par excellence* of women[5] is coffee – properly brewed coffee. Women drink together when their men are away and if they have remained single or are separated/divorced. Younger women drink in small groups at home, to mark a special occasion, while meeting to talk over 'business', or in preparation for going out (to dance and look the men over).

Brännvin and beer are not drinks for women. Ladies' drinks traditionally were sweet liqueurs or much diluted *groggs*. Contemporary women drink wine and other foreign beverages such as Campari, dry Martini and the like. Fads are common.

Socially, women are playing with dynamite when drinking. If femininity is related to alcohol at all, it is to its absence. There are no excuses allowed for women drinking too much. In this society, where overindulgence is the only known reason for aberrant behaviour, a lot of behaviour unrelated to the use of alcohol will be interpreted as the result of too much drinking.

DRINKING ALONE

Drinking alone should not be done. To drink alone is to be anti-social (by not wanting to share); it is commonly thought to be an indication of alcoholism. And alcoholism is shameful: to be labelled an alcoholic is a condemnation beyond words for a woman since women by definition do not drink and therefore cannot/should not become alcoholics. For men it is shameful as well: a man who cannot '*klara sin sprit*' (handle his drink) has shown himself to be a lesser man than the others who can. Possibly not a man at all – lately I have heard men gossiping about other men insinuating that those who are the worse for drink are homosexual as well.[6] They will be met with pitying contempt – and endlessly invited to drink. A known drunkard causes embarrassment to a group intent on drinking as a known total abstainer does. Both are reminders that one really ought not to drink. Both will be pressed to join in the drinking – the alcoholic because he is a '*stackars sate*' (poor devil) and the abstainer because people drinking abhor being watched by a sober fellow.

Outside society is another society consisting of the 'A-team', men who have no jobs, and who live on social security. They are very public in this society where most social life takes place in non-public places. The moral condemnation by the 'straight' people is ruthless and rests on three points: they are living off public funds ('my tax money is supporting someone else's hedonism'), they could handle their alcohol 'if they only wanted to', and 'there, but for the grace of God, go I'. The presence of the A-team keeps anxiety about alcohol alive.

FRIDAY NIGHT ON NORRA TORGGATAN 3[7]

Friday was cleaning day. I was part of the household of Ulla Hansson, a 35-year old woman who lived in a largish flat with her 15-year-old son. The flat overlooked the Old Square of the small town – once the site of open-air commerce, now a parking space serving modern shopping needs.

After cleaning it was time to do the shopping for the weekend. At the time I arrived in Torsby, in June 1976, the daily needs of the townspeople were catered for by three large stores. On Friday afternoons they would all have long queues as people waited in line to pay for their needs for the coming week.

The queue would be as long in *Systemet*. *Systemet* was housed in a modern building and had moved into the premises while I was doing field work. The shop was of a standard design, used all over the country: a long counter with five cash registers; brightly lit displays with many brands of wine, arranged according to the colour of the wine and price range. Very little wine was sold in this shop where the standard order would be for *brännvin* (of many different varieties), vodka and whisky. The atmosphere in *Systemet* would be hushed but tense. Massive men in their working clothes, not talking, looked as if their right to buy would be questioned any minute, reminiscent of the days when the cash registers were equipped with a random mechanism that would signal to every twentieth customer or so that they should identify themselves, just to make sure that no blacklisted persons slipped through the net, while saving the sales personnel the embarrassment of having to ask for identification. The sales company had had several campaigns to dissuade people from doing their shopping for the weekend on Fridays (on Saturdays *Systemet* is closed), but with little success. Swedes are conditioned to finish up their alcohol and it is difficult for most to keep drink at home. The only way to be sure there is something to drink on Friday, therefore, is to buy alcohol on Fridays.

Ulla avoided shopping for wine and spirits. Her position in the community was that of a veritable social outcast. Being seen in *Systemet* would be further confirmation of her imputed alcoholism. Instead I would go, or Carl, her man friend. Carl's walking was severely impaired by an old polio-damage and, come to think of it, he most probably sent someone from the firm where he was working, as an economically responsible person (*kamrer*). A handicapped person, particularly one associated with an imputed woman alcoholic, ought not to be seen at *Systemet* either.

Coming home from *Systemet* with a few bottles of white wine, I found Ulla preparing her specialty, a concoction of mussels, parsley, anchovies and garlic, for the evening. The recipe came from a well-known gourmet journal. Not only Carl but also Bertil, Carl's best friend and business partner, would be coming for the evening.

Bertil and Carl came straight from work, both by car. Carl had lived together with Ulla before I arrived in Torsby, but had recently moved 20 km south of Torsby to a house he had bought. Ulla did not want to move outside town and so had remained in their earlier flat together with Mats, her son from a teenage marriage. Bertil was in his late thirties, a school-friend of Carl, with whom he now ran a small firm. Bertil was one of many Torsby men who had never left home. His work as a building worker specializing in insulation took him all over the country, but he operated out of his parents' home and his mother looked after all his domestic needs, as she had all his life. Bertil had a very nice car, equipped with a powerful cassette player, and he loved listening to jazz. His other passion in life was fishing: fly-fishing for big-river fish, most of the time across the border in Norway.

Mats appeared shortly after the men arrived. These two men, particularly Bertil, acted as his fathers and mentors – and became even more so later on in his life.

Ulla had laid the table in one of the front rooms. With the food she and I had wine and the men beer and schnapps. Mats was not allowed anything, even though we all knew that he was already drinking with his friends when they went out 'dancing'. Drinks before eating does not occur in traditional settings. Instead, a proper Swedish dinner with guests is introduced by a course of a variety of pickled herrings (sill) with potatoes and schnapps, regardless of what is served afterwards. In our case, this would not be served since we were *en famille* and both men and Mats had had a proper lunch at midday.

A few decades ago, 'free drinking' in the company of women would be considered very improper. 'Free drinking' meant everybody drinking as they pleased. In Sweden, *brännvin* is served in schnappsglasses, small glasses in the shape of an inverted cone. To drink you had to *skåla*[8] with someone. In some circles, each schnapps was accompanied by a drinking song (short, humorous and to the point). The rounds of schnapps had their own names and women were not supposed to venture beyond *halvan* (the second round). The whole process of drinking was surrounded by rituals, more elaborate in some circles than in others, but all more elaborate than those of today.

After eating there had to be coffee. Coffee with an *avec*, brandy for the men, sweet liqueur or sherry for the women.

And after coffee, we would settle down to drinking. In this time and place we played cards, a variety of poker called 'Chicago', while drinking. Together with Carl we would have vodka mixed with soft drink – orange or tonic. We would now be thoroughly relaxed. In this circle card playing was not done for money – it was a pastime that could include all five of us with Mats as the most serious player. Carl and Bertil would maintain a proper male tone – showing off their wit, making jokes, talking about people. Ulla and I would, however, not play a hen-like role. The company would be too small and we all knew one another too well for that. All the same there would a subtle drinking competition between the men. To drink much without showing signs of being drunk was the game. And Ulla and I had to show that we were game too, that we were up to taking part in the male games. Drinking vodka with soft drink made this feasible since it was easy to dilute your drink rather more than the others did.

As the evening wore on, the card playing would diminish and there would be less general conversation and more dialogue. This is the time when men speak, lay down the armory that upholds their everyday male role play and talk to one another as human beings.

The kinds of conversation that men hold in this condition are different from the conversations they hold when sober. The bravado is gone; the distance, otherwise rigorously upheld, between male and female spheres of interest is lessened. Men bring up the worries and cares that they have. They may weep if they feel like it or burst out in anger – show the kinds of emotions that are not in harmony with the male façade. There is a certain eerie Jekyll-and-Hyde feeling about these dual-role performances. The one presupposes the other. Without the ideology of male control and management that belongs to the working week and sobriety, there would be no need for the inversion of behaviour during drinking times. Without the catharsis provided by drinking, the normal façade could not be upheld.

CONCLUDING REMARKS

To become a man in the Torsby community a boy must learn how to handle alcohol and to join in the two parallel discourses pursued by men, the one of control and self-sufficiency, and the other of community and mutual support.

During the regular working week control and self-sufficiency are the ideals to strive for if you are a working man. '*En bra karl reder sig själy!*' (A genuine man manages on his own.) To be seen to work hard – be hard – and to be recognized as capable under working conditions is necessary for a man's reputation and for his self-esteem. All of this is thought to be irreconcilable with intoxication.

Leisure time in the company of other men is another matter. Protected by the screen of alcohol a man can voice and show the emotions denied expression in the hard, cold light of regular time. He has stepped outside time. Feelings and behaviour thought to be irreconcilable with sobriety may be tolerated.

To grow up to be a man in the time, place and class I am portraying here is to learn to manage this game of split social personalities, through the judicious use of alcohol.

Womanliness, on the other hand, is simply not related to alcohol. Nor are relations between women mediated by liquor. Even though young women today drink a great deal more with less shame than previous cohorts it is an entirely different matter from male drinking.

In a comparative perspective, the absence of alcoholic beverages in everyday commensality is striking. There was a time when beer and *brännvin* were natural components of a regular meal in Sweden and when the relation between producer and product was as immediate as in wine-producing countries. The beginning of the end of this era was signalled in 1776 with the first Crown monopoly on distilling and came to a complete stop during the first decades of the twentieth century with the pass-book and rationing.

Today, and in living memory, alcohol is for special occasions, to the extent that the presence of wine and spirits also mark an occasion as special.

The popular ambivalence about drink is captured in these two aspects – that alcohol is necessary to signal joint joy and pleasure, and that alcohol is seen as the cause of most kinds of aberrant behaviour.

NOTES

1 The historical account is based on Henriksson (1963) and Sjögren (1903).
2 An elected parliament with representatives from the four estates: nobility, clergy, commerce and self-owning farmers. Government was not responsible to parliament, but only parliament could levy taxes and legislate.
3 Compared to France, the price of whisky is 3.5:1, vodka 3:1, and malt whisky 2:1. Also compared to France, per capita consumption in 100 per cent alcohol units is 1:2.5, and death by cirrhosis of the liver is 1:8 (Source: Ulf Nilsson, 'Skål för Europa', *Expressen*, 23 August 1990, p.14). The rule is that the alcohol content of a drink should be reflected in its price: the higher the alcohol content the higher the price. In an attempt to divert consumption to 'softer' drinks, wine is given a lower tariff. The two strongest of the three grades of beer available are also sold exclusively through *Systemet* (or *Bolaget*), the popular name for the chain of state-owned and run liquor shops.
4 There are a couple more catering mainly for lunch guests; they will close in the afternoon.
5 And of men, when alcohol is out of the question.
6 This is a new thing – the AIDS epidemic has apparently brought an articulation of homosexuality to this community.
7 3 North Square Street.
8 Raise your glass, attract someone's attention, look into that person's eyes, drink down your schnapps or take a drink from your wine glass, make eye contact again with the other person and salute with the glass, before putting down the glass in front of you.

REFERENCES

Bjerén, G. (1981) 'Female and male in a Swedish forest region: old roles under new conditions' in *Women: Work and Household Systems, Antropologiska Studier*, 30–31, pp.56–85.
Henriksson, A. (1963) *Svensk Historia*, Stockholm: Bonniers.
Nilsson, U. (1990) 'Skål för Europa!' *Expressen*, 23 August, p. 14.
Sjögren, O. (1903) *Sveriges historia*, Stockholm: Pröléen and Comp.

10 No fishing without drinking

The construction of social identity in rural
Ireland

Adrian Peace

In the small Irish community of Clontarf (a pseudonym), heavy alcohol
consumption is considered nothing untoward. For most men, any weekend
involves a substantial amount of drinking within several of its bars: a
proportion of these drink regularly throughout the week; and although at
weekends some men would be in the company of their wives, drinking is
for the most part a male preserve. Since the adult population of Clontarf is
only 450, the fact that no less than eight bars can survive, and in some cases
prosper, itself indicates that drinking is a major dimension of recurrent
income expenditure.

The concern of this chapter is to couple the analysis of drinking with
some exploration of how various social identities are constructed in Clontarf.
For whilst social anthropologists have often examined alcohol consumption
as a feature of generalized community experience (see the contributions to
Douglas (ed.) 1987), my concern is to examine drinking's contribution to the
reproduction of social identities within the community. Clontarf folk do not
consider it abnormal for men to drink heavily: this is considered an element
of the community's routine practices. But this is not to say that drinking is
not remarked upon: the quality of beers and spirits, the ambience of different
bars, changes in individual consumption patterns, the quirks of public house
owners, are just a few of the recurrent conversational topics. From this
discourse of drinking, constructions of identity emerge.

Fishermen always figure most prominently in this flow of drinking
discourse since they drink more frequently and more copiously than any
other fraction of the community: and the particular location in which they
reside and take their leisure is especially renowned for the role which
alcohol consumption plays. These features too are routinely remarked upon
and discussed: fishing and drinking are considered indivisible and there are
numerous markers of their interconnectedness. In this chapter I examine
this especially privileged relation between fishing and drinking and locate
their affinity within the material circumstances of production. It will be

argued that the relation has important consequences not only for the collective identity of pier folk but also the construction of gender relations within Clontarf. After detailing how the politics of fishing and drinking is related to the politics of gender, we will return to examining the role played by alcohol in this particular form of simple commodity production in rural Ireland.

'FISHING OUT THE PIER'

Despite its small size, Clontarf is exceptionally differentiated. Its constituent domains are the country, the village and the pier, each of which has a particular occupational concern, an exclusive population engaged in it, and an inescapably idiosyncratic ethos. The country is the preserve of farmers and farm families who possess their own small units of production: the relationship between a family and its farm is always a special and identifiable one; and each family's affairs are always considered private and hallowed. The village is dominated by several large, but not unified, families whose main concern is commerce. As the owners of general stores and public houses, they are especially prominent socially and politically in the village. But this domain is also the hub of community-wide traffic, and by contrast with the country is a very public place indeed where little is secret and much is commonplace.

Although these differences are pronounced enough, it is nevertheless the pier which is considered the most distinctive of the three domains: it is often said that 'things happen at the pier that couldn't happen anywhere else in Clontarf'. Central to this distinctiveness is the concentration of the harbour, the bars, and the domestic residences of pier folk within a few hundred yards' radius. A majority of regular fishermen reside here with their families in houses directly overlooking the harbour. The two bars mainly frequented by them stand, with all due symbolic moment, between the harbour and their domestic dwellings so that all fishermen must at least pass the bars several times each day.

Fishing out of Clontarf is a form of simple commodity production within a small urban industrial society. The boats are mostly between thirty and forty-foot wooden-hulled vessels and fibre glass dinghies (or 'punts'). The former require a crew of three and it is from them that most fishing is done throughout the year. Characteristically a three-man crew comprises the boat's skipper-owner and two others called sharemen. All three receive an equal share of the boat's catch with a further two shares reserved to cover improvements to the boat, new gear and the cost of fuel. Boats are privately owned and, in addition to this being the skipper-owner's major capital asset, it is the only source of his own and his dependents' livelihood as well as being the main focus for all fluid capital and labour. These small boats are sometimes tied up for days on end due to inclement weather, yet there is endless maintenance work to be done. Even when a boat is tied up, its owner will be on board discussing 'her' strengths, 'her' weaknesses, and 'her' foibles with other fishermen. The discourse about fishing is tangled, ramified, and never-ending, especially among owners.

The reputations of skippers and sharemen are wholly determined by the performance of their boats. An owner-skipper's standing is the subject of regular review as is that of a shareman who stays with a particular boat for some time. Usually between a dozen and a score large boats and punts are working out of the pier: since all (bar one) are restricted to a single day at sea at a time, each evening their boxes of fish are on the pier awaiting collection by a fish buyer. The success of a boat and its crew is therefore instantly and publicly estimable in a way that no other local population's output could possibly be. Insofar as the skipper owns the boat and is personally responsible for every decision taken on it, so his personal reputation comes under the closest possible scrutiny.

Relations between fishermen are consistently egalitarian and recurrently conflictual. By virtue of being self-employed men in possession of their own productive resources, an ethos of egalitarianism is inescapable. The idea that every man is as good as his neighbour is a consistent thread informing most important codes of interpersonal conduct. This is not to suggest that there are few material inequalities amongst Clontarf's fishermen (though neither are there marked disparities), it is rather to acknowledge that the emphasis on equality concerns moral attributes rather than material assets. The ethos is variously signalled by nicknames, greeting styles, the use of epithets and the sustained abuse of those who, despite all, insist on proclaiming themselves superior to others.

This itself creates conflict: but most is produced by other considerations. Fishermen fall out over how fishing should be done, they quarrel over details of the share system, they vie for harbour moorings, they accuse one another of incompetence, and when drift nets or lines of crayfish netting become inadvertently tangled out at sea, boat owners find themselves publicly at loggerheads. Once differences are in the public domain, they inevitably become wrapped up in matters of reputation and prestige from which many find it impossible to step down. Since there are always in this condensed arena of work, leisure and residence, dormant past tensions and volatile current ones in place, it does not require a spectacular addition to provoke escalation. The most telling index of this potential is the street brawl. Elsewhere in Clontarf, physical violence between grown men would be unthinkable: yet at the pier, every now and then, a fist fight breaks out and does much to reinforce the pier's image of a rough place inhabited by truculent residents.

Notwithstanding the tough, manual nature of fishing, it requires a great deal of knowledge to be pursued successfully. For a start there are the copious quantities of local knowledge about fishing conditions which older men have acquired over the decades: these focus on the movement of different fish at different times of the year, under different climatic conditions and in different locations (or 'marks'). Most men have favourite marks where they frequently fish, others will stay clear of particular locations – and these may be one and the same. More currently, there is the ever-changing information about other Clontarf boats which any skipper follows assiduously, connecting this information with relative size catches at the end of the day. Relevant, too, is the location of Irish, French, Spanish and English trawl fleets, for the arrival of these off-shore can spell drought conditions locally as the general area is 'fished out'.

Again, current knowledge concerning fishing authorities is indispensable, especially during the summer months of salmon fishing, for most boats the more lucrative period of the year. It would not be so were not every rule surrounding salmon fishing actually flouted; so it becomes imperative to be familiar with the current activities of the bailiffs. Of like consequence is up-to-date information about market outlets. The sale of fish here is not centralized (on the lines of, say, a cooperative arrangement), but divided between at least three independent buyers who compete for the clientage of boat owners and then sell directly to consumers in the regional market-place, or to other buyers, including overseas ones. Boat owners must therefore keep a weather eye open for all current prices inside and outside Clontarf in order to decide whether present arrangements with a buyer should be maintained or broken off. Similarly fluid are the relations between skippers and sharemen for there is no effective contract between them, only a verbal agreement to work together until such times as one party determines otherwise. As a result, skippers keep well abreast of how sharemen on other boats are performing, and sharemen are always well informed about the relative fortunes of every other skipper in Clontarf.

DRINKING TO SOCIAL DIFFERENCE

The pressures of private boat ownership, the uncertainty of personal reputations, the aggressive competitiveness of fishing, and the imperative of up-to-date knowledge are, then, some salient features of the occupation which economically and culturally dominates the pier. In combination they put men regularly and recurrently in Clontarf's bars so that drinking becomes as much a means of production as the boat and the gear to fish with. It is an occupational imperative among Clontarf's fishermen to maintain a solid footing in the discourse distilled in the community's public houses. The two bars adjacent to the harbour are the pre-eminent sites in which this discourse is composed, but two others in the village are also popular with some. Accordingly, fishermen are continually in motion between these bars and may well visit all four of them (and others besides) in the course of a night or a weekend of solid drinking. Especially in the village bars, fishermen rub shoulders with farmers, business folk, wage-earners and the unemployed: but by the end of a night's drinking, it is usually the case that fishermen have fallen in with their own. Be that as it may, it is a virtual cultural requirement that to be a fisherman it is necessary to drink well. As is the case in Houat, south Brittany, multiple constructions surround the notion of a 'real fisherman' (Jorion 1976), but the idea that an effective and successful fisherman could keep himself to himself and not drink well would be considered out of the question, whilst these are two quite common and expected characteristics among the community's farmers.

It is assuredly within the commensal setting of the bar that any fisherman constructs his personal reputation – or, one might say, chases it down since in this setting all reputations well proceed their bearers. Erving Goffman once wrote (1959:33): 'People are obliged not only to carry out their tasks and routines, but also *express* their competence in doing so'. It is in drinking sessions that a fisherman does this and thereby legitimizes his mode of operation. Fishing is a craft occupation requiring an inordinate amount of experience and knowledge which can be exercised in a wide variety of ways: there is no set programme for catching fish. A fisherman therefore articulates the discrete and particular rationale behind his way of doing things in conversation and debate with his peers, including even those major decisions which all have to take every year. When to cease salmon fishing, for example, and put down tangle nets is a decision which all owners of larger boats must take: but the transition often enough occurs over a two-month phase, such is the range of variables which has to be considered.

Since a skipper's ultimate decisions on major issues have fundamental ramifications not only for his family but also his sharemen and their dependents, so they warrant accountability; and this is exactly what tran-spires in extended drinking sessions throughout the year. Accordingly it is in the milieu of the bar that the reputations of skippers are made and unmade over stout and whiskey chasers. Of course, it is boxes of fish which ultimately determine any fisherman's worth; but it is also a central part of local belief that a good deal of fishing depends on luck. In order to account for a good spell in terms of personal ability and expertise rather than chance, any fisherman needs to provide his own account and explanation in the public milieu of the bar: and quite as important as the consolidation of his standing in such circumstances is the hardening of his self-confidence, by no means a negligible asset in this competitive location.

Evidently related to this consideration is the fact that the bar is the outstanding site in which to make conspicuous display of one's productivity. Although a boat's output is evident enough by virtue of being despatched from the pier, there are important exceptions. Fishermen go to great lengths, for example, to hide the quantities of salmon they have on board, likewise with crayfish, for these are the most valuable of catches and a boat owner known to be doing well at a particular mark can expect others to move in and crowd him out. (On secrecy in fishing, see contributions to Andersen and Wadell 1972, Smith 1977 and Pálsson 1982.) Considerable satisfaction can come from having effectively disguised the details of such successes whilst on the other hand publicly broadcasting one's high return through drinking heavily oneself and buying rounds for others. The early 1980s saw a relative decline in the returns from fishing with the result that expansively buying rounds fell into disrepair as a regular ritual. It is therefore now all the more noteworthy when a fisherman does so. It is following a sustained bout of high productivity that one expends more money than usual on oneself and one's closest associates – as when, for example, in 1988 one young fisherman on a share in a successful boat managed to spend well over £100 on spirits in a drinking spell which lasted two full days.

The important properties of alcohol are that it is publicly consumed and that it available in specifiable quantities (see Collman 1988, Chapter 6). Since fishermen well know what all others customarily drink, any marked variation is not only noted but some explanation is sought. Not all such changes, however, can be directly related to success in fishing. A frequent (but certainly not universal) claim amongst established fishermen is that, provided the essential requirements of the family are met, they are relatively indifferent to money, even contemptuous of it. Certain drinking sessions appear virtually set in motion to display precisely that. In late 1988 the most spectacular (and then, infamous) binge involved four brothers, all in middle age, with families to support. Together they consumed an exceptional quantity of stout and spirits from Friday afternoon through to the Sunday evening, breaking only for an occasional meal. The drinking session had taken off in impromptu fashion, as does all 'good crack' in Clontarf: but the pier population was assuredly impressed by the brothers' conspicuous indifference to their immediate financial circumstances. None of the four was fishing successfully, two were – if anything – performing badly.

It is in such sessions as these that men display their ability to hold their beer well and to demonstrate their physical toughness: a good deal of physical horseplay accompanies any serious drinking bout. As we have seen, this quality is indispensable to small-scale fishing out of Clontarf for there are none of the comforts which are now so widely available on modern trawlers (as described by Cohen (1986), for Shetland Island vessels). On most Clontarf boats in the early 1980s even the engine-driven hauler was a recent addition. In winter months conditions at sea can be acutely uncomfortable; and all fish processing is done at sea and by hand. Accordingly, to be a fisherman it is necessary to be hard. Less obviously, the chances of other fishermen driving over one's salmon nets, taking a knife to the top or bottom ropes of drift nets, or cutting away lines of lobster pots are now increasingly high, given the competitive nature of this occupational niche. One is less likely to be the target of such sabotage if it is well known that outright physical confrontation will result, and accordingly some readily demonstrate their physical prowess to signal that they should not be unduly provoked.

Yet above all else, it is the knowledge that is condensed, compounded, and constantly refined in the bars which is most essential to effective fishing over time. One simply does not get proper access to this scarce resource unless one's membership of the occupational cadre is established and ongoing. Even blow-ins who have brought new boats into the harbour have faced near-insuperable obstacles in their initial, and hostile, induction phase. So access to this resource cannot be other than as part of a generalized exchange process. One is expected to provide information which will be of value to an extended circle of others, quite as much as theirs will be to oneself. But this has to be done whilst observing other implicit codes for conduct at the pier, such as that which requires a primary sense of obligation to one's present crew, even though it is understood that its composition will be short-lived, or that which demands loyalty to one's close relatives, despite the fact that male siblings and cousins find themselves in direct competition with one another. The consideration which cannot be overemphasized is that all such information is frequently changing and needs to be quickly acted upon. The movement of shoals of fish is not only rapid but exceptionally unpredictable on this section of the Irish coastline. Unless a fisherman rapidly learns of their presence and acts on it, the opportunity is lost. Market prices change considerably and within relatively narrow periods of time: so too do selling opportunities to particular buyers inside and outside Clontarf. In the summer months, the sudden advent of bailiffs either over the horizon by boat or by the single main road into Clontarf can only be anticipated by access to an inter-community network of contacts which terminates locally in Clontarf's bars. Under such circumstances, there can be no effective alternative to being there in the bars regularly; whilst some specific, clearly demarcated information may be readily available, the great bulk of it is built into the routine flow of a wide variety of verbal encounters. One has to extract the information which one needs and act on it accordingly. It is for these reasons that a recurrent presence has to be maintained. Unless a fisherman makes a couple of visits to his favourite bar each day and spends in them several evenings each week, he is marginalized from that flow of drinking discourse on which his means of livelihood substantially depends.

THE BOUNDARIES OF PLACE AND GENDER

The processes described thus far are central to the reproduction of the pier's collective identity as a distinct domain inside Clontarf. Elsewhere I have described how a collective identity of Clontarf as a community finds consistent expression without undermining the sense of internal hetero-geneity (Peace 1986). Presently the important issue is that the inter-connected economic and social relations which turn upon drinking and fishing are themselves integral to the pier residents' distinct identity within the community at large. To sum up the major influences: in addition to the pier being physically distinct from the village and the country, fishing is its consciously paramount occupation and is pursued by a handful of promin-ent families concentrated there. The rough character of pier life, from physical aggression through to a notable earthiness in daily speech, is especially marked by comparison with the ambience of the other two domains. The role played by drinking in the social life of the pier is relatively pronounced too, and is at times condemned as reprehensible by villagers and farmers who consider themselves more restrained. Above all, as will now be evident, the drinking discourse focused upon pier bars is so very dense and detailed that it is beyond the capacity of non-fishermen to contribute to it. To a greater degree than the farmers in the country or business folk in the village (both of whose occupational discourses are far less notable), the sheer detail and volume of constantly changing informa-tion results in the fishermen realizing a distinct, bounded discourse around the pier domain which others find difficult to penetrate.

The same constellation of fishing–drinking relationships has a profound impact on the construction of gender relations inside the pier domain. The result is a marked divide between the work sphere dominated by men and the domestic sphere directed by women. Once again the prevalent con-sideration is relative for this distinction is not one which obtains elsewhere in Clontarf. On the community's agricultural properties, farmers and their wives cooperate closely, the latter frequently taking charge of milking, calf-rearing, and the raising of small animals for sale. Joint enterprise is even more pronounced amongst the commercial enterprises which predominate in the village. The three village bars, for example, are all family enterprises in which husband and wife cooperate to the full, not least to minimize the need for non-familial labour requiring wage-payment. As with the farms, public houses and village shops are run by pooling all available family labour so that sons and daughters are recruited as soon as possible into the routine operation of these enterprises.

By contrast it is not unusual for the wives of fishermen to claim that they know little about their husbands' work; a few pronounce their indifference. Even if this is not to be taken quite literally, within this particular form of commodity production there is no role occupied by women, nor evidence to suggest that in the past women processed fish on lines described for somewhat similar communities in the British Isles and beyond (Thompson 1983, Sider 1984). Contemporaneously, then, the pier woman's pre-dominant role is a service one, wholly embedded in and circumscribed by the parameters of the domestic household. Whereas the social relationships of men are focused upon the harbour and the bar, those of women are centred upon the home or, more strictly speaking, the relations between several domestic units which are concentrated together above the harbour.

In that most pier residents were born either in Clontarf or its vicinity, younger and middle-aged women frequently have their own or their husbands' parents residing nearby. Accordingly, in addition to the evidently major task of bringing up children, the first specific component of the woman's service role is that of providing for the aged, since the chief burden invariably falls on married women and requires a considerable number of resources to be devoted to their care (particularly since regional welfare facilities are located at a good distance from this small community). Also by virtue of being locally born, most women have a number of siblings resident in Clontarf or neighbouring settlements; and in this context the bonds between siblings are always intimate. Whether of the same gender or not, the relationship is wholly privileged by contrast with all others. And to these relatives are to be added the husband's siblings, with whom a woman is expected to be (minimally) on cordial terms, some of whom will be around the same age as the fisherman's wife and either have had children or are still in the child-bearing phase.

A pier housewife is thus typically surrounded by relatives to whom she is affinally or consanguineally related. For fairly evident reasons, her routine social network is dominated by the female relatives with whom she shares household chores, the minding of infants, escorting older children to school, and providing meals for all concerned. So when one talks with, or simply listens to, pier women from fishing families discussing their daily affairs, the indelible impression is that their domestic lives are about juggling with time. They are involved in a never-ending process of imaginatively and creatively structuring the hours of the day in order to mediate the competing pressures put upon them by children, husbands, parents and parents-in-law, as well as neighbouring siblings. If the point seems an obvious one, all that can be rejoindered is that it proved striking to this ethnographer since by comparison their menfolk are relatively indifferent to the clock. Apart from the haste of casting off from moorings at the commencement of a trip, and even that is an exercise subject to inordinate delay often enough, fishermen frequently have time on their hands whilst their wives struggle with its scarcity.

As one might anticipate, the production of tension and conflict between pier households is relatively frequent, whereas by contrast conflicts between farming families are not only few but also short-lived. Disputes between and within related households over children, money, property ownership, and sexual matters incline to be regular amongst pier residences. What is especially striking about them is that, whatever understanding there might be to keep such matters within family bounds, this proves virtually impossible to sustain. It is especially problematic to do so because disputes between women become so frequently interlinked with, and indissoluble from, disputes between their menfolk at the pier. One's neighbour may be the wife of one's husband's shareman: one's husband may be engaged in running battle at sea with one's brother who, with his family, resides hard by; one's friendship with a fish buyer's wife may be put at hazard because husbands are at odds over prices or payments; and so forth. As a result of such multiplex relations, conflicts between pier households become involved and intricate, and they do much to compound the pier's reputation as a disputatious locale. But whilst their husbands are able to engage in varied avoidance and distancing strategies under such circumstances, either by going out to sea or retiring to a village bar, women with their many responsibilities are less able to do so. Put simply, women have no extra-household milieu to which they can turn if they wish to put distance between themselves and the accumulating tensions of the pier.

Instead their characteristic response is to forge, and then to rely heavily upon, close friendships with one or two fellow pier residents. Whilst it is rarely the case for fishermen to exhibit special dyadic associations – but rather to concur with the interpretation of one who said 'Everyone here's your friend or your enemy, and in one week he may be your friend and in the next your enemy!' – their wives form special, enduring attachments which effectively become relations between confidantes. Whether based on friendships from school days, developed specifically in Clontarf, or rooted in siblingship or cousinhood, it is in such bonds that fishermen's wives find the resources to negotiate with the intensity of their micro-social world. It is in them too that they elaborate their own discourse of domestic politics by drawing upon and further compounding their characteristic intimacy with the pier. The state of various marriages, the financial circumstances of households, the careers of local associations, the intrigue of extramarital liaisons – these are some of the issues to be kept abreast of; and their detailed examining in its turn feeds through into their verbal encounters with parents, neighbouring relatives and other co-residents, in a seamless thread of talk and endless currents of conversation out of which the pier as a bounded domain is constantly being constructed.

OF DRAMAS, SAGAS AND DRINKING

To this extent, the discourse of domestic politics elaborated by pier women and the drinking discourse of their husbands are similarly constitutive of the social boundary which distinguishes their domain from the remainder of the community. The contrasting nature of the daily round of men and women is reflected in their myriad conversational encounters, yet each is equally pier-focused and is such as to reinforce the prevalent and prideful notion that 'We are pier folk and we are different'.

Contrasting as they may be, however, it is equally the case that these gender discourses are effectively complementary. Simply because the daily round creates some socio-spatial separation, it does not lead to their lives remaining distinct and separable (although that the one inexorably results in the other is assumed in the classic study by Dennis *et al.* 1958). At least in Clontarf, the experiences of spouses are wholly complementary at one level precisely by virtue of their being discrete at another, for in the quiet of the home their experiences can be knitted together in a comprehensive web of interpretation. Their mutual accomplishment is a shared cognitive map of their social domain. Ongoing events, some of which I would call dramas, others sagas, comprise the governing threads of their disjointed talk, for it is such events out of which the framework of pier politics is fabricated. In my terms, dramas incline to be variations on much the same themes, are of limited duration, involve restricted personnel, and they can be followed closely without requiring any active intervention. As the term implies, sagas occur on a politically grander scale and are temporarily extended also. Sagas engage a larger body of local figures, several issues are frequently at stake, they have long-term consequences, and they generate often heated exchange amongst the broader, attentive audience of pier residents.

The crucial point for emphasis at this point is that the pier, above all other locations in Clontarf and its wider locality, is the especial source of both dramas and sagas. And this is because – returning now specifically to the role of alcohol amongst the fishermen – of the distinctive relationship between drinking and fishing. What is critically common to both is that they are equally generative of the untoward, the unexpected, and the unforeseen event. In concert they thus present a formidable coupling.

Because of the limited ecological niche occupied by Clontarf fishermen, and the competitive circumstances in which their livelihoods are gleaned, scarcely a couple of days pass by without some drama – well worth broadcasting – having transpired. In the context of the pier bar, where a generalized camaraderie coexists constantly with specific enmities, sustained drinking sessions recurrently create their own highlights and dramatic developments. When therefore happenings out at sea are continuously fed into the flow of social interaction at the bar, an especially heady combination results. In other words there is a distinctively homological relationship between drinking and fishing: their correspondence is such as to produce irregular events, unpredictable happenings, uncertain relationships, and unanticipated consequences. In addition to the self-evidently transactional nature of relations within this sphere of simple commodity production, there is much else which defines reduction to such terms. Drinking and fishing create a specific cultural ethos in which uncertainty, luck, chance and capriciousness are always in attendance, and at times seem quite dominant.

Under such circumstances the fishermen's constant movement between Clontarf's bars, the way in which men drop in and drop out of several conversational encounters within the space of an hour, and at the end of a night's drinking will be comfortably 'full up' or somewhat inebriated (the local term is 'langers' or just plain 'pissed'), are open to interpretation as the most effective of improvisations which can come to terms with the uncertainties of their material circumstances. First, it is in the course of such apparent aimlessness that the individual fisherman is able to take rapid yet comprehensive stock of all those social relationships which are of consequence to him. Fishermen themselves often imply that as a way of life fishing would be unrivalled were it not for the fact that it produces such a complexity of relations with other men. But this is in the nature of the occupation, it has to be addressed, and it is through the extensive drinking in bars that this is substantively done. After a weekend's solid drinking, they emerge with a firm grasp on the fabric of social relations which are so determinant of the way in which they make their living.

In addition to this, it is in the context of drinking bouts that fishermen can effect the changes to their social relationships which customary codes of interpersonal behaviour do not facilitate under more normal circumstances. Notwithstanding their often-pronounced renegade activities, most fishermen are as much constrained by established standards of face-to-face conduct as anyone else. Accordingly they find it difficult, for example, to break off the association with a shareman because of his unsatisfactory performance out at sea, or to repair a breach with another skipper when the conflict between them has evidently run its course. Heavy drinking sessions in crowded bars provide precisely the appropriate circumstances for such modifications to interpersonal dealings: for whilst, say, a fisherman would find it impossible to walk up to a rival on the pier and forthrightly suggest that bygones should be bygones, the offer of a drink between somewhat inebriated men surrounded by their pushing, shoving, and loud-talking peers would be hard to turn down, whatever the nature of past differences. (See Faris 1973 and Firestone 1967 for similar argument.)

Finally, it is in such settings and with several rounds of drink behind them, I propose, that fishermen are able not only to take stock of the social relations around them but also to evaluate reflexively their own particular circumstances within that social field and their own social selves. Here in particular it warrants repetition that all fishermen possess their own means of production, that they thus accord themselves a high degree of self-esteem, and that their social reputations are of tremendous importance to them. This being so, it is of real consequence to the self-esteem of the fishermen to be present in the bars and to demonstrate their capacity to hold their liquor well in the company of their peers. Following a night or a weekend of sustained conversation and sustained alcohol consumption, the individual can emerge with a reinforced sense of his productive worth and with his social self fully intact, despite the temporary setbacks and occasional failures to which all fishermen are subject time and again. When fishermen are doing badly for some while then, as we have seen, their public reputations become subject to considerable buffeting: such is the inherent nature of their occupational relationships. But by socializing effectively and drinking hard and well – and in knowing well that he can do both regardless of immediate circumstances out at sea – he is able to retain full confidence in his calibre as a fisherman and in his sense of self as a member of the pier domain.

To express the point somewhat differently, the proposition is that, as fishermen imbibe heavily and become somewhat inebriated (bearing in mind that this is a matter of phenomenal degree), they do not thereby lose control over their immediate circumstances or indeed abandon their sense of judgement. On the contrary, it is precisely under such circumstances that they are in a position to grasp effectively the fluid and complex realities of their world in a more comprehensive fashion than is usually the case. As the drink flows, as tongues loosen, as masks fade and the camaraderie takes over, so the experiential realities of fishing out of Clontarf come into clear view. Far from the individual's judgement becoming, as one might say, clouded or dull through alcohol, the fisherman's sense of not only the social worth of his fellows but more importantly his social self becomes, in fact, more acute and keen than is possible at other times. In short, a significant role of alcohol in Clontarf's pier domain is to provide opportunities for the fisherman to be especially reflexive when at the centre of those social relations which not only determine his livelihood but are also pivotal to the way in which he constitutes his own social identity.

ACKNOWLEDGEMENTS

I am obliged to Jojada Verrips, Nigel Rapport and Roy Fitzhenry for their comments on an earlier draft of this chapter. The chapter has previously appeared in *Maritime Anthropological Studies* (1991) Volume 4 No 2.

REFERENCES

Andersen, R. and Wadell, C. (eds) (1972) *North Atlantic Fishermen*, St John's: Institute of Social and Economic Research, Memorial University of Newfoundland, Papers No 5.

Cohen, A.P. (1986) *Whalsay: Symbol, Segment and Boundary in a Shetland Island Community*, Manchester: Manchester University Press.

Collman, J. (1988) *Fringe Dwellers and Welfare: The Aboriginal Response to Bureaucracy*, Queensland: Queensland University Press.

Dennis, N., Henriques, F. and Slaughter, C. (1958) *Coal is our Life*, London: Tavistock.

Douglas, M. (ed.) (1987) *Constructive Drinking: Perspectives on Drink from Anthropology*, Cambridge: Cambridge University Press.

Faris, J.C. (1973) *Cat-Harbour – a Newfoundland Fishing Settlement*, St John's: Institute of Social and Economic Research, Memorial University of Newfoundland, Studies No. 3.

Firestone, M. (1967) *Brothers and Rivals: Patrilocality in 'Savage Cove'*, St John's: Institute of Social and Economic Research, Memorial University of Newfoundland, Studies No 5.

Goffman, E. (1959) *The Presentation of Self in Everyday Life*, New York: Doubleday.

Jorion, P. (1976) 'To be a good fisherman you don't need any fish', *Cambridge Anthropology*, Vol. 3, No 1, pp.1–12.

Pálsson, G. (1982) 'Territoriality among Icelandic fishermen', *Acta Sociologica* 25: 5–13.

Peace, A. (1986) '"A different place altogether": diversity, unity and boundary in an Irish community' in A.P. Cohen (ed.) *Symbolizing Boundaries: Identity and Diversity in British Cultures*, Manchester: Manchester University Press.

Sider, G. (1986) *Culture and Class in Anthropology and History: A Newfoundland Illustration*, Cambridge: Cambridge University Press.

Smith, M.E. (1977) *Those who Live from the Sea: a Study in Maritime Anthropology*, St Paul: West Publishing Co.

Thompson, P., Wailey, T. and Lummis, T. (1983) *Living the Fishing*, London: Routledge & Kegan Paul.

Name index

Abu-Lughod, L. 50, 52, 68n
Agar, M. 3
Aguilera, F. 74, 75
Ahlström-Laakso, S. 4, 5, 17, 27n
Allen, P. 25n, 130n
Altman, Y. 71
Andersen, R. 172
Anderson, P. 24n
Anderson, R.K. 24n
Arensberg, C.M. 4

Bales, R.F. 4, 24n, 26n, 75
Barrows, S. 130n
Barth, F. 148
Barth, M. 102
Barûdî, S. 38
Bashir, A. 84, 86, 98n
Beck, S. 6, 25n, 130n
Bennett, L. 4, 24n
Bianquis-Gasser, I. 18
Biris, C. 112
Bjerén, G. 8–10, 17, 19, 21, 24n, 159
Bloch, M. 16, 26n, 98n, 127
Blum, E. 26n, 98n
Blum, R. 26n, 98n
Boissevain, J. 129n
Bonnefoy, Y. 106
Bourdieu, P. 19, 27n, 28n
Brandes, S.H. 4, 7, 10, 25n, 130n
Braudel, F. 113
Brown, P. 97n, 98n
Bruun, K. 2, 24n, 25n
Bunzel, R. 1, 24n
Buonaventura, W. 39
Bynum, C.W. 97n

Campbell, J.: (1964) 4, 17, 19, 25n,
98n, 99n, 123, 128n, 139n; (1966)
26n
Caplan, P. 25n
Carstairs, G.M. 24n
Chelebi, K. 36–7
Christian, Jr., W.A. 18
Clinard, M.B. 25n
Collier, J.F. 76–7
Collman, J. 172
Colson, E. 8, 24n
Comaroff, J. 50
Cooper, M.A. 26n
Corbin, J.R. 74, 75
Corbin, M.P. 74, 75
Cowan, J. 9, 25n, 48–9, 68n, 69n, 130n
Cyprian, St 86

Danforth, L.M. 97n, 110, 128n
Davies, P. 2, 24n
Davis, J. 25n, 129n
Dennis, N. 177
Dennis, P.A. 25n, 27n
Dimas, V. 118
Dimen, M. 25n, 123
Dimitriou-Kotsoni, S. 128n
Dolgin, J. 22
Douglas, M.: (1966) 81, 148, 152;
(1975) 17; (1987) 2, 3, 6, 48, 71,
167
Driessen, H.: (1983) 7–8, 25n, 71, 74,
77, 78n, 130n; (1984) 75; (this
volume) 9–11, 17
Drower, E.S. 17, 26n
Dubisch, J.: (1983) 128n; (1986)

Subject index